D1561563

DATE DUE

Modernist Alchemy

Also by Timothy Materer

Wyndham Lewis the Novelist

Vortex: Pound, Eliot, and Lewis

The Letters of Ezra Pound and Wyndham Lewis (editor)

Selected Letters of Ezra Pound to John Quinn (editor)

Cornell University Press   *Ithaca and London*

Timothy Materer

Modernist Alchemy

Poetry and the Occult

BRESCIA COLLEGE
LIBRARY
65033

Copyright © 1995 by Cornell University

All rights reserved. Except for brief quotations in a review, this book, or parts thereof, must not be reproduced in any form without permission in writing from the publisher. For information, address Cornell University Press, Sage House, 512 East State Street, Ithaca, New York 14850.

First published 1995 by Cornell University Press.

Printed in the United States of America

⊗ The paper in this book meets the minimum requirements
of the American National Standard for Information Sciences—
Permanence of Paper for Printed Library Materials, ANSI Z39.48-1984.

Reprinted by permission of Harcourt Brace & Company and Faber and Faber, Ltd.: Excerpts from "Choruses from 'The Rock,' " "Journey of the Magi," "A Song for Simeon," and "The Waste Land" in *Collected Poems 1909–1962* by T. S. Eliot, copyright 1936 by Harcourt Brace & Company, copyright © 1964, 1963 by T. S. Eliot. Excerpt from *The Cocktail Party,* copyright 1950 by T. S. Eliot and renewed 1978 by Esme Valerie Eliot. Excerpts from *The Family Reunion,* copyright 1939 by T. S. Eliot and renewed 1967 by Esme Valerie Eliot. Excerpts from "Little Gidding," "Burnt Norton," "East Coker," and "The Dry Salvages" in *Four Quartets,* copyright 1943 by T. S. Eliot and renewed 1971 by Esme Valerie Eliot.
   Reprinted by permission of HarperCollins Publishers, Inc. and Faber and Faber, Ltd.: Excerpts from "Ouija" from *The Collected Poems of Sylvia Plath* by Sylvia Plath and edited by Ted Hughes, copyright © 1960 by Ted Hughes; copyright renewed. Excerpts from "Mystic" from *Winter Trees* by Sylvia Plath, copyright © 1963 by Ted Hughes; copyright renewed. Excerpts from "Elm" and "Lady Lazarus" from *Ariel* by Sylvia Plath, copyright © 1963 by Ted Hughes; copyright renewed. Excerpts from "Ariel" from *Ariel* by Sylvia Plath, copyright © 1965 by Ted Hughes; copyright renewed. Excerpt from "Lyonnesse" from *Winter Trees* by Sylvia Plath, copyright © 1972 by Ted Hughes. Excerpts from "Dialogue over a Ouija Board," "Snakecharmer," "Crystal Gazer," "The Ravaged Face," and "Sonnet to Satan" from *The Collected Poems of Sylvia Plath,* edited by Ted Hughes, copyright © 1960, 1965, 1971, 1981 by the Estate of Sylvia Plath; editorial material copyright © 1981 by Ted Hughes.

Library of Congress Cataloging-in-Publication Data

Materer, Timothy, 1940–
   Modernist alchemy : poetry and the occult / Timothy Materer.
      p.   cm.
   Includes bibliographical references (p.   ) and index.
   ISBN 0-8014-3146-8 (alk. paper)
   1. American poetry—20th century—History and criticism.   2. Occultism in literature.   3. Alchemy in literature.   4. Modernism (Literature)   I. Title.
PS310.O33M37   1995
811'.50937—dc20   95-34932

For My Family

Contents

Illustrations

Preface

All our secrets are formed from an image.
—George Ripley, *Opera Omnia Chemica* (1649)

Anyone who writes about occultism might be suspected of occasionally turning over a tarot card or perhaps of contacting a deceased relative now and then. Thus authors of books on the subject sometimes begin by stating that they themselves do not necessarily believe in occult phenomena, but they usually stop short of denying their possible validity. Occult phenomena are often thoroughly documented, and it is customary to maintain an open mind. My reading of works on occultism has, however, convinced me that phenomena well documented in one book or article are later exposed as frauds in another. When it comes to supernatural experience, even scientists and scholars are all too willing to jump to conclusions; and the number of frauds, from professional hoaxers to friends who claim to "guess" one's astrological sign, is legion.

Interest in the occult may be labeled intellectually suspect or the sign of a budding neurosis. Why then should the occult fascinate so many writers? One cannot fully understand why occultism is attractive to any particular person, because it seems to be a conceptual scheme that particularly appeals to unconscious motivations. One can speculate, however, that a fascination with occultism often arises in reaction to an increasingly scientific and secular culture. According to Mircea Eliade, occultism has grown as the mainstream churches have come to consider social relevance their distinguishing virtue. In my own case, perhaps I miss the traditional ritual, terminology, and sacramentalism (the orthodox equivalent of "magic") of my childhood religion and find an analogue to it in literary occultism. One may feel that, as Oscar Wilde wrote of Robert Browning's mysticism, "We have so few mysteries left to us that we cannot afford to part with one of them."

Writers on this subject also need to define what they mean by *occultism* before discussing its influence. Although I have used terms such as *mysticism, supernatural,* and *magic* in ways that suggest that they are all equivalent to the term *occult,* they are in fact only loosely related. For example, a book titled *Henry James and the Occult* (1972) is basically a study of James's interest in séances and spiritualism. Taken by itself, spiritualism is not necessarily "occult." As we will see, Ann Braude argues that spiritualism in nineteenth-century America was not occult, because contacting the dead was a democratic procedure that required no secret spells or priestly caste. Yet when spiritualism became associated in the 1890s with Helena Blavatsky, and séances communicated secret wisdom from spiritual masters, it surely became part of the occult movement. As the word *occult* denotes, the key quality is something hidden or secret. The dominance of a print culture over an oral one, however, eliminated true secrecy. The titles of Madame Blavatsky's *Isis Unveiled* (1877) and *The Secret Doctrine* (1888) suggest the paradoxical nature of the occult. Blavatsky did not think that publishing a "secret doctrine" for all the world to read made it any less occult. Although many would read her words, she assumed that few would understand. (This assumption could be inferred from her contempt for most of her disciples.) The marks of occultism are seen when spiritualism is linked to secret wisdom or (as in Blavatsky's works) draws widely and indeed indiscriminately from sources such as Hermeticism, Indian mysticism, the Cabala, Gnosticism, and Neoplatonism.

The mixture of distinct strains of spiritual experience as well as secrecy characterizes the occult. Although it is common to refer to an "occult tradition," *tradition* can be a misleading word in this context. Phrases such as "the Christian tradition" and "the Neoplatonic tradition" denote material that is vast but relatively well defined. Established religions such as Judaism and Christianity are synoptic and synthesize their borrowings; occultism is comparatively eclectic and juxtaposes rather than harmonizes its disparate elements. If one spoke of the Jewish tradition, it would include the Cabala without necessarily implying occultism. If the cabalistic doctrine of emanations is given a Neoplatonic interpretation, however, then the unorthodox, untraditional quality of occultism emerges. I have more to say about "tradition" in Chapter 1. But for now I simply assert that occultism is distinguished both by its secrecy and its untraditional mixture of spiritual beliefs.

The heterodoxy of occultism suggests a third distinguishing quality —disreputableness, which is in part the result of its mélange of spiritual traditions. For certain temperaments, the very scorn directed at occultism by agnostics and mainstream believers alike is an attraction. W. B. Yeats's code name in the Order of the Golden Dawn was Demon Est Deus Inversus. Occultism is usually seen as an inversion or direct challenge to Christian doctrine; for example, occultism may emphasize the feminine or androgynous nature of the deity in defiance of Christianity's God the Father.

Embracing occultism is therefore inherently rebellious. Doing so helped W. B. Yeats and Sylvia Plath express their dismissal of conventional religion. Ted Hughes believes that the current ridicule of occultists is analogous to the persecution of Renaissance occultists Giordano Bruno and John Dee, and so he experiences a sense of adventure in using its concepts. In Hughes' poetic world, as in Ezra Pound's, an original thinker is invariably ridiculed or persecuted. H.D. (Hilda Doolittle) thought the repressed concepts she discovered in occultism awaited liberation by the poet; for her, they were the true alchemical gems. Robert Duncan and James Merrill found in the occult art of alchemy a forgotten understanding of sexual identity that tolerated rather than repressed androgyny and homosexuality. From Yeats and Pound to Duncan and Merrill, alchemy provides a symbolic system that helps poets to explore their own art. Like alchemy, poetic art refines the base matter that the unimaginative overlook.

Secrecy, eclecticism, and rebelliousness characterize the occultism to which these poets are drawn. But I have not yet named occultism's most dramatic quality: the belief in spiritual forces and entities that transcend and yet are directly apprehensible to humanity. Magical practices that exert the power of mind over matter, as well as revelations of transcendent wisdom or future events, depend on the tangible existence of the supernatural. The cry of the occultist is Yeats's in "The Second Coming": "Now I know!" In occultism ethical behavior counts for nothing compared to a personal gnosis, which comes through direct experience rather than faith. This gnosis helps to account for occultism's obscurity; for it represents a discourse among true believers through a symbolic code only the enlightened can grasp.

If one could imagine an occultist church, each member would be at least a bishop; and some might consider themselves the very god they worshiped.

Occult belief in supernatural revelation is a perennial attraction to poets. The ancient connection between poetry and religious ritual suggests a natural link between poetry and occultism. Fiction is not only less ancient but less marked by this ritual function. The secret language of symbolism through which occultism speaks has an inherent attraction for poets. Moreover, the occult image is not merely a symbol, but in a transformation that is the poet's dream the symbol creates what it signifies. The effect of great poetry is so profound that it may indeed seem magical and thus inspire belief in the supernatural. Of course the language of fiction also has such power, but it does not usually work through images in the concentrated way of poetry. There are modern occultist novels (leaving aside the "horror" genre of such writers as Stephen King and Anne Rice), for example, those of Charles Williams and Carlos Castaneda. But generally novelists who treat occultism are interested in exploring its psychological basis, as in John Fowles's *The Magus* or Umberto Eco's great anatomy of occultism, *Foucault's Pendulum*. Occult concepts and symbols seem to be used most powerfully in the art of poetry.

My intention in this book is to show how occult lore and ritual inspire modern poets, from Yeats to Merrill, who are nevertheless aware and often skeptical of their history and premises. These poets deal with the problem of belief and disbelief with a modernist sophistication and self-consciousness that is neither merely credulous nor merely skeptical. The book is not a survey of occultism in modern poetry but a discussion of some poets whose use of it reveals a modern recovery of discarded beliefs and modes of thought. I conclude with James Merrill because his attempt to suspend both doubt and belief fulfills a poetic style that Yeats initiated in modern English poetry. Merrill's radical skepticism refuses to resolve antitheses and is paradoxically receptive to spiritual beliefs.

TIMOTHY MATERER

Columbia, Missouri

Acknowledgments

Grateful acknowledgment is made for permission to quote from the following sources:

Excerpts from the following works by Robert Duncan are reprinted by permission of New Directions Publishing Corporation: *Bending the Bow*, copyright © 1968 by Robert Duncan. *Ground Work: Before the War*, copyright © 1984 by Robert Duncan. *Ground Work II: In the Dark*, copyright © 1987 by Robert Duncan. *The Opening of the Field*, copyright © 1960 by Robert Duncan. *Roots and Branches*, copyright © 1964 by Robert Duncan.
Reprinted by permission of New Directions Publishing Corporation: Excerpts from *Collected Poems, 1912–1944* by H.D. Copyright © 1982 by the Estate of Hilda Doolittle. Excerpts from *Hermetic Definition* by H. D. Copyright © 1972 by Norman Holmes Pearson.
Reprinted by permission of Viking Penguin, a division of Penguin Books USA Inc., and Faber and Faber, Ltd.: Excerpts from *Cave Birds*, by Ted Hughes and Leonard Baskin. Copyright © 1978 by Ted Hughes for text, © 1978 by Leonard Baskin for illustrations.
Reprinted by permission of Alfred A. Knopf Inc. and Faber and Faber, Ltd.: Excerpts from *Selected Poems: 1946–1985* by James Merrill. Copyright © 1992 by James Merrill.
Reprinted by permission of New Directions Publishing Corporation and Faber and Faber, Ltd.: Excerpts from *Collected Early Poems* by Ezra Pound. Copyright © 1976 by the Trustees of the Ezra Pound Literary

Property Trust. Excerpts from *Personae* by Ezra Pound. Copyright ©️ 1926 by Ezra Pound. Excerpts from *The Cantos of Ezra Pound*. Copyright ©️ 1934, 1938, 1948, by Ezra Pound, ©️ 1972 by the Trustees of the Ezra Pound Literary Property Trust.

Reprinted by permission of Alfred A. Knopf Inc. and Faber and Faber, Ltd.: Excerpts from *Collected Poems* by Wallace Stevens. Copyright ©️ 1954 by Wallace Stevens.

Reprinted by permission of Simon & Schuster and A. P. Watt Ltd.: Excerpts from *The Poems of W. B. Yeats*, edited by Richard J. Finneran. Copyright 1928, 1933, 1934 by Macmillan Publishing Company. Copyrights renewed 1956, 1961, 1962 by Bertha Georgie Yeats.

An early version of Chapter 5 appeared as "Robert Duncan and the Mercurial Self," *Sagetrieb*, 9 (spring/fall 1990), and an early version of Chapter 6 appeared as "Occultism as Source and Symptom in Sylvia Plath's 'Dialogue over a Ouija Board,'" *Twentieth Century Literature*, 37 (summer 1991). Revised sections of the following articles were used for Chapter 8: "The Error of His Ways: James Merrill and the Fall into Myth," from *American Poetry*, Volume 7:3, ©️ 1990 Lee Bartlett and Peter White, McFarland & Company, Inc., Publishers; and "Death and Alchemical Transformation in James Merrill's *The Changing Light at Sandover*," *Contemporary Literature*, 29, ©️ 1988, by permission of The University of Wisconsin Press. The following was incorporated into Chapter 3: "W. B. Yeats, T. S. Eliot and the Critique of the Occult in *Four Quartets*," *Yeats Eliot Review*, 10 (winter/spring 1989):1–4. I thank the editors for permission to reprint. I also thank Colin McDowell for collaborating with me on an article on Ezra Pound and W. B. Yeats in *Twentieth Century Literature* (1985) which influenced this book.

The writing of this work was facilitated by a research leave granted by the Provost and the Research Council of the University of Missouri–Columbia and by the support of the University of Missouri Research Council. I am grateful to James Merrill for permission to use and quote from his papers at the Olin Library, Washington University, St. Louis, and Kevin Ray, Curator of Manuscripts, for assistance in using them. I thank Patricia Willis, curator of the Pound Archive at the Beinecke Library, Yale University, for her help and encouragement, and the staff at the Crofton Library, University of California–Berkeley, for assistance in using their Robert Duncan collection. I am grateful for the help of William French, Leon Surette, Akiko Miyake, Vincent Sherry, Roger Gilbert, and Greg Foster and for the support of Bernhard Kendler. My wife, Barbara, gave me invaluable help in preparing the final typescript. My children, Andrew the teacher, Susan the explorer, and Nick the alchemist, all contributed to the chemistry of this book.

T. M.

Abbreviations of Works
Cited in the Text

Robert Duncan

Bow	*Bending the Bow*
FC	*Fictive Certainties*
Field	*The Opening of the Field*
GWBW	*Ground Work: Before the War*
GWII	*Ground Work II: In the Dark*
Roots	*Roots and Branches*

T. S. Eliot

CPP	*The Complete Poems and Plays: 1909–50*

H.D. (Hilda Doolittle)

CP	*Collected Poems: 1912–44*
HD	*Hermetic Definition*
Tribute	*Tribute to Freud*

Ted Hughes

CB	*Cave Birds: An Alchemical Cave Drama*

James Merrill

CLS   *The Changing Light at Sandover: Including the Whole of the*
         Book of Ephraim, Mirabell's Books of Number, Scripts for the
         Pageant, and a New Coda, The Higher Keys
REC   *Recitative: Prose by James Merrill*

Sylvia Plath

LH   *Letters Home: Correspondence, 1950–1963*
SP   *The Collected Poems*

Ezra Pound

Cantos   *The Cantos of Ezra Pound*
CEP   *The Collected Early Poems of Ezra Pound*
GB   *Gaudier-Brzeska*
LE   *Literary Essays of Ezra Pound*
Personae *Personae: The Shorter Poems*
SR   *The Spirit of Romance*
Trans   *Translations of Ezra Pound*

Wallace Stevens

WS   *Collected Poems*

W. B. Yeats

Auto   *The Autobiography of William Butler Yeats*
Poems   *The Poems: A New Edition*
Vision   *A Vision: A Reissue with the Author's Final Revisions*

Modernist Alchemy

Introduction:
Literary Occultism

Credo quia impossibile est.

—Tertullian

For, though no person, you can damn
So, *credo ut intelligam.*
—W. H. Auden on Mephistopheles, *New Year Letter*

When Alice in *Through the Looking Glass* tells the White Queen that no one can believe impossible things, the Queen replies that sometimes *she* has believed six impossible things before breakfast. Alice needs the ability to believe the impossible if she is to understand the looking glass world, and so do poets who write of the occult, which takes them into worlds as strange as Alice's. As Lewis Carroll knew, faith may be described as believing the impossible. The White Queen is echoing the second-century Christian Tertullian, who said he believed in Christ's incarnation because it was impossible—a miracle. An entirely reasonable belief would not be a belief. Insisting on the paradoxical nature of religious truth, Kierkegaard thought Tertullian's epigram almost defined the nature of belief.[1]

The poets discussed in this book, however, are not believers in any usual or orthodox sense. Yeats's mixture of skepticism and naïveté is characteristic of occultists. He would imply at times that his occult beliefs were the center of his life, at other times, that he valued them only for the metaphors they furnished his poetry. Depending on their orientation, critics like to emphasize one side or another of Yeats's vacillation. His statements, however, should be not taken literally but recognized as a feature of occult rhetoric. Occultists may seem to dismiss their beliefs when challenged, and discuss them freely only with other believers. This cautiousness is evident in the interviews James

Merrill has given about his long poem *The Changing Light at Sandover*, which he based on transcripts of nearly thirty years of Ouija board sessions: the firmness of his belief in the reality of these sessions varies with the skepticism of the interviewer.[2] Unlike Yeats, though, and like the American poet Robert Duncan, Merrill generally adopts a skeptical and ironic tone when discussing his occultism despite the years he has devoted to exploring its doctrines.

A type of modernist irony does accompany the most successful use of occult doctrines by twentieth-century poets. Some modern poets, however, use these doctrines without any obvious signs of irony. H.D. (Hilda Doolittle)'s belief in astrological predictions and invocations of the dead seemed unqualified and unshakable. She felt no need to argue for the reality of what was so deeply real to her, even when her occult beliefs were challenged by Sigmund Freud himself. Although Sylvia Plath was not a devoted occultist like H.D., when she writes of occult experience, it is with the same absolute conviction of its reality. Ezra Pound, who often ridiculed Yeats's occultism, was like Yeats in mixing skepticism with credulity. He dismissed any challenge to his own occult beliefs by saying that they were only for the elect and, by their nature, incomprehensible to the ignorant multitude. Both Pound and Ted Hughes adopted the pose of a magus or shaman with secret knowledge. Like Yeats and unlike Pound, however, Hughes argued that certain occult phenomena have been publicly verified.

In all these varieties of belief in the impossible, one feels the relevance of another religious tenet as basic as Tertullian's. The medieval philosopher Saint Anselm said that he believed in order to understand: *credo ut intelligam*. Like Tertullian's phrase, Anselm's suggests that one wills a belief that, as a result of believing it, only then seems intellectually coherent. To the agnostic, this process seems highly suspect. Thus critics accuse Yeats of believing in ghosts only because their imagined reality inspired his poetry. Belief is necessary to the writing of works like *A Vision* or "Supernatural Songs." Without her belief in séances with the dead, or his in the Ouija board, H.D. could not have written *Trilogy* or Merrill *The Changing Light at Sandover*. The creation of such works calls for more than Coleridge's "suspension of disbelief"; the phrase is too negative. Some kind of active belief was required to create Plath's world in "Dialogue over a Ouija Board" or Hughes's in *Cave Birds*. I. A. Richards thought that the question of belief or disbelief need not arise, *"unless the logical context of our ideas is in question."*[3] It often is in question for occult poetry; the poets who write it suspend neither belief nor disbelief but believe in order to create. This quality is perhaps clearest in Merrill, who is constantly questioning, within the poem itself, the reality of the events in the *Changing Light* trilogy but who finds them utterly real as he experiences them. Yeats referred to such an experience as being "overwhelmed by miracle as all men must be when in the midst of it" (Vision 25). These poets cannot believe that such experiences are psychological delusions, though that suspicion haunts them, nor that they are simply aesthetic visions.

But how seriously can we, as readers rather than creators of poems, take such beliefs? Readers might well question the sincerity, maybe at times the common sense, of writers who profess occult beliefs. In her book on the American religious lyric, Elisa New says that to study such lyrics is to be "thrust out of the theoretical universe we've come to know" with its assumptions about "the equation of literariness and an intrinsic skepticism of language." She argues that certain poems by Emily Dickinson, Hart Crane, and Robert Frost challenge such assumptions and even seem to resist the "disenchantments of irony." New writes that these affirmative poems are "driven not so much by the Nietzschean will to power on which current theories rely as by what William James called 'the will to believe.'"[4] If New is right about the resistance of readers to poems that develop from the tradition of Christian faith, one might expect still greater resistance to those that develop from occultism. In *The Birth of Modernism*, Leon Surette indeed assets that a "scholarly phobia of the occult" has led critics to misinterpret modern writers as "skeptical relativists" (161) and so to obscure the influence of occultism on the development of modernism.

Critics have resisted granting modern poets their occult donnée, much as New says they have resisted understanding that Dickinson and Crane wrote religious lyrics. The two cases are related because occult poets are also religious in their curious way. They are, for example, religious in the root sense of pursuing rites or rituals such as Yeats's invocations, Plath's exorcisms, and Merrill's séances. What I consider the most interesting occult poetry does not, however, resist what New calls the "disenchantments of irony." The type of irony we see particularly in James Merrill is related to what Alan Wilde has termed "suspensive irony." In *Horizons of Assent*, he maintains that modernist irony registers the disparity between the past and the present, or between an ideal world and a depressingly real one, without any hope of healing the breach. In contrast, postmodern irony is "suspensive: an indecision about the meanings or relations of things is matched by a willingness to live with uncertainty" (44). This kind of irony allows the possibility of "enclaves of value" (148) within our lives in which "the gaps and discontinuities of twentieth-century literature, heretofore the mark of absence or negation, become instead the sign of a not yet constituted presence" (186). In the prose writers Wilde discusses, for example, Donald Barthelme and Stanley Elkin, this "presence," or the possibility of it, is a non-transcendent, entirely human value. On the contrary, Yeats, Hughes, and Merrill create signs of a transcendent or divine presence. Thus the irony in these poets is different from the kind Wilde describes. In Barthelme or Elkin, irony is a response to a world with no permanent values; but in the poets analyzed here, the irony is directed more at the self than at the world. Although these poets posit a transcendent presence in the universe, they generally maintain an ironic attitude toward their own ability to sense it. According to Richard Rorty, Kierkegaard thought that Hegel would have been a greater philosopher if he had demonstrated his awareness of "his own finitude . . . by an ironic gesture rather than by putting forward a claim."[5] We often find such a gesture in these poets and particularly in Yeats and Merrill.

The success of literary occultism depends on the artist's ability to penetrate an uncanny world. Belief in the occult world is necessary, yet at the same time, a modern poet who lacks a sense of irony when exploring this world may seem hopelessly naïve. An ironic stance helps the occult poet negotiate the difficulty by acknowledging, as Yeats does, that his occult doctrines may be "mummy truths" or by admitting, as Merrill does, that his description of the supernatural world resembles bad science fiction. Wilde, in his description of suspensive irony, is echoing John Keats's description of "Negative Capability," which can also help us define the particular kind of suspensive irony the occult poet may employ. Keats said the artist needs to be "capable of being in uncertainties, Mysteries, doubts, without any irritable reaching after fact & reason. " A poet who lacks this gift might as a result "let go by a fine isolated verisimilitude caught from the Penetralium of mystery."[6] The "Penetralium of mystery," an appropriately enigmatic term (in Latin, an inner room or secret place), describes the world the poets in this book explore. The very nature of occult exploration means that the poet will remain in uncertainties, mysteries, and doubts.

In "Meditations in Time of Civil War," Yeats writes that his life has been spent on the "half-read wisdom of daemonic images" (Poems 206). I return often to this line because it condenses the pathos of the quest for wisdom through the occult. Yeats must be content with uncertainties, but he concludes "Meditations" with the statement that this wisdom will or must "suffice." In a clever play on words, Richard Ellmann writes that Yeats possessed "Affirmative Capability." Ellmann thinks this altered term is more appropriate to Yeats because "it begins with the poet's difficulties but emphasizes his resolutions of them."[7] The term *negative capability*, however, is just as applicable because Keats as well as Yeats is concerned about the way intellectual skepticism, "the irritable reaching after fact and reason," might prevent the poet from affirming what can only be a "verisimilitude" as opposed to a "truth." Yeats rebelled against his father's positivistic skepticism, which dismissed all the "verisimilitudes" in a rigorous but constricting search for the truth in an age of science. As the verities of society and religion no longer seemed eternal, Yeats knew that the "verisimilitudes" would have to "suffice the ageing man as once the growing boy" ("Meditations," Poems 206).

The problem of achieving negative (or affirmative) capability was still more severe for a post-Freudian generation that understood the psychological seductiveness of religious beliefs. James Merrill faces this problem of belief frankly at the beginning of *The Changing Light at Sandover*. He suspects that his occult experiments are a "mistake" and, like Yeats in "All Souls' Night," fears the mockery of his readers. This anxiety suggests the special relevance of the subtitles for Part 3 of the poem ("Scripts for the Pageant"): "YES," "&," "NO," which are derived from the use of these terms on the Ouija board. Merrill said, in an interview, "The YES and NO came to be especially telling, the more I realized how important it was—not only for the poem but for my own mental balance—to remain of two minds about everything that was happening. One didn't want to be skeptical or merely credulous. Either way would have left us in reduced circumstances" (Rec 53). In another interview about the trilogy, Merrill insisted on the "doubleness of its source" and that "the point remained, to be always of two minds" (Rec 51–52). The epic (or mock-epic) range of *The Changing Light* would not be possible without this mental balancing act. Admirers of *Sandover* praise its sureness of tone, which varies from sublime to charmingly silly; and this doubleness, or openness to contradictory impulses, is basic to Merrill's sophisticated poetic manner.

There is also something defiant in Merrill's tone, which resembles Yeats's defiance in "All Souls' Night" when he asserts he has truths to tell "whereat the living mock" (Poems 230). Not only is Merrill writing poetry that may lead a reader to question the sincerity of his beliefs, but he is also writing out of a distinctly unorthodox "tradition." Within the poem, Merrill admits his discomfort with what he calls its spiritualistic "Popthink":

> all this
> Warmed-up Milton, Dante, Genesis?
> This great tradition that has come to grief
> In volumes by Blavatsky and Gurdjieff?
> (CLS 136)

In contrast, Wallace Stevens handled such material in what many would consider a more intellectually respectable manner. For example, he used occult alchemical imagery to represent the necessary fiction, the angel in the "lapis-haunted air" (WS 404) of *Notes Toward a Supreme Fiction*; and he used the imagery of a mystic marriage in *Notes* and other poems to represent the dialectic of reality and the imagination. No beliefs are implied by his use of this imagery. When Stevens uses the Yeatsian image of the polar dragon in "The Auroras of Autumn," he reminds us that it represents no "master of the maze" but the projection of an ordinary snake in an earthly glade. His alchemical marriages do not carry the portentous significance they have in the poetry of Ezra Pound and Ted Hughes. A "mystic marriage" (WS 401) in Stevens is conceived in terms of "as if":

> As if, as if, as if the disparate halves
> Of things were waiting in a betrothal known
> To none.
> (WS 464)

Yet such a complete suspension of belief in using these materials would have been impossible for Yeats, Pound, and H.D.; it would have robbed Plath's work of her unique intensity, and Merrill's trilogy would be unimaginable without it. These poets could not have written their style of poetry with their degree of conviction on the basis of the intellectual beliefs of a Stevens, who spoke approvingly of pressing away "from mysticism toward that ultimate good sense which we term civilization."[8]

Certainly Stevens himself displays the "negative capability" of the great poet when he turns away, in *The Auroras of Autumn*, from the psychic projections in the heavens to praise the "scholar of one candle" who tolerates uncertainties. Yet he forecloses the possibility of a world that transcends the human world. In the *Auroras*, the lights in the heavens are not "a spell of life, / A saying out of a cloud" as they could be for Yeats and Pound. Stevens's opinion of Yeats's spirits and the astrological speculations of *A Vision* may be inferred from his description in *Notes Toward A Supreme Fiction* of the "primitive astronomy" of a visionary "Arabian . . . With his damned hoobla-hoobla-how" (WS 383). Stevens's modernism is characterized by his skeptical and ironic sensibility. For Richard Ellmann, Helen Vendler, and many other critics, such a sensibility expresses the true spirit of modern poetry. This critical orientation helps explain Ellmann's and Vendler's attempts to sanitize Yeats's occultism by saying it was actually a form of aestheticism.

We have seen that Surette in *The Birth of Modernism* maintains that distaste for the occult and mystical has led modernist critics to interpret Pound and Eliot, for instance, as far more skeptical than they are. Surette contends that the critics undervalue the heritage of occultism because "scepticism and relativism are undoubtedly the two definitional dogmas of modern enlightened academic humanism." For example, he argues that critics have generally ignored the religious dimension of *The Waste Land* to emphasize instead the poem's place "within the Nietzschean enterprise of 'calling into question' all religious faith" and that Pound was in fact credulous about occult beliefs though skeptical about Christian ones.[9] The critical tendency Surette describes systematically reduces mystical beliefs to aesthetic positions. This skeptical relativism is of the kind Stevens defines in praising the good sense that turns away from mysticism. If one believed that "negative capability" depended on such a skeptical suspension of belief, then neither Keats, Yeats, nor Pound would have that capability. But there is another kind of skepticism that does not foreclose belief in the transcendent. Just as irony may be the protective covering of a believer as well as an agnostic, skepticism may prepare the way for belief as well as disbelief. Jeffrey Perl has analyzed this skepticism in T. S. Eliot, whom he describes as recognizing "his own irrational prejudices and those of his age" and questioning his "disbelief as well as belief."[10] (Eliot himself described his persona Eeldrop as a "sceptic, with a taste for mysticism."[11]) Eliot's description of the "demon of doubt" in his essay on Pascal describes the kind of mental flexibility that one finds in Merrill's remarks on the "YES & NO" of poetic creation. He writes that this demon is "inseparable from the spirit of belief" and that therefore the skeptic's relation to his beliefs is a "systole and diastole, [a] movement to and from, of approach and withdrawal."[12] In Eliot, skepticism is dialectically in relation with belief and the capability to be open to a transcendent faith.

Eliot is drawing on a tradition of Christian skepticism that runs through Montaigne (whose *Apology for Raimond Sebond* deeply influenced Eliot), Pierre Bayle, and Kierkegaard. This tradition recognizes that one cannot rationally verify beliefs in God or the afterlife; yet neither can one disprove them. Kierkegaard argues that, if one reaches a point of skeptical despair because no moral or religious principle can be established, there are only two outcomes, both of which involve the will rather than the reason. As Richard Popkin describes this state, "One can either *will* to doubt everything, or *will* to believe something."[13] Popkin seems to echo William James' phrase in his essay "The Will to Believe." James's thesis is that our "passional nature" may validly decide whether to doubt or believe if a proposition cannot by its nature be decided intellectually. The adventurous character of creative thinking is open to all possibilities and repudiates the will-not-to-know when one is faced by what James calls a "momentous" choice. An adventurous thinker would not risk a loss of truth because of a fear of error. James seems to echo Anselm's *credo ut intelligam* when he claims that there are "cases where a fact cannot come at all unless a preliminary faith exists in its coming." He concludes his essay with a metaphor that appeals to this spirit of an adventurous quest for truth: "We stand on a mountain pass in the midst of whirling snow and blinding mist, through which we get glimpses now and then of paths which may be deceptive. If we stand still, we shall be frozen to death. If we take the wrong road, we shall be dashed to pieces."[14] The implication is obvious: we must will to act and act on our beliefs.

In the poets examined in these chapters, we discover a will to believe and sometimes as well the return of repressed religious impulses. Merrill admits in one interview, "I must have some kind of awful religious streak just under the surface" (Rec 44), and in another he admits his occultism could be described as a "displaced religion" (70). His discomfort at this "streak" is obvious even in these brief phrases. Yet these poets have all approached—as Eliot said of Yeats—"the religious sources of poetry." They have all challenged the disbelief of the modern age. From Yeats to Merrill, Stevens's "as if" is countered by Merrill's "YES & NO," in which the yes of belief balances the no of doubt.

This receptivity to experience also characterized Sigmund Freud, who was among the great explorers of occult phenomena. Freud con-

sidered occultism, which he defined as a belief in "the real existence
of psychical forces other than the human and animal minds with
which we are familiar," as an expression of the "loss of value" society
experienced after World War I. He considered it an attempt to compensate in a spiritual world for the diminished attractiveness of
earthly existence and deplored its tendency to reimpose "the old religious faith" or the "superseded convictions of primitive peoples."[15]
Yet Freud himself would not entirely dismiss occult beliefs and remained, like many other late nineteenth-century thinkers, seriously
interested in occult phenomena. He became a member of the Society
for Psychical Research in 1911 even at the risk of embarrassing the
psychoanalytic movement. Although Peter Gay, in his *Freud: A Life for
Our Time*, virtually dismisses Freud's interest in the occult, Freud's
colleague and first biographer, Ernest Jones, devoted an entire chapter
to Freud's interest in occultism because he thought it illustrated "better than any other theme the explanation of his genius." Jones found
a key to Freud's genius in what he called his "exquisite oscillation
between scepticism and credulity."[16] In his chapter titled "Character
and Personality," he analyzed Freud's "tolerance of anxiety" and his
"plastic and mobile mind, one given to the freest speculations and
open to new and even highly improbable ideas." (Similarly, T. S. Eliot
praised William James, another member of the Society for Psychical
Research, for his "curiously charming willingness to believe anything
that seemed preposterous to the ordinary scientific mind.")[17]

Jones's chapter on Freud's occultism is an extended illustration of
this intellectual openness. Jones himself recalled Freud telling him
late-night stories about clairvoyant patients or visits from the dead,
seeming to enjoy shocking Jones with his apparent credulity and quoting Hamlet's words that "there are more things in heaven and earth
than are dreamed of in your philosophy" (3:381). Freud's "exquisite
oscillation" is found in such works as "The Uncanny" (1919), "Psycho-analysis and Telepathy" (1921), and "Dreams and Occultism"
(1932). In "The Uncanny," for example, there is no hint that uncanny
experiences have anything but a psychoanalytic explanation; but two
years later in the privately delivered paper "Psycho-analysis and Telepathy," Freud told a group of colleagues (including Ernest Jones)
about incidents that impressed him with the reality of telepathy, including a visit he made to a medium. The comments on the possible
reality of these events were made privately because he was worried,
particulary after his quarrel with Carl Jung in 1912–13, about the damage a link between occultism and psychoanalysis would do to the

latter's status as a science. In "Dreams and Occultism," he wrote that there was "a heavy weight of probability" in favor of telepathy and excused himself to Jones by saying that "finally one must show one's colors" (3:406).

Freud's admission of the reality of telepathy may seem a relatively minor endorsement of occultism compared with believing in astrological predictions or the reality of spirits. But as Freud said himself, in relating the anecdote about Saint Denis walking "quite a distance" after his decapitation, it is the first step that counts.[18] Freud knew how serious any least admission of his interest in occultism could be because "all our instinctive prepossessions" seem to be against psychoanalytic insights while occultism is "met half-way by powerful and mysterious sympathies."[19] Nevertheless, Freud was open to occultism just as he was to other beliefs that have been contemptuously dismissed—for example, that dreams are deeply meaningful.

Freud is an excellent guide to understanding occultism not simply because he was a psychoanalyst but also because he understood from the inside the thought processes of occultists. Although Ernest Jones leaves *Totem and Taboo* (1913) out of his account of Freud's writings on occultism, this work in fact best demonstrates Freud's insight into the magical thinking that constitutes occultism. For our purposes, the key chapter is the third, "Animism, Magic, and the Omnipotence of Thoughts." Animism is the belief that the world is peopled with "innumerable spiritual beings both benevolent and malignant" who control both natural phenomena and human actions. Yet animism is not merely a belief but a "system of thought, and indeed the most basic and complete system that mankind has developed" among the three systems humanity has produced: "animistic (or mythological), religious and scientific. Of these, animism, the first to be created, is perhaps the one which is most consistent and exhaustive and which gives a truly complete explanation of the nature of the universe."[20] Of course Freud believed that the scientific view of the universe is the accurate one, but he realized that it is the least appealing, whereas animism has the primitive appeal that attracts us with "powerful and mysterious sympathies." The judgment that animism is a "complete system" also relates it to occultism. Of the poets we study here, Yeats and Merrill particularly develop a systematic explanation of a universe in which human fate is entirely dependent on the actions of daemons or spirits.

Animism resembles occultism not only because it deals with the spirits of the dead (and indeed arises as a system to combat human-ity's dread of death) but also because the "technique" associated with it is magic (91). Believers in animism use magic to gain control over the spirits, thereby imposing their will on the world and even tri-umphing over death. Freud compares such magic to art because our civilization credits the "omnipotence of thought" only in "the field of art. . . . People speak with justice of the 'magic of art' and compare artists to magicians" (90). The artist draws on the primitive feelings found in animism just as the magician draws on them to demonstrate a power over spirits. But there is a second and even closer affinity between magic and art: both work through the association of ideas. For example, the destruction of a carven shape of a person will stand for the destruction of that very person, or the anointing of a knife will alleviate the pain of a wound made by the knife. In this association of ideas, Freud identifies two principles—similarity (as in the carving) and contiguity (as in the weapon); in literary art, the principles would be termed *metaphor* and *metonymy*. The artist is thus linked with the shaman, and magic with literary technique—just as an occultist would wish.

Poets of the occult, like the priests of animism, deal with primitive fears and beliefs through the magical techniques of metonymy and metaphor. For this reason, as I suggested in the Preface, occultism seems to flourish more among poets than among fiction writers. John Milton said that poetry was more "sensuous and passionate" than prose.[21] In this context, I would say that poetry is more primitive and magical, and prose fiction more skeptical and analytic. For example, in Merrill's novel *The Seraglio*, the protagonist's use of the Ouija board is clearly a sign of the deepening neurosis that leads to his self-castration. In *The Changing Light at Sandover*, occultism is not simply or skeptically regarded as a symptom because the experience is so deeply real to the Ouija board players.

On the basis of Freud's analysis in *Totem and Taboo*, the two essential characteristics of occultism seem to be a belief in a world of spirits and a belief in magic as a way to gain both knowledge of and power over this world, including the power to escape death. The crucial dif-ference between the animistic or religious world view and the scien-tific is that the latter accepts the finality of death. Freud of course prefers the scientific view, which "no longer affords any room for human omnipotence; men have acknowledged their smallness and submitted resignedly to death and to the other necessities of nature" (88). Yet the poets I discuss would consider even the finality of death an open question. Yeats expresses this belief in the omnipotence of his thoughts in "All Souls' Night":

> Such thought—such thought have I that hold it tight
> Till meditation master all its parts.
>
> (Poems 230)

This mastery allows him to envision everything from hell to heaven ("where the blessed dance"). We have seen, however, that Yeats acknowledges the unsatisfying nature of his devotion to reading "daemonic images," and indeed "All Souls' Night" ends with the ominous note that the thought Yeats holds so tightly binds him like the wrappings of a mummy. Yeats's grand pronouncements, like the revelation of "The Second Coming," are always qualified so as to show that he is not tempted for long by a claim to omnipotence or omniscience; he is too ironically aware of his own limitations. Ezra Pound glories in the role of the spiritual magus, more even than Yeats, but he too admits his ultimate powerlessness. Such admissions from these poets recall, sometimes through direct allusion, Shakespeare's Prospero breaking his staff and preparing for death.

A later generation of poets, represented by Plath, Hughes, and Merrill, are particularly haunted by Shakespeare's characterization of Prospero in *The Tempest*. As Frank Kermode was the first to observe, Shakespeare drew upon Heinrich Cornelius Agrippa's *De occulta philosophia* in his characterization of Prospero as a magus. Frances Yates places Prospero in a still wider context in arguing that the inspiration for his character was the Renaissance occultist John Dee, whose "Occult Neoplatonism," according to Ted Hughes, had a profound influence on Shakespeare.[22] D. G. James, like Yates, believes that Prospero's great renunciation of his "rough magic" is the "ending to the history of magic and the occult in Western Europe."[23] Perhaps magic and the occult were never again so widely believed in and feared. But the current of occultism continued underground in England throughout the eighteenth and nineteenth centuries, and this book shows how it has surfaced powerfully among twentieth-century poets in English.[24] If Prospero's speech does not quite carry the cultural weight that Yates and James find in it, however, it does sum up both occultism's glorious dreams and its inevitable failure to transcend the human. The attraction of the "omnipotence of thoughts" is found in Prospero's description of his powers, which includes the control of thunder and earthquake and culminates in the power over life and death: "graves at my command / Have wak'd their sleepers, op'd, and let 'em forth / By my so potent art (5.1.44–50). He resigns his powers, however, with equal conviction:

> But this rough magic
> I here abjure . . . I'll break my staff,
> Bury it certain fadoms in the earth,
> And deeper than did ever plummet sound
> I'll drown my book.
>
> (5.1.50–57)

The Tempest provides a touchstone to help us assay the poetic achievements of literary occultism. Ted Hughes's comments on *The Tempest* in his *Shakespeare and the Goddess of Complete Being* demonstrate the fascination the play can have for a poet. As the most self-conscious of the occult poets, however, James Merrill shows the sharpest insight into *The Tempest* through the references to it in *The Changing Light at Sandover*. The last chapter of this book concerns Merrill because he summarizes so brilliantly the course of literary occultism and because he understands its silliness as well as its sublimity. If poetry is magic, then the poetry of the occult is rough magic that, as Prospero learns, may threaten one's humanity. In Umberto Eco's *Foucault's Pendulum*, a character realizes just before his death by cancer that the language of occultism can metastasize like cancerous cells (567). Merrill is clearly aware of the rhetorical inflation and obscurity inherent in the overdetermined language of the occult. But his poetry is neither an implied defense of occultism, like Yeats's or H.D.'s, nor a criticism of it, like Eliot's. Nor does he draw on it as uncritically as Pound or Hughes. He both celebrates the imaginative power that modern poets have discovered within it and treats it with a sustained irony that transforms its nature. Without losing his rationality, or his humor, he believed in occultism in order to understand and use its creative power.

Occultism is a cyclic phenomenon, and the 1990s seem to be one of its highpoints, as were the 1890s. Some knowledge of its history and intellectual reputation helps one to appreciate what the occult poets make of it. A character in Eco's *Foucault's Pendulum*, remarking on the growing number of occult book shops and publishers, accounts for the phenomenon by avering that in an "age of confusion" readers will

"gobble up anything that's hermetic . . . anything that says the opposite of what they read in their books at school" (261). The number of
occult and New Age bookstores in America doubled in the 1980s;
occult titles increased tenfold for some publishers; 900 numbers offer-
ing psychic advice and occult World Wide Web pages are proliferat-
ing. The fashion for New Age books, videos, seminars, "meditation
kits," and the like is a "megatrend" for the twenty-first century.[25] Such
material draws on dozens of cultures and religions to produce a mixture of spiritualism, astrology, telepathy, divination, alchemy, and
numerous other mythical rites and occult practices. If there is a distinction between occult and New Age movements, it might be that
the New Age lacks a vision of evil and is less concerned with magical
power over people and events.[26] Eastern mysticism and Western occultism are the ingredients of these movements because they are by
definition out of the mainstream even though popular occultism may
reinforce a mainstream political ideology. Their popularity arises from
a cultural alchemy that presents age-old doctrines in versions that
seem new and entertainingly strange.

The suggestion that these movements are the result of an "age of
confusion" echoes Freud's explanation for the popularity of occultism.
A harsher version of his basic criticism of occultism appears in Theodor Adorno's "Theses against Occultism," where he states flatly that
"attraction to the occult is a symptom of the retrogression of consciousness" (7). Without a conventional belief or religion, but unable
to bear the void of unbelief, the occultist invests faith in a "pseudo-
rational" system that allows for the localization of "free-floating anx-
ieties in some definite symbolism."[27] The "little wise men, who
terrorize their clients behind their crystal balls, are toy models of the
big ones, who hold the fate of mankind in their hands." Occultism
thus resembles totalitarian systems, which foster dependence on themselves and rationalize painful social conditions. In capitalist society,
occultism offers a way out of the organizational net of constant de-
mands and challenges of a society ruled by a "hierarchical business
set up."[28] People may thus be given an illusory sense that there is a
way to escape the net. An occult system, such as W. B. Yeats's theory
of the phases of the moon in *A Vision*, is as deterministic as a modern
bureaucratic political system because one's character is determined by
these phases. Yet Yeats expounds this system to give his readers the
illusion that they somehow understand (if not control) the workings
of the system. (He said *A Vision* allowed him "to hold in a single
thought reality and justice" [25].) According to Adorno, occult sys-

tems, such as the astrology features in newspapers, give to society's victims an impression that there is some hidden meaning that makes sense of their lives, "while at the same time corroborating that this sense can neither be sought in the realm of the human nor can properly be grasped by humans." This ungraspable quality, presented as axiomatic, protects occultism from genuinely rational criticism. From Adorno's perspective, occultism "enhances disillusion by surrendering the idea of the human even more completely to blind nature than it actually is."[29] Yeats's *A Vision* illustrates the tendencies Adorno criticizes in its exposition of the phases of the moon and in Yeats's claim, when expounding a particularly abstruse doctrine about cyclic recurrence, that "this cannot yet be understood" (137).

Christian thinkers criticize occultism on much the same ground as philosophical skeptics. T. S. Eliot might have considered the recovery of an old or primitive faith, even if it wore an occult mask, better than no faith at all. But in *Four Quartets* he dismissed occultist claims to "converse with spirits" or "riddle the inevitable / With playing cards" as merely "Pastimes and drugs, and features of the press" (CPP 135–36). His explanation for their popularity resembles Freud's in that such beliefs are especially important "when there is distress of nations" (136). W. H. Auden is another Christian poet who considered occultism a fraud. Beyond his amusing dismissal of Yeats's occultism as "Southern Californian," he had a serious objection that it deflected concern away from real-world psychological problems.[30] The medium in the Auden-Kallman opera *Elegy for Young Lovers*, who was modeled on Yeats's wife, is psychologically ill; and her cure coincides with the disappearance of her visions. Nevertheless, Auden himself became fascinated with the occult, especially in later life, and it is not so surprising as some critics thought to see him play the role of spirit control in Merrill's *Changing Light*.[31] Eliot also had an enduring fascination with occultism despite his explicit rejection of it.

As Freud considered occult beliefs a reaction to the disillusion caused by World War I, Eliot in *Four Quartets* believed it was a reaction to the moral confusion caused by World War II. The violent deaths of millions of people in war intensified interest in spiritualism and the occult. For example, H.D. said that she communicated in 1945 with deceased Royal Air Force pilots through table tapping.[32] Yet the enormous popularity of occultism in the final decades of the nineteenth and twentieth centuries has come at times of relative stability. Freud's explanation for occultism's appeal even to a stable society was that, in an age of great scientific achievement, occultism was "a part of the tentative approach to the great revolution toward which we are heading." This was to be a peaceful revolution based on human enlightenment, and even Freud (by 1921) was willing to allow occult studies a place in the avant-garde.[33]

To approach the challenge of a new age, the Society for Psychical Research was founded in England in 1882 and focused research into spiritual phenomena among the century's intellectual elite, including Freud, William James, the future prime minister of England A. J. Balfour, and scientists such as Sir Oliver Lodge, an eminent physicist who demonstrated the existence of radio waves.[34] The society exposed many frauds, including H. P. Blavatsky's claims to be receiving spirit messages at her headquarters in Madras, India. Yet when the society could not disprove a psychic phenomenon, it seemed to substantiate it; and some members, Oliver Lodge, for example, went on to write books (in Lodge's case, after the death of his son in World War I) that attempted to reconcile scientific and spiritual phenomena through psychic research.

This intellectual interest was reflected on the popular level by the growth of spiritualist societies. Spiritualism has been distinguished from occultism because it is not concerned with secret knowledge or magical powers. The spiritualists generally offered contact with a beloved son or grandmother rather than a magus like Blavatsky's Mahatma Koot Hoomi or Yeats's Leo Africanus. In her book *Radical Spirits*, Ann Braude emphasizes the movement's egalitarian elements: "Spiritualists believed that there was nothing mysterious about spirit communication, that it required no special knowledge, and that it was equally accessible to everybody" (178–79). Nevertheless, from the time of Blavatsky's visit to America in 1873, spiritualism and theosophy seemed to grow stronger together. The spiritualist movement began in America in 1848 and soon spread to England, which had a national spiritualist organization by 1891. The American medium D. D. Home was particularly famous for his well-attested (yet fraudulent) levitations. Robert Browning's portrait of Home in "Mr. Sludge, 'The Medium'" (*Dramatis Personae*, 1864) shows how spiritualism spoke to and shamelessly used religious doubts:

> As for religion—why, I served it, sir!
> I'll stick to that! With my *phenomena*
> I had the atheist sprawling on his back,
> Propped up Saint Paul, or, at least, Swedenborg!
> (664–67)

Although "New Age" is a current term, it also expresses the feeling in the second half of the nineteenth century that vast material and spiritual changes were imminent, a sense heightened in the 1890s by the simple fact that a new century would soon begin.

It was also in America that Blavatsky and her supporters founded the Theosophical Society in 1875. Plagiarizing on a grand scale, she published compendiums of occult lore in *Isis Unveiled* (1877) and *The Secret Doctrine* (1888). Her work focused the occult movement because it brought together so many of its obscure religious and mythological sources. If spiritualism supplied access to the spirit world; and occultism, the rituals to control its power—then Theosophy supplied the intellectual background (such as it was) for a New Age. Blavatsky's work, for example, helped inspire Yeats to found the Hermetic Society in Dublin in 1886. Her *Secret Doctrine* particularly excited Yeats because, as Northrop Frye wrote, "Whatever else it may be, [it is] a very remarkable essay on the morphology of symbols. " Frye noted in 1963, as Braude has more recently, that spiritualism and occultism provided an area where women could assert their individuality and authority. Frye defends Blavatsky's "charlatanism" as "less a reflection on her than on the age that compelled her to express herself in such devious ways."[35] Even Ezra Pound, in a surprising juxtaposition, defended Blavatsky as an occultist Gertrude Stein, "dealing in Upanishads rather than Picassos. and knowing, nacherly, more of the subject than rural yokels [of] 1900 or 1880."[36] Despite his condescension, Pound also sees Blavatsky's value as a pioneer.

Her talent for synthesizing myths and symbols from world mythology accounts for her impact on poets and thinkers in Germany as well as England. Yeats's trust in Blavatsky was not destroyed when the Society for Psychical Research discovered that her shrine in India, where objects materialized mysteriously, actually contained secret panels and that spirit messages from the Mahatmas did not drop from thin air but were lowered on threads from cracks in the ceiling. She ignored such charges or brazened them out. Her answer to plagiarism charges was that the mental vibrations of the Mahatmas, who dictated to her, and those of the plagiarized authors had unfortunately crossed. In 1887, Yeats joined Blavatsky's Theosophical Lodge in London, which she established after being forced by the scandal to leave India. Immediately after the scandal in 1884, she also founded the Theosophical Society in Germany, where her influence was as catalytic as it was in America and where her notions of the spiritual evolution of a superior Aryan race, as well as the secrecy and elitism natural to her movement, fit developing political tendencies.[37] Blavatsky's impact in France, however, was relatively slight, perhaps because occultism had already been so thoroughly absorbed into the literary tradition.

Midcentury France had at least three major writers who drew upon the themes and sources of occultism and powerfully influenced English writers: Honoré de Balzac, Gérard de Nerval, and Victor Hugo. In the trilogy he called *Le livre mystique* (1831–35), Balzac created characters who are initiates into occult mysteries. *Louis Lambert* dramatizes the tension between the seer and the artist which so obsessed Yeats. In Balzac's Swedenborgian novel, *Séraphita*, the title character seems a woman to men and a man to women because s/he is a spiritual being whose ascension at the fable's close gives mystical powers to the two lovers of Séraphita. In *Le voyage en Orient* (1851), Nerval drew from his studies of Pythagorean, Orphic, and Gnostic texts to create personae like Balzac's, who are occult initiates but who feel less conflict in their roles than Louis Lambert. In the sonnets that deeply impressed poets as different as T. S. Eliot and Robert Duncan, *Les chimères* (1854), Nerval used cabalistic and alchemical imagery to develop a masterpiece of occult poetry in which even the obscurity, as in *The Waste Land*, contributes to the poem's mysterious appeal.[38]

Victor Hugo not only drew on occultism in his poetry but also became deeply engaged in occult practices in the 1850s, when spiritualism was beginning to develop in France. A friend introduced him to "table turning" while he and his family were in exile on the Island of Jersey. Hugo was not only troubled by his political exile but also was still grieving for the death of his daughter Léopoldine in 1843. During a séance in Jersey, he believed that he contacted his lost daughter and communicated with her through raps on a table in a code developed for the occasion. (Adèle Hugo kept a record of these sessions in *Journal de l'exil*.) These sessions remind one more of James Merrill's Ouija experiments in *The Changing Light at Sandover* than of Mrs. Yeats's automatic writing, because the spirits of Moses, Mohammed, Shakespeare, and many other famous men flocked to Hugo as they did to Merrill. In particular, Hugo's *Les contemplations* and *Dieu*, which were both written during the period in Jersey, drew upon these séances. The spirits not only gave Hugo "metaphors for poetry," as in Yeats, but the content of long philosophical poems, as in Merrill's *Changing Light*.

The heritage of these writers influenced the mystical tone of French Symbolist poets such as Mallarmé and Verlaine and, through the Symbolists, the poets of England. Edmund Wilson thus entitled his study of early-twentieth-century English literature, *Axel's Castle*, after the play by August de Villiers de l'Isle-Adam about a Rosicrucian initiate who seemed to Wilson the representative type of the modern artist. As William York Tindall observed, a simple description of the play's hero shows why it so deeply affected Yeats. Count Axël lives "in exile from the world in his Gothical castle in the Black Forest, pursues Rosicrucian studies, attempts the 'Great Work' of alchemy, practices magic," all the while speaking "eloquently of Hermes Trismegistus, Paracelsus, and the Magi."[39] More even than Louis Lambert, he is the model of the true artist/seer and never more so than when he and his beloved (also a Rosicrucian) commit suicide rather than consummate their love because the experience could never equal its intensity in their imaginations. Frank Kermode believed that occultism went ✓ "hand in hand with the Romantic movement in France" and that the modern conception of the image as "autotelic, liberated from discourse, with coincident form and meaning" could not have developed from Romantic and Symbolist aesthetics without "a rapprochement between poet and occultist. Magic came, in an age of science, to the defence of poetry."[40]

Surette's *The Birth of Modernism* describes the way the interpretation of modernism by Wilson, Tindall, and Kermode, which emphasized its occult and Symbolist heritage, was displaced by the views of critics who neglected or ignored this heritage. Surette argues that this "scholarly phobia of the occult" has also obscured the significance of the "non-canonical" nineteenth-century occult writers—Blavatsky, Eugène Aroux, Abbé Barruel, Friedrich Creuzer, Artur de Gobineau, Edouard Schuré—who deeply influenced the understanding of myth inherited by modernist authors. They conceived of myth as the record of encounters with the spirit world rather than as the embodiment of the cultural ideas or the consciousness of a people. Surette believes that critics have also ignored the way Friedrich Nietzsche's *Birth of Tragedy* was given an occult interpretation by the English writers G. R. S. Mead, A. R. Orage, and Allen Upward, who in turn influenced the conception of myth that Pound, Yeats, and Eliot inherited. Surette's reinterpretation of these minor but influential writers enforces Kermode's sense of the closeness between the Symbolist and occult movements.

The work that introduced T. S. Eliot to French Symbolism interpreted the movement as a mystical as well as an aesthetic doctrine. Arthur Symons's *The Symbolist Movement in Literature* (1899) held that symbolism began when "God named the world into being."[41] His opening essays discussed Nerval and Villiers de l'Isle-Adam. He summarizes some key elements in occultism as he praises Nerval for realizing the "central secret of the mystics" (17) transmitted through Pythagoras and the Smaragdine Tablet of Hermes down through Jakob Böhme and Emanuel Swedenborg. Symons observes of Villiers de l'Isle-Adam that "questions of magic began, at an early age, to preoccupy him, and, from the first wild experiment of *Isis* to the deliberate summing up of *Axël*, the 'occult' world finds its way into most of his pages" (23).

Symons dedicated *The Symbolist Movement* to Yeats because the Irish poet was the "chief representative of that movement in our country" (xix). Yeats transmitted the occult/symbolist movement that Symons describes to some of the greatest poets of the twentieth century, and the strongest link in this transmission is between Yeats and Ezra Pound. Yeats met his mistress Olivia Shakespear in 1895 through occult circles in London. She wrote plays on occult subjects with Yeats's friend Florence Farr, who was also a member of the Order of the Golden Dawn; and she was the friend of Dion Fortune, who reorganized the Golden Dawn after Blavatsky's death. Shakespear also translated a seventeenth-century occult text that Yeats and Pound were to study when they spent the winters together at Stone Cottage.[42] She introduced Yeats to Pound in 1909. Shakespear's daughter Dorothy became the wife of Ezra Pound, and Dorothy's close friend Georgie Hyde-Lees became Yeats's wife.

Pound's interest in the occult, however, predated his meeting with Yeats. In writing of Pound's influence on her in 1905–7, H. D. recalled an "avalanche of Ibsen, Maeterlinck, Shaw, Yogi books, Swedenborg, William Morris, Balzac's *Séraphita*, Rossetti and the rest of them."[43] Pound's introduction to occultism may have come from the concert pianist Katherine Ruth Heyman, whom he met and fell in love with around 1904. She was known as the "high priestess of the Scriabin cult," who not only performed the Russian composer's music but proselytized his mystical beliefs.[44] When Pound met Olivia Shakespear in London, he was thus already well read in the spiritualism that absorbed both her and her daughter. In his correspondence with Dorothy, he is informed enough to suggest esoteric texts to her and to explain the nature of "real symbolism, Cabala, genesis of symbols."[45] They both admired Madame Blavatsky's former secretary, G. R. S. Mead, and explored his works together.[46] Although Pound and Yeats were both serious students of occultism, they were, however, drawn to different elements of it.

T. S. Eliot was a critic of Yeats's occultism as early as 1919, and despite some decidedly occult elements in his poetry, his importance to the history of literary occultism lies in his criticism of it as a dangerous heresy. Although he was undoubtedly dogmatic when he dismissed Yeats's spiritual world as "the wrong spiritual world," his disparagement of the occultist's "reckless desire for the absolute" raises an issue that Yeats himself knew was central to his art and life. Eliot's concern with occultism is central not only to *The Waste Land* but also to his later poems and plays, as he searched for a language that could adequately approach what he called "the religious sources of poetry."[47] Despite his formal disapproval of it, Eliot could appreciate occultism in modern poetry as a sincere attempt to revive a religious sensibility.

H.D. was at once both more serious and more playful than Ezra Pound with occultist properties. Like Yeats, she believed in ghosts and tried to contact them through séances. She was more sophisticated, however, than either Yeats or Pound about the occultism's psychoanalytic dimension. Pound disapproved of her consultations with Freud, but through them H.D. gained a deeper sense of her role as a poet, or maker of symbols, which strengthened her later poetry. Although her use of archetypal symbols might seem to dispose her to Jung's theories, she in fact distrusted Jung and admired Freud as a modern "alchemist." Her insights into Freud help demonstrate why Freud is a better guide than Jung to the significance of occultism. Freud helped H.D. understand the meaning of her visions and their characteristic symbolism without inhibiting her ability to use them poetically. Her debate with Freud ultimately strengthened her belief in a spiritual world and psychic powers. Her occultism was an "alchemy of the word" that never limited its importance to poetic symbol making. Unlike Pound, who simply drew heavily upon occult beliefs and symbols, both H.D. and Yeats may be described as true occultists.

As the major source of occultism in modern poetry in English, Yeats's theory and example inspired the generation that included Pound, H.D., and Eliot. The second generation of poets to feel Yeats's influence were Robert Duncan, Ted Hughes, Sylvia Plath, and James Merrill. Although they possessed a post-Freudian sophistication about religion and myth, they all embraced occultism in some of their most ambitious poems.

As Robert Duncan tells us in his essay "Occult Matters," he grew up in a family that belonged to a group that was an American analogue of Yeats's Golden Dawn. Duncan's understanding of occultism helped him to appreciate H.D.'s career in his *The H.D. Book*, a work-in-progress that spanned the years 1966–81. Duncan not only was one of the first critics to recognize the importance of H.D.'s later works, especially *Trilogy*, but also perceptively argued that H.D. was never merely an "imagist" poet. The image associated with the movement of 1912, which charged language with "sensory impression," was to Duncan "generically different" from the image Pound, Eliot, and H.D. developed in their later poetry. Duncan notes that imagism arose at a time when Pound was learning from Yeats and Mead and that the "movement" was not an "isolated literary affectation or strategic front but the first phase of certain generative ideas in poetry," which included a renaissance of theosophical ideas which "brought back the matter of old mystery cults."[48] Duncan did not consider himself, as he did Yeats and H.D., an occultist. In speaking of the "matter" of the mystery cults, he meant that occultism provides a "matter of poetry" much as Arthurian lore provides the "matter of Britain." No poet uses this "matter" with greater confidence, and sidesteps so gracefully the problem of poetry and belief, as Robert Duncan. Having been raised in a family to whom indeed occultism was a family heritage, he uses its doctrines and motifs with unprecedented assurance.

Ted Hughes also learned occult lore, and even the use of magic crystals and tarot cards, during his childhood in an isolated region of Yorkshire. His study of anthropology at Cambridge University introduced him to what Duncan calls "the matter of old mystery cults," which no modern poet has exploited more fully than Hughes. His reading of Jung enlarged his understanding of these cults and deepened his knowledge of alchemy. Although Sylvia Plath was always fascinated by tarot cards, her interest in occultism was limited until she met Hughes. When she married him, she wrote to her mother that she and her husband would become "a team better than Mr. and Mrs. Yeats—he being a competent astrologist, reading horoscopes, and me being a tarot-pack reader, and, when we have enough money, a crystal-gazer." (The two poets hoped to contact Yeats's spirit on a trip to Ireland in 1962.)[49] They employed the Ouija board as well as tarot cards and crystal gazing to provide subjects and inspiration for their poetry. But occultism eventually played an even larger and more ominous role in their lives, especially in Plath's case, as it came to mean more to them than a source of poetic exercises. Compared with Plath's, Hughes's occultism seems tame; but his cultural reach is much wider, making them an interesting study in contrasts as poets of the occult. Hughes's poetry also contrasts revealingly with Duncan's because, despite occultism being as natural to his background as it was to Duncan's, Hughes succumbs to the temptation that Duncan avoids of taking on the rhetorically inflated role of a magus.

James Merrill's occultism in *The Changing Light at Sandover* is unique because he not only uses occult doctrines and devices but also self-consciously meditates within his poetry on the implications of this use. Although Yeats is also self-conscious about his occultism, he does not make this awareness a major theme of a poem as Merrill does in his embarrassed admission about working in a "great tradition that has come to grief." Although he admits within his trilogy that treating an occult subject is an "error," he values his errors for the reason that Robert Duncan gives in "The Truth and Life of Myth." In poetry as in Freudian dream analysis, nothing can be dismissed or mistaken: "Mistakes themselves mark the insistence of meanings in other meanings. . . . The analyst has redeemed as revelation of what he calls the subconscious or the Id all the despised and exploded errors from the dormitories of the soul that men had dismissed as irrational" (47). The "occult" is the "irrational," and Duncan and Merrill want to redeem whatever they find of merit within it—that which makes it the "matter of poetry." Despite the passage of more than a century, Merrill's sense of the way occultism may free the imagination resembles Robert Browning's. Although Browning's "Mr. Sludge, 'The Medium'" devastates the medium's pretensions, the poet recognizes that the medium and the poet resemble one another. Mr. Sludge is quite sincere when he says:

> I've told my lie,
> And seen truth follow, marvels none of mine;
> All was not cheating, sir, I'm positive!
> . . . .
> I tell you, sir, in one sense, I believe
> Nothing at all,—that everybody can,
> Will, and does cheat: but in another sense
> . . . .
> That every cheat's inspired, and every lie
> Quick with a germ of truth.
>   (1309–25)

Mr. Sludge compares himself as a medium with the artist who, for example, makes up fictions about Greeks doing impossible feats before Troy; and Browning seems at least sympathetic to Sludge's argument that the medium's revelations also contain a measure of "creativeness and godlike craft!" (1469). Merrill takes this comparison of the medium and the poet into the modern era by arguing that both figures liberate the unconscious mind. Although he admits that exploring the occult world is a probable "error," a trip into what Eliot called the "wrong spiritual world," this transgression into unexplored areas of the poet's psyche may be the essence of poetry. As Yeats wrote,

> My rhymes more than their rhyming tell
> Of things discovered in the deep,
> Where only body's laid asleep.
>
> (Poems 50)

Daemonic Images:
From W. B. Yeats to
Ezra Pound

I was lost in that region a cabbalistic manuscript
... had warned me of; astray upon the Path of the
Chameleon, upon Hodos Chameliontos.
—W. B. Yeats, *The Trembling of the Veil*

1 W. B. Yeats is a classic case of a writer who turns to occultism as a compensation for a lost traditional faith. Although his family was Protestant, his father was a skeptical rationalist deeply influenced by John Stuart Mill, Charles Darwin, and Auguste Comte. In his *Reveries over Childhood and Youth*, Yeats wrote, "Father's unbelief had set me thinking about the evidences of religion and I weighed the matter perpetually with great anxiety, for I did not think I could live without religion" (Auto 15). Occultism was so crucial to Yeats's resistance to his father's intellectual power that he dated his break from that influence from the time he began to study "psychical research and mystical philosophy" (59).

Because his grandfather was a Church of Ireland minister, Yeats might have adhered to Protestantism if he could not do without religion, or he might have converted to Roman Catholicism, like his fellow poets Ernest Dowson, Lionel Johnson, and Oscar Wilde. But embracing occultism allowed the son to defy the father, much as spiritualism in Ann Braude's view helped women to defy a male world.[1] For Yeats, occultism represented a total break not only with his father's rationality but also with his respectability. In 1894 J. B. Yeats described his son's occultism as "hot and credulous." In 1915 he wrote to him with characteristic sharpness: "A mystic is a man who believes what he likes to believe and makes a system of it and plumes himself on doing so."[2] This warning, which New Agers might ponder, did not dissuade Yeats from writing *A Vision*, a book easily as strange as one of Blavatsky's volumes.

Northrop Frye's attempt to make Blavatsky more respectable by viewing her works as aesthetic rather than mystical productions ("a morphology of symbols") is echoed in the criticism of Yeats's occultism. Early critics, for example, David Daiches and Yvor Winters, deplored Yeats's occultism, and W. H. Auden and George Orwell ridiculed it.[3] Allen Tate and R. P. Blackmur intelligently speculated on the problems Yeats's occultism posed for the poet's readers, but less serious critics simply ignored those problems; and none put the issue as acutely as J. B. Yeats when he said of the poet, "I must feel to my core that he has a vigorous character and an intellect clear as crystal. Otherwise I am soon tired of his melodious verses."[4] Richard Ellmann and Helen Vendler set a new stage in Yeats studies by interpreting his mysticism as in reality an aesthetic vision. In 1963, Vendler frankly stated that she interpreted *A Vision* in terms of "aesthetic experience" rather than "esoteric doctrine." Her purpose of defending Yeats's late plays from the "charge of incomprehensibility" is achieved at the cost of simplifying them in terms of ordinary and not visionary experience.[5] Similarly, Ellmann claims of Yeats's occultism that Yeats seems credulous only for an "artistic effect."[6] It may be true that one responds to Yeats's system as an aesthetic rather than a religious construct, but one cannot assume that Yeats, or any creator of an occult system or religion, was solely engaged in an aesthetic creation.

Poets hope to be heretical and provocative, but their scholars ("learned, respectable bald heads," as Yeats called them [Poems 140]) want them to be as learned and respectable as they are. In *The Identity of Yeats* (1964), Ellmann dissociates Yeats from a disreputable occultism when he questions whether we should in fact place Yeats in the occult tradition, or rather, as it was "renamed by one critic, the Platonic tradition" (xvi). The critic is F. A. C. Wilson, in his *Yeats's Iconography* (1960), who himself tried to make Yeats seem more respectable by equating his occultism with Platonism. Ellmann goes further than Wilson, however, in dissociating Yeats from occultism. He first uses Wilson's research to equate Yeats's occultism with Platonism, then cites the poet's claims in "The Tower" that he mocks Plato's and Plotinus' thought (Poems 198) to prove that he rejected Platonism and—therefore—occultism. Ellmann avoids the question of whether Platonism can really be equated with occultism; and he disregards the possibility that Yeats's emotional renunciation of Plotinus and Plato merely expresses a revulsion to aging rather than a considered intellectual belief.

Ellmann also uses sleight of hand when he cites Yeats's breaks with Madame Blavatsky and MacGregor Mathers of the Order of the Golden Dawn as evidence that Yeats was not a true believer; for it was Blavatsky who dismissed Yeats from the Theosophical Lodge for magical experiments that she thought might hurt the reputation even of her organization. The incidents in the winter of 1889–90 which led to his ouster are described by one of Blavatsky's biographers. Yeats was directing a paranormal research committee in which the researchers tried to resurrect a flower from its ashes with the help of an air pump and, in another experiment, tried to move a needle in a glass case through psychokinesis.[7] Because these experiments reflected badly on the Theosophical movement, Blavatsky told Mead to demand Yeats's resignation.

Similarly, Yeats's quarrel with Mathers in 1900 was strictly internecine strife among occultists, who quarrel just like orthodox believers. Occultists are continually distinguishing themselves from others who seem to them betrayers of the movement's true spirit. After Blavatsky died, for example, the Theosophists immediately broke into two groups over the issue of who was truly channeling the insights of Mahatma Koot Hoomi. Yeats's quarrel with Mathers was in no sense a break with the Order of the Golden Dawn itself. The order finally did split in 1903 into one group led by Yeats and Algernon Blackwood, another led by A. E. Waite, which included Charles Williams and Evelyn Underhill.[8] It is true that Yeats could adopt a skeptical pose. When he wanted to avoid arguments or win over a skeptical audience, he would say his occultism gave him "stylistic arrangements of experience" (Vision 25) or "metaphors for poetry" (Vision 8). (Even so, we should recall that in the Romantic and symbolist tradition, "metaphor" was in itself magical.)[9] We will see a similar strategy of selective and ironic disavowal in James Merrill. Yeats never implied that occultism gave him nothing more than figures of speech.

Against Yeats's many self-defensive statements, one must balance such declarations as "I believe in the practice and philosophy of what we have agreed to call magic, in what I must call the evocation of spirits."[10] (Part 2 of "The Tower" is a powerful example of such evocation.) There is also the evidence of Yeats's forty years of membership in the Golden Dawn. He reached the highest degree a mere mortal can attain, Adeptus Minor, and was known as Frater D.E.D.I. (Demon Est Deus Inversus, or the Devil is the reverse of God). A series of books introduced a new phase of Yeats criticism in which occultism is granted its central importance in his poetic career: G. M. Harper's *Yeats's Golden Dawn* (1974), M. C. Flannery's *Yeats and Magic* (1977), James Olney's *The Rhizome and the Flower* (1980), Graham Hough's *The Mystery Religion of W. B. Yeats* (1984), Kathleen Raine's *Yeats the Initiate* (1986), and Frank Kinahan's *Yeats, Folklore, and Occultism* (1988).

Although they are a welcome balance to the aesthetic interpretation of Yeats's occultism, some of these works are weakened by an implausible attempt to make occultism respectable. Olney's elaborate argument that there is an "alternative" Western philosophical tradition, stemming from the pre-Socratic philosophers and shared by both Yeats and Jung, in effect robs Yeats's beliefs of their unorthodoxy and rebelliousness. As Wilson tries to remake Yeats's occultism into Neoplatonism, so Olney remakes it into a "Heraclitian" or a kind of "perennial philosophy"—all wisdom, little ritual, and no magic. Kathleen Raine goes to the extreme of welcoming Yeats's occultism as a tradition that only now can be understood: "What seemed to many at the time (comparing Yeats with Eliot) his weakness, his willful obscurantism, we can now see as a source of his strength and of his lucidity in the New Age we are entering" (5). On the contrary, I believe that Yeats's obscurity, or even his crankiness, is an undeniable and engaging element of his work which cannot be wished or explained away.

The exception within this new trend in Yeats criticism is Graham Hough's lectures on Yeats's "mystery religion," which argue that Yeats's poetic heritage is too complicated "to find a single uniting thread or a single essential idea at the root of it" (8). As he acknowledges, Hough's understanding of occultism builds on an early study of literary occultism, Denis Saurat's *Literature and the Occult Tradition* (1930). Saurat contends that the tradition's miscellaneous and raffish qualities help account for its attraction: "Occultism is the place of refuge of all vanquished religions and philosophies. It contains, for the poets, in contrast to the orthodox culture of their time, a whole world of artistic possibilities" (62). Hough distrusts the word *tradition*, however, because it means "something handed down." It may therefore suggest something rather orthodox which could imply "a strain of sectarian self-righteousness that is as alien to Yeats as it is to the spirit of poetry" (8). Hough borrows from Wittgenstein the term *family resemblances* to suggest the kind of affinity among the unorthodox, countertraditional doctrines and beliefs that make up occultism. Writing one of the finest explorations of Yeats's "magic," R. P. Blackmur also stresses the tentative, fragmentary quality of Yeats's ideas when he describes the "dogmas of magic" as heresies that cannot be accepted except on their own authority as a "fragmentary insight" with "only the momentary unity of association."[11] Occult doctrines, like archaic sculptures or the *Corpus Hermeticum* itself, seem to derive their fascination and authority from their fragmentary nature. To deprive occultism of its heretical status, or worse yet make it into the new mainstream, would rob it of its glamour. As Yeats knew, occultism conveys little or nothing if it does not shock, surprise or puzzle the mind.

For Yeats, occultism in poetry was above all a search for secret wisdom and power through the agency of "daemonic images." In his autobiography *The Trembling of the Veil* (1922), his description of his occult investigations always involves the contemplation or transference from mind to mind of some elemental symbol such as the sun, the moon, or dancing figures. In the section entitled "Hodos Chameliontos," or "The Path of the Chameleon," he speaks of exercises in which "image called up image in an endless procession" (181). Yeats's poetic goal was to unify these images into "some articulation of the Image" (184). The word *image* is capitalized to indicate one that is charged with archetypal and magical power. In his "Vorticism" essay, Pound also capitalizes the word when it refers to such a unifying image—in this case, specifically a sphere. In describing Dante's *Paradiso*, Pound says that the "form of sphere above sphere, the varying reaches of light, the minutiae of pearls upon foreheads, all these are parts of the Image" (GB 86). Yeats's poem "Byzantium" is about an attempt at creating such a unifying image. Although the poem concludes with the image of the sea, the "images that yet / Fresh images beget" emerge from it and overwhelm the poet with their phantasmagoria. It seems that, for Yeats, occult images are inherently fragmentary and produce only the "half-read wisdom of daemonic images" (Poems 206).

Because he assumed that the modern poet could not articulate an image as fully as could the poet of Dante's era, Yeats recognized as much as Eliot or Pound did the poetic validity of the fragmented image. Nevertheless, Yeats disdained Eliot's and Pound's conviction that "the imagery of common life" could be raised to "first intensity."[12] He condescendingly described Eliot's poetry as the "accurate record of the relevant facts."[13] Why write about rat's feet on broken glass or newspapers in vacant lots when one could write about images that are inherently powerful, such as golden birds, rough beasts, and starlit domes? Yet the divergence between Yeats and Eliot is not so great if one compares Yeats with the poet of "Ash Wednesday" rather than of early lyrics like "Preludes." Although Pound and Eliot revolutionized poetic imagery, their later works show that they did not abandon traditional images such as the rose.

In the case of the imagery of Pound and Yeats (Eliot's imagery is considered in Chapter 3), Pound's modernism and his invention of imagism has led critics to make an excessively sharp distinction between their poetic techniques. Pound himself, it is true, was the first to make this distinction between Yeats and the modernist poets. In 1913, he explained that the poetic theory of Ford Madox Ford (Hueffer) was in "diametric opposition" to Yeats's: "Mr. Yeats has been subjective; believes in the glamour and associations which hang near the words. . . . Mr. Hueffer believes in an exact rendering of things."[14] This distinction is relevant to Pound's famous description of Yeats in the 1948 *Pisan Cantos* (Canto 83) "dawdling" around Notre Dame Cathedral in Paris, "in search of whatever" and pausing "to admire the symbol / with Notre Dame standing inside it" (*Cantos* 528). As a symbolist poet, Yeats is "in search" of correspondences in the outer world with an inner reality. The "whatever" in Yeats's mind might be the archetype of the Mother goddess or a theory about the medieval age. The reality of the cathedral is meaningless to Yeats unless it interprets or corresponds to an inner, spiritual reality. Pound's implied criticism is that the "whatever" discovered by "dawdling" is not precise enough to achieve an imagist "exact rendering of things." He suspects that Yeats imposes rather than discovers poetic form. The criticism is extended by relating Yeats to the Gothic structure of Notre Dame Cathedral (Ford thought Yeats was a great poet but a "gargoyle"). The passage goes on to contrast this symbol with some carved mermaids in the Santa Maria Dei Miracoli in Venice, where the stone carvings of mermaids or sirens by Tullio Romano have the naturalness and precision Pound also praises in Canto 76 (460).

Critics of both Pound and Yeats have developed this contrast of the two poets' conceptions of the symbolic to a misleading extreme that has obscured their mutual fascination with daemonic images. Commenting on the Notre Dame passage, Richard Ellmann maintained that in Pound's poetics "symbols interfered with experience instead of letting experience coalesce into its natural pattern." This distinction leads Ellmann to a perceptive but excessively sharp contrast of the poets. According to Ellmann, Pound believed the poet's task was "to probe, experiment, accumulate until things—some things at any rate—shone with their intrinsic light. . . . Pound's view of experience is as 'improvisatory,' as informalist, as Yeats's is formalist."[15] Pound's best critics agree with Ellmann. Hugh Kenner's reading of the Notre Dame passage also contrasts Pound's "exact rendering" of experience with Yeats's symbolism, which "infected much of his verse with significance imposed on materials by an effort of will."[16] Donald Davie wrote that Kenner's remark "makes the essential point" and added, "Yeats can see Notre Dame as an artifact, a presence created in masonry and sculpture, only inside the symbol, only for the sake of what it answers to in him, not for what it is in itself."[17]

This contrast of an imagist with a symbolist corresponds to the contrast critics also make between Pound's focus on political and economic reality and Yeats's on occultism and the afterlife. My argument, however, is that (1) even though Pound might ridicule aspects of occultism, such as "psychical research," he respected its "wisdom tradition" and sense of "true symbolism"; and (2) that even if Pound lost interest in occult matters with the growth of his Confucianism and economic interests, that interest revived at the time of the *Pisan Cantos* and especially when he was at St. Elizabeths.[18] These arguments are developed in Chapter 2, whereas here our concern is with how Yeats's and Pound's shared interest in occultism is reflected in their imagery.

The images of the gyre and the sphere in Yeats's poetry have been thoroughly discussed by his critics. Yeats himself expounded on these forms in Book 1 of *A Vision*. The sphere represents all of reality and may also symbolize "changeless eternity." Gyres or vortices are formed out of "circles diminishing," which generate the constant change of ordinary reality (Vision 67–68). One finds this image cluster in "Meditations in Time of Civil War," where the sphere and its gyres are implied in the reference to the Primum Mobile which makes "the very owls in circles move" (Poems 203). The rotation of the great sphere is diminishing into (as well as causing) the gyres of the birds. The gyres may also be caused by the loosening of the circle of perfection. In "The Second Coming," the "widening gyre" of the falcon's flight symbolizes the approaching dispersal of the unity of a civilization. In *A Vision*, Yeats explains how all things fulfill their allotted places in the unfolding of the universe: the "final" cycle is the Platonic Year, with the smaller cycles that constitute the whirling gyres. In "Chosen," he symbolizes his final meditative state as the condition where his persona struggles "on the track / Of the whirling Zodiac" and finds fulfillment when the "Zodiac is changed into a sphere" (Poems 272–73). But even in *A Vision*, Yeats can say little about the sphere; for "no man can say" what might occur when "the sphere, the unique intervenes" (263). Richard Ellmann notes perceptively that Yeats only occasionally mentions the sphere in his verse "because it had come to seem a remoter ideal" than it had been in his youth, when he often used its equivalent symbol, the rose.[19]

This symbolic complex of gyre and sphere is as natural to Ezra Pound's poetic universe as it is to Yeats's. Pound first used the gyre image in the 1908 poem "Plotinus." In a Browningesque monologue, Plotinus speaks as one who has traveled through the "node of things" and through "the vortex of the cone" to become "an atom on creation's throne" (CEP 36). Pound's many references to Plotinus in the *Cantos* have encouraged some scholars to place Pound, as they have Yeats, in a Neoplatonic tradition. But Plotinus appears in this poem, as he does in Yeats, as a master of occult knowledge rather than a founder of a school of philosophy. The vortex image, which was to become so important to Pound in 1915, is indeed found in Plotinus's *Enneads*.[20] But Pound's own footnote to the poem cites another occult master as a source, not precisely of the vortex image but of the Yeatsian "cone" image: "The 'cone' is I presume the 'Vritta' whirl-pool, vortex-ring of the Yogi's cosmogony. The sonnet tho an accurate record of sensation and no mere (not) theorizing is in close accord with a certain Hindoo teacher whose name I have not yet found" (CEP 296). Pound's note implies that he is something of a master himself, that Plotinus's experience corresponds to his own.

Pound thus credits both Western and Eastern thinkers as the source of his image, employing the cultural synthesizing that was common to Yeats and indeed all the occultists of the time. Blavatsky wrote in *The Secret Doctrine*, "The law of Vortical movement of primary matter, is one of the oldest conceptions of Greek philosophy, whose first historical sages were nearly all Initiates of the Mysteries. The Greeks had it from the Egyptians, and the latter from the Chaldeans, who had been the pupils of Brahmins of the esoteric school" (119). Pound's own source cited in his footnotes to "Plotinus" confirms the universality of vortices and "vorticism" by passing over all of the above to include a "Hindoo teacher" he chose not to identify.

Although Eva Hesse suggests that the teacher is Patanjali,[21] he is actually a "Yogi Ramacharaka." Pound himself recommended Ramacharaka's series of "little blue Yoga books" to William French during his studies with him at St. Elizabeths Hospital in the 1950s.[22] These seem to be the same "series of Yoga books" Pound once gave to Hilda Doolittle—as described in her *End to Torment* (23). In his *Advanced Course in Yogi Philosophy and Oriental Occultism*, Ramacharaka uses the word *vritta* precisely as Pound uses it in his note to "Plotinus": "Mind-substance in Sanscrit is called 'Chitta,' and a wave in the *Chitta* (which wave is the combination of Mind and Energy) is called 'Vritta,' which is akin to what we call a 'thought.' ... *Vritta*, when literally translated means 'a whirlpool or eddy in the mind,' which is exactly what a thought really is."[23] This is the same "'Vritta' whirl-pool, vortex-ring" of Pound's note, and the Yogi is also a source for Pound's conception of the atom: "The Yogi teaching is that the 'ultimate atom' of Matter is really a 'little whirlpool' *of* ether."[24] We will see this vortical movement in Canto 2.

As "Plotinus" offers Pound's first poetic use of the vortex image, "Histrion" offers an early version of the sphere, in which alchemical imagery emphasizes its perfection: "'Tis as in midmost us there glows a sphere / Translucent, molten gold"(CEP 71). "Before Sleep" contains lines descriptive of gyres that are almost as geometric as something out of *A Vision*; "A Song of the Degrees" mentions "the golden disc." But the most important use of gyre and sphere before the *Cantos* occurs in the poem "Phanopoeia," with its "swirl of light" that follows the poet/alchemist while a "silver ball forms in [his] hand." As the sphere takes on the celestial color of the sapphire, the "swirling sphere has opened / and you are caught up to the skies" (Personae 167–68). In the use of the sphere imagery, as in many other instances of shared occult interests, Pound is far freer than Yeats in using the sacred symbols.

When Pound illustrated the effect of the imagination's form-making power, he chose a Yeatsian image of a rose, a "rose in the steel dust" (Canto 74:449). As he grew dissatisfied with the "static images" of the imagist movement, he sought a term for a "patterned" or "dynamic" image and so developed the name of the movement meant to supersede imagism: vorticism. A vortex was not only a dynamic image but also a creator of form. In his 1914 essay "Vorticism," he spoke of the vorticist image and vorticist form as producing "equations" for the emotions. In his "I Gather the Limbs of Osiris," the metaphor is also scientific when he imagines that "words are like great hollow cones of steel. ... charged with a force like electricity, or, rather, radiating a force " (34). In his "Cavalcanti," although he compared "magnetisms that take form" to a rose, it is a rose that a "magnet makes in the iron filings" (154). Hugh Kenner and Donald Davie cite Pound's scientific terminology to stress his modernity and to correlate his art with the world of forms and energies explained by the physical sciences.[25]

But Pound's theory of poetic form is as mystical as it is scientific. For example, in the same passage in which he describes vorticist "equations," he also describes "analytical geometry" as "the thrones and dominations that rule over form and recurrence. . . . In like manner are great works of art lords over fact, over race-long recurrent moods." (The use of the words *race* and *moods* suggests Yeats's direct influence.) He represents the equation for a circle as "the universal, existing in perfection, in freedom from space and time" (GB 91–92). When he depicts poetic forms as magnetisms, he regrets that we cannot conceive them, as a medieval philosopher would have, as forces "that border the visible" in a "world full of enchantments" (LE 154).

Pound's use of so many Yeatsian images is as much the result of the poets' common use of occult symbols as it is of the older poet's influence. Yeats's rotating cones, gyres, and spheres are related to Pound's vortex, and Yeats's conviction that Pythagorean number ratios control aesthetic form recalls Pound's "equations." The link between a "scientific" and a "mystical" view of form may be found in the kind of images the Theosophists used to express spiritual experiences. The kind of magnetic or vibration patterns Pound refers to were discussed by the Theosophists Annie Besant and C. W. Leadbeater in *Thought-Forms* (1901). Just as magnetism or vibrations can generate geometric patterns in sand or dust, so can our thoughts generate patterns in "etheric matter." Examples of such patterns in *Thought-Forms* are a variety of vortices, gyres, and spheres (Figure 1).

Whether Pound was influenced directly by Theosophical thought-forms is not crucial to my argument because the influence of such ideas was widely diffused. For example, the influence of the English Theosophists returned to England through Kandinsky's "On the Spiritual in Art." Besant's and Leadbeater's *Thought-Forms* influenced Kandinsky's theory that emotions were vibrations that can be expressed visually. Kandinsky's ideas reached the vorticists through Edward Wadsworth's translation of "On the Spiritual," which appeared in BLAST No. 1 (1914). Pound borrowed from Kandinsky freely and without acknowledgment for his BLAST statement (entitled "Vortex") about vorticist art. His formulation that the vorticist uses the "primary pigment" of a particular art ("IF SOUND, TO MUSIC; IF FORMED WORDS, TO LITERATURE; . . . COLOUR IN POSITION, TO PAINTING") is lifted from Kandinsky's description of art's "eternal language": "in literature—

Figure 1. Thought-Forms, from Annie Besant and C. W. Leadbeater, *Thought-Forms*, 1901.

the word, in music—sound, in sculpture—volume, in architecture—line, in painting—color."[26] Similarly, when Pound writes of a Gaudier-Brzeska sculpture that the "spherical triangle" is a "central life-form" of vorticist artists, he is borrowing Kandinsky's conception of the triangle as a symbol of "spiritual life" (GB 137).

In addition to painting and sculpture, photography was influenced by such Theosophical concepts. The most important photographer in this manner is the artist Pound referred to (in a presentation copy of his *Gaudier-Brzeska*) as "Magister," Alvin Langdon Coburn.[27] Coburn's photographs, whether of urban scenes or portraits of famous men, emphasized circular and spherical forms—turning a view of St. Paul's dome, for example, into something as mysterious and evocative as Yeats's "Byzantium" (Figure 2). His "Pythagorean" conception of the

Figure 2. A. L. Coburn, *The Embankment, London*, 1906; St. Paul's Cathedral is in the background. Courtesy of George Eastman House.

"spiritual significance of a geometrical truth" is expressed in his pictures of familiar yet transfigured objects (54). Another important photographer was the Italian Anton Giulio Bargaglia, who wrote in his *Fotodinamismo futurista* (1911) that he wanted to express reality as "vibration" (13). Bargaglia influenced futurist painters Giacomo Balla and Gino Severini. In turn, the vortical designs in paintings like Balla's *Spherical Expansion of Light* influenced profoundly the English vorticists. In the vorticist journal BLAST, however, Wyndham Lewis characterized the Italian futurists as childishly fascinated with modern technology, obscuring futurism's occult background much as the occultism of Pound's imagism and vorticism has been obscured. Unlike Lewis, Pound acknowledged Kandinsky's importance as an artist, but he also obscured his debt to Kandinsky when he praised a Renaissance

Figure 3. Constantin Brancusi, *Sculpture for the Blind: "Beginning of the World,"* 1916. Courtesy of the Philadelphia Museum of Art: Louise and Walter Arensberg Collection; © 1995 Artists Rights Society (ARS), New York/ADAGP, Paris.

alchemist, John Heydon, as having discovered "long before our present day theorists . . . the joys of pure form . . . inorganic, geometrical form" (GB 127).[28]

Pound held to Lewis's view of vorticism as a purely English development relatively uninfluenced by futurism or Kandinskian mysticism. As he said of vorticism in his essay on Brancusi (1921), "the metaphysic of Brancusi is outside and unrelated to vorticist manners of thinking" (LE 444). What Pound means by Brancusi's "metaphysic" is implied in the following description of the sculptor's ambition of "getting all the forms into one form; this is as long as any Buddhist's contemplation of the divine love." Of Brancusi's ovoids (Figure 3), he writes that "one might consider them as master-keys to the world of form—not 'his' world of form, but as much as he has found of 'the' world of form" (443).

Pound is not so esoteric in his interpretation of Brancusi as is Yeats, who wrote that the "ovoids of bright steel / Hammered and polished by Brancusi's hand" were magical evocations of spirits (Poems 571).

(As sculptures such as "The Sorceress" show, Brancusi could indeed think of his works as totemic magical figures.)[29] Pound, in contrast, explains the effects of these ovoids by employing his mathematical/ mystical conception of form in his Brancusi essay: "Brancusi is meditating upon pure form free from all terrestrial gravitation; form as free in its own life as the form of the analytic geometers; and the measure of his success in this experiment . . . is that from some angles at least the ovoid does come to life and appear ready to levitate" (LE 444). The occult and mystical aspects of Brancusi's art, which Pound cautiously refers to, were ignored by art critics before Radu Varia's *Brancusi* (1986). Varia exaggerates occultism's influence by improbably suggesting that Brancusi may have been an initiate of a secret society, but he does clearly demonstrate the impact on Brancusi of his early reading of Blavatsky (a French translation in 1904) and how it influenced his lifelong treatment of spherical and spiral motifs.[30] The Brancusi drawings reproduced by Varia include spiral designs (Figure 4) that resemble the diagrams in Yeats's *A Vision*.

Brancusi used such designs, as did Yeats, to express the secret patterns of human destiny. Varia's explanation of why Brancusi experimented with the ovoid form after 1909 is expressed in virtually Yeatsian terms because the two artists share a theosophical vocabulary: "The ideal representation of the sphere—its absolute form— plunged into the vibrant current of the world, is caught by tormenting, deforming life forces. . . . The sphere is to being as the ovoid is to existence. It was inevitable that Brancusi, preoccupied only by pure forms, should be captivated by the ovoid, with its self-evident cosmological flavor, rather than by the sphere, which belongs to the domain of abstraction" (137). This distinction between the two forms is like Yeats's distinction between the gyre and the sphere. The sphere was approached and contemplated through the gyre and ovoid forms because, as Ellmann wrote, it was a "remoter ideal."

As in Yeats's poetry, there is a natural relation between the sphere and the vortex image in Pound's. The earliest use of the vortex or cone image in the *Cantos* appeared in a canceled 1915 draft in which, as James Longenbach writes, Pound "flaunts his visionary prowess" as he sits at the "low point of a cone" with his thoughts reaching beyond the heavens.[31] Although this explicitly Yeatsian passage was not retained, *The Cantos* explore similarly geometric imagery as Pound searches for what he described in a 1927 letter to his father as "the divine or permanent world" within the seeming chaos of nature and history.[32]

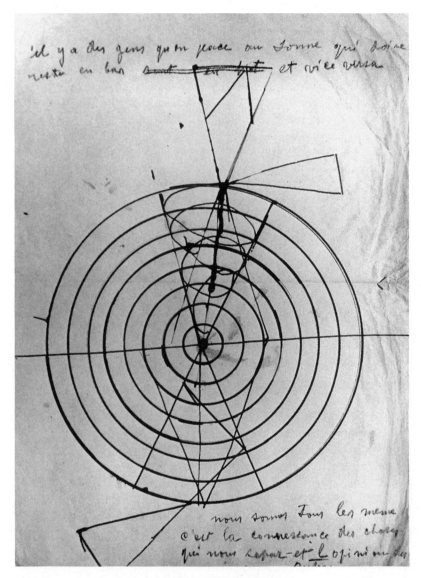

Figure 4. Constantin Brancusi, *The Pyramid of Fate*, 1925. © 1995 Artists Rights Society (ARS), New York/ADAGP, Paris.

Yeats believed that this quest for a divine world was parallel to his own. In "A Packet for Ezra Pound," the preface to the revised edition of *A Vision*, he correlated his speculations with Pound's in *The Cantos*. Richard Ellmann believes that this dedication of *A Vision* to Pound was "half a jest" and a defiance of Pound's anticipated disapproval of Yeats's investigation of the afterlife and of hidden historical patterns.[33] Leon Surette thinks otherwise: that the "Packet" is meant to identify the similarities in their poetic work. He argues that both *A Vision* and *The Cantos* are "metahistorical works" that reflect on the true history of the world as revealed in various obscure texts and in the careers of mythical and historical figures.[34] Yeats's theory that the phases of the moon determine human fate is of course alien to Pound. But his conception of historical cycles and archetypal personalities is not unlike Pound's in *The Cantos*. Yeats wrote "A Packet" in 1928 while he and his wife were visiting the Pounds in Rapallo. His comments in it demonstrate that Pound had described to him the same conception of *The Cantos* as a search for the "divine world" as in the 1927 letter to the elder Pound. Yeats described this conception as a fugue in which "fixed elements," which Pound compared with the signs of the Zodiac, and "archetypal persons" are intertwined with rapidly changing "modern events" (Vision 5). Leaving these archetypal persons until the next chapter, we look now at how the fixed and changing elements are seen in *The Cantos*'s symbolism of sphere and vortex.

Canto 1 begins with the prospect of a sea voyage through "spiteful Neptune," but soon we see "waves taking form" in Canto 2: "And So-shu churned in the sea, So-shu also, / using the long moon for a churn-stick" (9). There has been much controversy about this So-shu, but this entity might best be regarded as a demiurge who churns the waves to make a generative vortex.[35] In Indian myth, the sea is churned to form the elixir of life, generating at the same time the constellations from chaos. Traditional illustrations of the Mahabharata (one of the works Pound read aloud to Yeats at Stone Cottage in 1913–14) show a serpent emblem of spiral motion turning the world axis.[36] In Canto 25, the waves become crystal and form into a crystal sphere: "and saw the waves taking form as crystal" (119). Earlier, the reader has heard of "the NOUS, the ineffable crystal" (Canto 40:201) and seen in the *Pisan Cantos* "Serenely in the crystal jet / the bright ball that the fountain tosses " (Canto 76:449). The phrase "no cloud, but the crystal body" (76/457) is related to the phrases "the sphere moving crystal, fluid," "the crystalline, as inverse of water" (457), and "within the crystal, went up swift as Thetis" (459). Even in the Pisan prison camp, Pound wrote that "the crystal can be weighed in the hand / formal and passing within the sphere" (459) to suggest that the perfection of the sphere is still achievable. At one point in Canto 76, he says of an experience in the "gemmed field": "nor is this yet *atasal*" [divine union] (457–58). But by the Canto's conclusion he uses a repeated image of a butterfly escaping his tent through the smoke hole (461, 462) to suggest at least the possibility of the soul's flight (*psyche*, or "soul," is also a Greek word for "butterfly"). Both here and in Canto 92, the butterfly is the Dantean image (*Purgatorio*, 10.125) of the soul seeking the vision of God. In a remarkably condensed image, the butterfly flies through a "smoke hole" that recalls the scene of the alchemical laboratory in Goethe's *Faust* (Part 2).[37]

Canto 29 links Yeats, who appears as the "Lusty Juventus," to the gyre and sphere imagery. Juventus describes the "replica," or mental image, of Yeats's system of interpenetrating cones, which represent the dynamics both of the mind and of historical cycles:

> He said: "Ten thousand years before now ...
> Or he said: "Passing into the point of the cone
> You begin by making the replica.
> Thus Lusty Juventus, in September.
> (Cantos 142)

The ideas of the eternally young Juventus are declaimed in a setting that contrasts his vitality to the moribund society that ignores him— indicated by references to the homes of a church elder and the funeral director. (The still-vital old man of this passage, who says "'What I know, I have known'" [142] seems, however, to be G. R. S. Mead.)[38] Juventus explicates ideas that are crucial both to Pound and to Yeats. For example, he teaches that " 'matter is the lightest of all things ... whirled in the aether'" and that " 'light also proceeds from the eye'" (143), which recalls Pound's description in "Cavalcanti" of "the radiant world where one thought cuts through another with clean edge, a world of moving energies" ... (LE 154). The conclusion of Juventus's disquisition describes the effect of a mystical sphere in the same terms that Pound uses in "Phanopoeia":

> "In the globe over my head
> "Twenty feet in diameter, thirty feet in diameter
> "Glassy, the glaring surface—
> "There are many reflections
> "So that one may watch them turning and moving."
> (Cantos 143)

Although, in the specification of the exact diameter of the enlarging sphere, there may be some satire on Yeats's pedantic precision, this passage and the entire Canto is a tribute to Yeats's ageless vi-

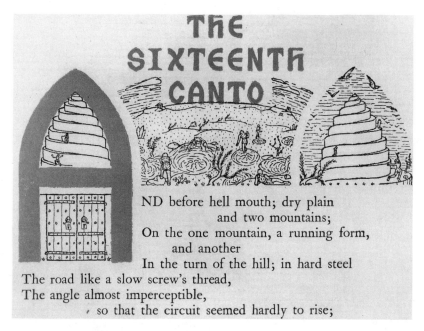

THE SIXTEENTH CANTO

ND before hell mouth; dry plain
    and two mountains;
On the one mountain, a running form,
    and another
    In the turn of the hill; in hard steel
The road like a slow screw's thread,
The angle almost imperceptible,
    ⸱ so that the circuit seemed hardly to rise;

Figure 5. Henry Strater, Illustration for Pound's Canto 16, from *A Draft of XVI Cantos,* 1925. Courtesy of Cornell University Library, Rare and Manuscript Collections.

tality. Even though Juventus is apparently in the "September" of his years, he is more vital than Arnaut, the other major poet in this Canto. "Arnaut" is a satiric portrait of T. S. Eliot, with whom Pound visited the Provençal castle of Excideuil in 1919. Though Arnaut is also associated with spiral imagery, Pound implies that he is unable to grasp its significance. He stands before "the wave pattern cut in the stone / Spire-top alevel the well-curb," but all he has to say is, "I am afraid of the life after death" (Cantos 145). A photograph of the wave pattern, reproduced in Hugh Kenner's *The Pound Era* (337), stands for the kind of elemental image, like the spire-top and tower of the castle, that Yeats and Pound are quick to recognize. Arnaut, to the contrary, with no apparent understanding of the Yeatsian cycles of the soul, is preoccupied with the fear of death. We see a similarly favorable judgment on Yeats's vitality and perceptiveness in Canto 113. Like Yeats, Pound uses the image of the gyre or spiral not only as a general symbol of spiritual development but also to indicate his own spiritual progress. The gyre is a Yeatsian "winding stair" in the opening of Canto 16, especially if we see it in context with Henry Strater's illustration of the Canto in the

1925 *A Draft of XVI Cantos* (Figure 5). As in Dante, the ascent from hell is by a spiral path.

A spiral flight out of a spiritual hell also occurs in the late Cantos. Amid references to Chinese, Manichean, and Mithraic religious rites, Pound in Canto 90 describes his release from despair through the agency of a feminine creative force.[39] This force is named Isis Kuanon in a double reference to the Egyptian goddess Isis and the Chinese Buddhist goddess of mercy Kuan-Yin. The refrain of the following passage, "m'elevasti" (you have raised me), is based on Dante's grateful acknowledgement to Beatrice in Canto 1 of the *Paradiso* (75): "*mi levasti*" (you raised me). In Canto 90, Pound's Beatrice is referred to by the Latin word for a prophetess, *sibylla*:

> Sibylla,
> from under the rubble heap
> m'elevasti . . .
> out of Erebus, the deep-lying
> from the wind under the earth,
> m'elevasti . . .
> from the cusp of the moon,
> m'elevasti. . . .
> (Cantos 606)

On the surface of these beautiful lines, nothing suggests the spiral nature of the ascent from the "deep-lying" hell. Yet the spiral pattern is inherent in the experience narrated, even though it is not expressed as explicitly as it might have been by Yeats. The pattern becomes clearer near the end of the Canto, when the spiral path is marked out amid references to the freeing of two characters from the Greek underworld, Tyro and Alcmene, who together with the knights (*i cavalieri*) referred to in the *Purgatorio* (14:109) ascend in a "crystal funnel of air" (Cantos 608). The ascent is paralleled by the movement of the "blue serpent," which glides from its "rock pool." Pound uses the serpent image much as Yeats does in "The Poet Pleads with the Elemental Powers." Yeats's persona laments that the serpent who guards the pole or pivot of the universe is unable to guard his Beloved: "The Polar Dragon slept, / His heavy rings uncoiled from glimmering deep to deep" (Poems 72). In Canto 91, however, the intervention of the Sibylla enables the viper and blue serpent to stir into new life. The following passage from the Canto represents a similar vitalizing force through the union of earth and sky: "The natrix glides sapphire into the rock-pool. / NUTT overarching" (616). "NUTT" is the Egyptian goddess Nut, whose body stretches above the earth in an arc from horizon to horizon. The two lines in Pound thus describe the serpentine swirl of the rock-pool surmounted by the hemisphere of the heavens: an emblem of gyre and overarching sphere that again reveals the natural relation of these symbols.[40]

The imagery of vortex and sphere also pervades *Rock-Drill, Thrones de los Cantares* (1959), and *Drafts and Fragments of Cantos CX–CXVII* (1969). In Canto 106, Pound returns to the spiral ascent of his goddesses and queens. Selena, goddess of the moon, and Arsinoe, an Egyptian Queen,[41] are set amid imagery that implies this ascent: "jasmine twines over capitols [*sic*] . . . So late did queens rise into heaven" (Cantos 755). A more explicit spiral pattern than the twirling jasmine appears a few lines later in a passage that asserts the creativeness of the poetic mind. Pound's moonlight prefigures the coming solar revelation in the power of the mind ("God's eye") to perceive beauty and meaning. The moon's reflected light, imagined as the goddess Selena, reveals the "wave-swirl" in the sea, the proportions of colonnades and trees, and the beauty of a ritual dance ("Xoroi"):

> Selena, foam on the wave-swirl
> > Out of gold light flooding the peristyle
> > Trees open in Paros,
> > > White feet as Carrara's whiteness
> In Xoroi.
> > God's eye art 'ou.
>
> > > > (755)

Cantos 91 and 106 reprise the imagery of "the sphere moving crystal, fluid" that had earlier achieved fullest expression in Canto 76. Canto 91 begins with the poet invoking an alchemical "body of light [to] come forth / from the body of fire" (Cantos 610). The poet is rewarded by the appearance of "The GREAT CRYSTAL," with the "Crystal waves weaving together toward the gt / healing" (611), where "healing" carries its root meaning "to make whole"—in terms of the imagery, to join the solar and lunar aspects of humanity. In Canto 106 of Pound's final volume *Drafts and Fragments* (1969), he characterizes this union of sun and moon as "that great acorn of light bulging outward" (755), where the lunar and earthly acorn reflects the solar and transcendent light. In later Cantos, the image is referred to simply as "the ball of fire" (108:764), but its culmination occurs in Canto 116:

> I have brought the great ball of crystal;
> who can lift it?
> Can you enter the great acorn of light?
> (795)

The reference here is to the Cantos themselves, as several critics have noted; but it must also be to the vision of coherence Pound has discovered throughout his poem and which he believes is valid for his readers as well, if only they can follow him: "These concepts the human mind has attained. / To make Cosmos—" (795).

Pound's increasing use of occult imagery and ritual in the late Cantos brought his poetics still closer to those of Yeats. So it is fitting that in *Drafts and Fragments* he withdraws the criticism of Yeats made in the Notre Dame passage of Canto 83 of the *Pisan Cantos*. To understand the context of this retraction in Canto 113, we need to see how characteristic the whole Canto is of Pound's later poetic style. The Canto opens with an image of the sun moving through the twelve signs of the zodiac: "Thru the 12 Houses of Heaven . . . Pater Helios turning" (Cantos 786). This Canto examines the poet's restless mind ("the mind as Ixion, unstill, ever turning") within this context of Yeatsian cyclic movement. To those who follow "Pater Helios" into the light the poet says, "God's eye art 'ou, do not surrender perception" (113:790). But ignorance of everything from religious ritual to civic responsibility is threatening this perception: "'that kind of ignorance' said the old priest to Yeats / (in a railway train) 'is spreading every day from the schools'" (789). In Canto 113, Yeats's perception stands against this ignorance. Once again Yeats notices the symbol, but all that matters now is that he has been perceptive enough to notice it. The line about Yeats is framed by a reference to Plotinus ("the body is inside the soul—") and one to Mithraic rites ("the bull by the force that is in him—") and preceded by light imagery that helps us understand the significance of the symbol Yeats saw. The poet who noted the symbol, whatever it was, has demonstrated the perceptiveness of one who was preeminently "God's eye":

> the lifting and folding brightness
> the darkness shattered,
> the fragment.
> That Yeats noted the symbol over that portico.
> (89)

Forrest Read writes that this passage "reverses the spoof of *Pisan LXXXIII*," but he does not develop the implications of this reversal for Pound's late poetry.[42] The passage, with its reference to Plotinus, asserts the priority of the spiritual over the physical. The body is significant only as the manifestation of the soul, just as the portico is significant only because of the symbol that surmounts it. If this interpretation is correct, it indeed reverses Pound's spoof on Yeats admiring a "symbol / with Notre Dame standing inside it." Could Pound be saying that Yeats was right in valuing the symbolic power of the Cathedral over—in Donald Davie's phrase—"what it is in itself"? There is a similar emphasis on the primacy of the spiritual over the material in an allusion to the Na Khi ritual in Canto 112: "without ²Mùan ¹bpö / no reality" (Cantos 784). Without the concept, there is no way to perceive reality. "What it is in itself" is nothing at all. The passage from Canto 113 is too fragmentary to support the argument that Pound has adopted Yeats's view of the relationship of the object and its symbol. Nevertheless, Pound clearly praises Yeats as a poet who renews sacred symbols, like those over the portico, and who is aware of "the lifting and folding brightness." As Pound puts it in the lines that precede his final reference to Yeats in this Canto, both poets have their minds "set on that light / saffron, emerald, / seeping" (Cantos 789).

The complex of occult images represented by the gyre and sphere gave both Pound and Yeats the means of expressing their sense of a divine pattern in the world, one in which conflicts are alchemically resolved. Until he "tried to write Paradise" (Cantos, 120:803) in the late Cantos, Pound was more inclined than Yeats to believe that the "great crystal" was attainable. In Canto 116, Pound weighs his achievement as Yeats had in "Man and the Echo," but Pound seems to give more weight to the possibilities of the "one clear view" when he writes that he has "brought the great ball of crystal." Yeats understood better than Pound the burden of expressing the "half-read wisdom of daemonic images." Pound never outgrew Yeats as a poetic master. Despite the originality of his imagist poetry, which helped modern poetry to focus on ordinary experience, he shared with Yeats an obsession with images that are signs of a richer, hidden reality. Both Yeats and Pound reached the stage where they could say with Shakespeare's Prospero that they were ready to drown their book and think of death. As Prospero tells the audience in the Epilogue to *The Tempest*:

"Now my charms are all o'erthrown,
And what strength I have's mine own,
Which is most faint."

(1–3).

In contrast to Pound, however, Yeats always understood that the revelations are ever fragmentary and that we must return to the faint strength of human perceptions. The exultation of "Now I know!" is always followed by the darkness dropping again, and the daemonic images give only "half-read wisdom." Pound expresses this realization only after the humiliations described in the *Pisan Cantos* and the despair of the late Cantos. And even in the late Cantos there is an element of dogmatic assertion in Pound's belief that he has brought the "great crystal" into consciousness. Yeats established for modern literature the role of the poet as prophet or magus of occult wisdom. But it was Pound who played that role to the hilt. The consequences of this role for Pound and his poetry are the subject of Chapter 2.

Ezra Pound
as Magus

O Sages standing in God's holy fire
. . . .
. . . be the singing masters of my soul.
—W. B. Yeats, "Sailing to Byzantium"

We have seen that the poetry of both Yeats and Pound drew upon the "daemonic images" of occultism. Although Yeats directly influenced Pound's treatment of the image, the similarity in their poetry was more the indirect result of their sharing in this stock of images. The conception of the poet as a magus is inherent in this imagery. Like the magi of old, the poet, for Yeats and Pound, is one who can "read the signs" and transmit to initiates the secret wisdom incomprehensible to "shallow wits" (Yeats, Poems 207).

In considering how Pound and Yeats differ in what they took from the mélange of doctrines that makes up occultism, one might say that Pound tended to follow G. R. S. Mead's strain and Yeats, Blavatsky's more exotic one. Mead founded the Quest Society in 1909 in part to distance himself from his former association with Blavatsky. He felt about the Theosophists as A. E. Waite felt about the Order of the Golden Dawn in 1903 when he wrote it was "capable of a mystical instead of an occult construction." Mead was contending with members who, like Yeats, argued that it must "remain a Magical Order."[1] Mead claimed never to have "preached the Mahatma-gospel . . . and its revelations. I had believed that 'theosophy' proper meant the wisdom-element in the great religions and philosophies of the world"[2] The distinction is crucial to understanding Ezra Pound's interest in occultism and distinguishing it from Yeats's. Pound's skeptical remarks about Yeats's occultism, for example, are directed at Yeats's naïveté about séances and "spooks," as when he wrote about his stay with Yeats at Stone Cottage in 1913–14: "Yeats will amuse me part of the time and bore me to death with psychical research the rest."[3] Pound did not write, as Ellmann has claimed, that Yeats would bore him by discussing the "occult." The term *psychical research* referred to Yeats's search, of which even Madame Blavatsky disapproved, for evidence of an afterlife.[4]

The "psychical research" bored him but not the "wisdom-element" in the authors Yeats was reading at the time: Paracelsus, Agrippa, and Swedenborg. Pound was intensely interested in the correlation Yeats found between the Fenollosa Noh plays and spiritualism. As Pound wrote of the occult elements in these plays, "Some will be annoyed at a form of psychology which is, in the West, relegated to spiritistic séances. There is, however, no doubt that such psychology exists."[5] Here he uses the relatively new word *psychology* in a way that blurred the distinction (as Freud had complained) between a rigorous exploration of the psyche and "psychical research." He also used it lecturing before Mead's Quest Society, which became Chapter 5 of *The Spirit of Romance*, titled "Psychology and the Troubadours." His future wife, Dorothy Shakespear, suggested playfully about the lecture, "Say you're a re-incarnation so you *know*." She then added with genuine seriousness, "Are you? do you?" To Dorothy, Pound could also be quite serious about such ideas. Writing to her about a friend who had committed suicide, he implied that the friend was so pure that she had escaped the wheel of reincarnation and entered straight into Buddhahood: "M. is by now a small, fat, brown god sitting in a huge water-lily.... Said image may sound ridiculous, but it is a great comfort to one, and is so unanswerably true that I don't dare mention it to anyone else."[6] He used the image of the babe "sitting in the lotus" in "Post Mortem Conspectu" (Personae 78).[7]

In his Quest Society lecture on the troubadours, Pound spoke of the mysticism that underlies not only Provençal poetry but all literature: "I believe in a sort of permanent basis in humanity, that is to say, I believe that Greek myth arose when someone having passed through delightful psychic experience tried to communicate it to others" (SR 92). The term *delightful* protects Pound from seeming too credulous about psychic experience, as he stresses its delight rather than its revelatory power. He says that such myths may be considered "aesthetically" or "you may probe deeper." The chapter was not, as James Wilhelm believes, an "aberration" in Pound's study of romance lit-

erature but an indication of a major line of his early poetic development.[8] The essay is an exciting jumble of speculations on Dante, Greek
poetry, Spinoza, "ascetic yoga," and the troubadour's lady as "a sort
of *mantram*" (SR 97). There are also impassioned statements about our
"kinship to the vital universe" and a "universe of fluid force," with
below it "the germinal universe of wood alive, of stone alive" (92).
But even these speculations, Pound tells us in his excitement, may
have to be revised: "A recent lecture by Mr. Mead on Simon Magus
has opened my mind to a number of new possibilities" (91). He here
glimpses what he records in Canto 91 about the magician Simon Magus and his mistress Helen of Tyre as a type of artist and muse.[9] It is
a legend similar to the one Yeats tells in his story "The Tables of the
Law," about a beautiful young virgin discovered in a brothel.

These "new possibilities," Pound thought, had to be sorted out before he could embark on his *Cantos*. When he began spending his
winters with Yeats in Stone Cottage, he not only learned from Yeats's
occult studies but also introduced Yeats to some works he himself had
discovered, such as Lodovico Sinistrari's nineteenth-century treatise
De Daemonialitate, et Incubis et Succubis. James Longenbach's *Stone Cottage* shows how these winters with Yeats reinforced Pound's interest
in the occult. Longenbach concludes that occultism was important to
Pound because it suggested a way of enhancing visionary power (as
seen in his letter to Dorothy Shakespear) and confirming an aristo-
cratic status for what Mead called the "initiate in Secret knowledge."
Occultism, as Longenbach writes, "provides the artist with an esoteric
language and practice that distinguishes him from the rest of humanity." He shows that the early Cantos, with their record of visionary
experiences and places "full of spirits," are deeply influenced by
Yeats's occultism.[10]

But Yeatsian occultism of course first appears in Pound's early lyrics, especially in the use of a persona who seeks or possesses mysterious spiritual power. However critical he was of Yeats's interest in
magical practices, Pound was intensely interested in the conception of
the poet as a magician or alchemist. In Yeats such a persona may be
termed a *magus*. The Greek word *magos* denotes both a magician and
member of a priestly caste that understands occult arts. The "wise
men" of the Gospel of Matthew were astrologers from the East,
though later Christian tradition made them seem more respectable by
calling them "three kings." Yeats thought that the Theosophists and
members of the Golden Dawn were descended "from the same stock
of Magi."[11] In his early poetry, spiritual questers such as the Wander-

ing Aengus, King Goll, and Fergus find that melancholy, estrangement and even madness accompany whatever wisdom they acquire. His definitive characterization of such questers after esoteric wisdom appears in "The Magi." They are the "pale unsatisfied ones" who are perpetually "hoping to find once more" (Poems 126) the intensity of a new revelation. In Yeats, the search for occult knowledge is curiously like the search for faith in a Christian poet like T. S. Eliot. Although there are moments of insight and fulfillment, the emphasis seems to be on the dark night of doubt and spiritual barrenness that precedes such moments.

In the dialogue poem "Ego Dominus Tuus," Ille (who Pound said was really "Willy" Yeats)[12] invokes a master who he hopes will interpret for him the "magical shapes" (gyres and spheres, no doubt) that he is tracing in the sands and so "disclose / All that I seek" (Poems 162). The poem expresses the desire for such knowledge—not, as we will find so often in Pound's work, the satisfaction of having understood it. The drive to make the "magical shapes" is described as an "unconquerable delusion" (160), and it seems likely that the characters written in the sand will be washed away before they are interpreted. In a companion poem to "Ego Dominus Tuus," "The Phases of the Moon," the spiritual master Michael Robartes scorns the poet in his tower for discovering only "mere images" (Poems 163) and refuses to grant him the wisdom he seeks. Although "mere" has the archaic sense of "pure," in Robartes's mouth it carries the modern sense that the poet is "merely" a seeker of images—and will not achieve the wisdom the poet fondly hopes images bring. As the sixty-year old man of "Among School Children" knows, images "break hearts" (Poems 217). The one relatively full portrait of a magus in Yeats's poetry is that of Ribh, the strange Christian monk who discourses on pre-Christian Hermetic thought. In "Supernatural Songs," Ribh discourses on Hermetic theories of the Trinity, Swedenborgean ideas on sex among spirits, astrological notions of human fate, Yeatsian historical theories, and a teaching that hatred of God can lead one to God which comes straight from one of Mrs. Yeats's ghostly "communicators." In "Ribh in Ecstasy" the magus claims "My soul had found / All happiness in its own cause or ground" (Poems 285), but the sequence ends with the admission that "Hermits upon Mount Meru or Everest" finally know only the "desolation of reality" (289).

Although such moments of fulfillment are necessarily brief, magi like Ribh are nevertheless driven to seek them. In "The Second Coming," the reader of the apocalyptic signs cries, "Now I know," thanks to his vision of the "image out of *Spiritus Mundi*" (Poems 187)—even though the darkness has already dropped. Yeats learned that his revelations could come only through "mere images." In "Nineteen Hundred and Nineteen," he is "satisfied" with comparing the soul with a swan because the image allows the soul to see a mirrored "image of its state" (Poems 208). The satisfaction will not last, however, just as the Magi did not remain satisfied with the revelation of Bethlehem. Yeats's mature judgment of a life spent seeking secret wisdom appears, as we have seen, in the concluding lines of "Meditations in the Time of Civil War." In a poem filled with his central occult images, such as the "magical unicorns" of Phase 15 and the "brazen hawks" of Phase 1 of *A Vision*, the poet confesses with a bitter echo of Wordsworth's "Intimations" ode:

> The abstract joy,
> The half-read wisdom of daemonic images,
> Suffice the ageing man as once the growing boy.
> (Poems 206)

This bitter tone is largely absent from Pound's characterization of the magus because Pound, far more than Yeats, emphasizes the power of the magus. If the question arises of whether the magus's knowledge leads to power, Pound's answer is more likely to be positive—at least until *The Pisan Cantos* (1948). In his early work, his theories about a tradition formed by spiritual masters influence his prose and poetry about the troubadours of Provençe. He wrote in the *Spirit of Romance* of a time when "a man feels his immortality upon him. As for the effect of this phenomenon in Provence, before coming to any judgment upon it we should consider carefully the history of various cults or religions of orgy and of ecstasy" (94–95). His conception of these cults was influenced by a French Rosicrucian, Sâr Péladan (1858–1918), who wrote *Le secret des troubadours* (1906). Péladan claimed that the troubadours drew on a secret religious tradition of Greek origin and that this cult of poets, as Pound himself put it, sang "allegories in praise of a mystic extra-church philosophy or religion, practised by the Albigenses, and the cause of the Church's crusade against them."[13] According to Peter Makin, the influence of Mead and Péladan worked in tandem. Mead's influence emboldened Pound to speak, as someone who "knew," of a troubadour cult, and Péladan gave him "the idea of an esotericism and a sect." Leon Surette observes, however, that

Péladan was just one of a "babble of occult and mystical speculators and revisers of history."[14]

Pound's poem "The Flame" is a heady distillation of his theories about Provençe. The title refers to the visionary power of the troubadours, which made the flame of love into a religious ecstasy. Such a vision is symbolized by magical stones. The gods are in "places splendid, / Bulkwarks of beryl and of chrysoprase" (a line that echoes Yeats's "The Shadowy Waters" [Poems 416]); and the "dark secret" of such wisdom is addressed as "Thou hooded opal, thou eternal pearl" (Personae 49).[15] In "The Flame," the Provençal poets themselves assert that they were engaged in no mere political or verbal game but expressed a secret wisdom known to poets throughout history (as in the "tales of Oisin"): "We who are wise beyond your dream of wisdom, / Drink our immortal moments; we 'pass through' " (Personae 48). Passing through the "bonds and borders" of the ordinary world, the "Ever-living" (a term Pound also lifts from "The Shadowy Waters") whisper their vision through the veils that obscure them (Personae 48). Like Blavatsky in her conception of spiritual initiates or adepts (her Mahatmas), Pound believed that spiritual masters guide mortals, who may become initiates of the "wisdom philosophy" on the road to enlightenment. Here again, Yeats's dedication of *A Vision* to Pound, despite Richard Ellmann's opinion, seems quite serious inasmuch as they both believed that such masters are the source of spiritual wisdom and—a basic assumption of *A Vision*—that history is largely a record of their actions.[16]

This theory of what Olivia Shakespear's friend Dion Fortune called the "esoteric orders" of spiritual masters implies or depends on the doctrine of reincarnation.[17] That doctrine is central to Yeats's poetry from *The Wanderings of Oisin* (1889), with its Blavatsky-like conception of a "cyclic pilgrimage," to the late play *Purgatory* (1939), where a woman is trapped in the afterlife reexperiencing a violent scene that bars her rebirth.[18] No one escapes the wheel of creation until the karma of many lifetimes has been burned away. The few who do purify themselves escape the cycle of creation, unless they choose to return to help others. Thus Yeats hoped to meet "the mysterious one who yet / Shall walk the wet sands by the edge of the stream" and interpret "All that I seek" (Poems 162). He would be a spiritual master like the fictional Michael Robartes or the "actual" Leo Africanus, who came to Yeats through the mediumship of his wife.

Pound was well acquainted with traditional theories of reincarnation. In *The Spirit of Romance*, he translated a Latin poem by Andrea

Navigeri on the reincarnation of Pythagoras (226). In *Guide to Kulchur*, he wrote, "Romantic poetry . . . almost requires the concept of rein- carnation as part of its mechanism. No apter metaphor having been found for certain emotional colours" (299). Pound's own early roman- tic poems use this metaphor repeatedly, and in "Histrion" it is com- bined with a second occult image drawn from alchemy: "'Tis' as in midmost us there glows a sphere / Translucent, molten gold" (CEP 71). Various "Masters of the Soul," for example, Christ or Dante, are incarnated through these spheres. In "Plotinus," this particular "mas- ter of the soul" makes "new thoughts as crescent images of *me*" as he enters the souls of new avatars (CEP 36). In a note to this poem, Pound wrote that it was "an accurate record of sensation" and "no mere (not) theorizing" (CEP 296), as if to suggest his own status as a master of spiritual experience.[19] This status, moreover, suggests how tempera- mentally ready he was to believe that the poet was always at odds with society. He claimed that members of these cults were always persecuted but that they survived "in Provence, and survive today— priests, maenads and the rest—though there is in our society no pro- vision for them" (SR 136). (When Pound's interest later becomes more economic than mystical, he will complain that society's economic con- ditions make no provision for the artist.) Yeats's influence on this in- carnation motif is particulary clear in Pound's poem "Masks," which holds that myths are the tales of "souls that found themselves among / Unwonted folk that spake an hostile tongue," which includes "old wizards" or a soul who can still remember "the star-span acres of a former lot" and sings of it when "carnate" (CEP 34). In "Und Drang" (III), the poem's persona asserts, in a Yeatsian line that he "was Aen- gus for a thousand years" before his inspiration, "she, the ever- living," abandoned him (CEP 168–69).

Pound's early volume, *A Quinzaine for this Yule* (1908), which con- tains the key poem "Histrion," is organized around this theme of the influence of spiritual masters. Bruce Fogelman notes that the title of "Prelude: Over the Ognisanti" refers to the Ognisanti area of Venice, but the reference is more specifically to All Saints Church in Venice, which gives the area its name.[20] Pound's "saints" are not the orthodox ones of the church but the spiritual and poetic masters "high-dwelling 'bove the people here, / Being alone with beauty most the while" (CEP 59). The "I" of this introductory poem will simply record the songs of these "shades": "I transcribe them following" (59). The "fol- lowing" are the poems of *Quinzaine*. The volume's theme appears par- ticulary in "Histrion" and in "Beddoesque," where the "new-old runes and magic of past time" are caught from "the whole man-soul" (CEP 70). The poem claims that those who practiced the "'mantra' of our craft" are individuals only for a short time before they return to the "great whole liquid jewel of God's truth" (70).

The spiritual masters in *Quinzaine* include "Lucifer Caditurus" (CEP 66–67), who resolves to know as much as God knows whatever the cost; "Sandalphon" (67–68), the "angel of prayer" in the Talmud; and the "Purveyors General," who discover "new tales, new mysteries, / New songs from out the breeze" (62). These spiritual entities join the personae of Pound's *A Lume Spento*: Plotinus, Prometheus, Swinburne ("Salve O Pontifex!"), the "fool" in "Marlin," the "wizards" of "Masks," and the speakers of "Anima Sola," "Aegupton," and "The Tree." They become (in Yeats's phrase) the "singing masters" of Pound's soul. Chief among these is the legendary alchemist Paracelsus, who speaks in a poem published in *Canzoni* (1911): "Being no longer human why should I / Pretend humanity or don the frail attire?" (CEP 148).

It is significant that Paracelsus, the most enlightened of Pound's magi, is an alchemist. Pound shared with Yeats, not to mention Goethe and Rimbaud, a fascination with alchemy as an analogue of poetic art. In "Rosa Alchemica," Yeats's persona writes that he discovered that alchemy "was no merely chemical phantasy" and that the alchemists "sought to fashion gold out of common metals merely as part of an universal transmutation of all things into some divine and imperishable substance" (*The Secret Rose*, 126). Yeats's critics have fully explored his use of alchemy, from the wandering Aengus's "silver apples of the moon [and] golden apples of the sun" (Poems 60) to the "masterful images" (347) that grow out of base matter in "The Circus Animals' Desertion."[21] But Pound's use of alchemy has been less explored even though it was one of his longest continuing occult interests. Through the tradition of alchemy, he developed his conception of the "master of the soul" as poet as well as magus.

Pound published his poem "The Alchemist" in 1920 with the note that it was "unpublished 1912." The note implied that the poem had been abandoned rather than finished, and this impression was strengthened by the publication of the longer manuscript version of the poem in the *Collected Early Poems* (225–29.) His difficulty with this poem suggests not only his uncertainty about the theme of alchemy but also the challenge it posed to him as a writer. It was by exploring the art of alchemy that Pound developed his own poetics. In his essay "Brancusi," he spoke of an artist's belief "in a sort of elixir or philosopher's stone produced by the sheer perfection of his art; by the alchemical sublimation of the medium; the elimination of accidentals and imperfections" (LE 442).

"The Alchemist" is an amalgam of alchemical and troubadour elements. The mixed nature of the poem is evident in its subtitle, "Chant for the Transmutation of Metals." Although chant is not a traditional part of the alchemical process, chants to invoke the aid of spirits (such as the "manes" referred to in the poem) were common to magical rites. To Pound, it was as natural to add a magical chant to the alchemical process as it was to compare the rhythmic praise of the lady in Cavalcanti's poetry with a Hindu *"mantram"* (SR 97). In the introduction to his translations of Cavalcanti's poems (1910), Pound wrote, "The science of the music of words and the knowledge of their magical powers has fallen away since men invoked Mithra by a sequence of pure vowel sounds" (Trans 24). "The Alchemist" is part invocation and part mantra. The way these two mystical elements support the alchemical subject is suggested by another passage from *Cavalcanti:* "The equations of alchemy were apt to be written as women's names and the women so named endowed with the magical power of the compound" (18). The lady of courtly poetry could thus assume "all the properties of the Alchemist's stone" (SR 90 n. 2). These kinds of comparisons and the cultural synthesizing they presuppose became basic to *The Cantos.*

G. R. S. Mead's conception of the psychological goal of alchemy informs Pound's concept of alchemy. According to Ian Bell, Mead conceived "a model of alchemy as a ritual expression of psychic progress, 'a ladder of ascent from earth to the light world' that led finally to . . . a 'bringing to birth of a man's perfected subtle body.'"[22] The alchemist's stone would give its possessor the power over natural processes which Pound begs from the courtly ladies invoked in the opening lines of "The Alchemist." The women mentioned in the poem are drawn from Romance and classical literature and placed in a paradisiacal setting ("under the larches of Paradise") that will be alluded to in Canto 94:

> Saîl of Claustra, Aelis, Azalais . . .
> As your voices, under the larches of Paradise
> Make a clear sound.
>
> (Personae 70)

This rather Pre-Raphaelite feminine chorus is asked to watch over the process that will bring the light of gold out of elemental darkness:

Under night, the peacock-throated,
Bring the saffron-coloured shell,
Bring the red gold of the maple,
Bring the light of the birch tree in autumn
Mirals, Cembelins, Audiarda,
Remember this fire.

(Personae 70–71)

These lines describe the alchemical process with brilliant concentra-
tion. "Peacock-throated" alludes to the stage of the alchemical transmutation known as the *cauda pavonis*, or "peacock's tail." When the
alchemical vessel of glass displays the rainbow of colors associated
with the peacock (Figure 6), the final stage of the process is about to
begin. "Night, the peacock-throated" refers to both the beginning and
the ending of the process. The *cauda pavonis* indicates that the four
traditional stages of the transmutation of the gold (or alchemist's
stone) out of the *prima materia* has been successful. These fiery stages
are alluded to through the four colors associated with the night, the
birch tree, the saffron shell, and the maple. The poem ends as the
invoked *manes*, or spirits, "Guard this alembic" and "draw together
the bones of the metal" (72) into the alchemical *filius philosophorum*.
The alchemist has created new life.

The gathering of these elements culminates in an alchemical marriage. This pattern of mystic marriage of male and female, or solar
and lunar, elements is a recurring one in Yeats's poetry and also in
that of H.D., Robert Duncan, Ted Hughes, and James Merrill. Pound's
marriage of sun and moon is achieved by invoking the ladies in the
poem under the Provençal title of "Midonz": "Midonz, with the gold
of the sun" (Personae 71). These women are then associated with the
Greek goddess Latona, who is the mother of both the sun god Apollo
and the moon goddess Artemis: "Pallor of silver, pale lustre of Latona" (71–72). The Provençal Midonz is also the womb of new life.
She is impregnated by the alchemist himself, who represents the seminal element of fire.

"The Alchemist" is a tour de force of alchemical lore, but there is
more than just its designation as "unfinished" to suggest that Pound
was dissatisfied with its theme. In a poem he published soon after he
finished "The Alchemist," he was openly skeptical of alchemy as a
magical art. In "Xenia," a sequence of lyrics that appeared in *Poetry*
in 1913, he wrote of the alchemical alembic as a "glass subtly evil."
The six-part sequence describes the regeneration of "an ugly little man

Figure 6. The alchemical peacock's tail (*cauda pavonis*), from an eighteenth-century manuscript.

Figure 7. Mercury as hermaphrodite, from J. D. Mylus, *Philosophia reformata*, 1622.

/ Carrying beautiful flowers," who appears in Part 1 out of the "over-hanging gray mist," into the alchemical homunculus ("O soul of the captive") in Part 5.[23] The poem culminates in an apostrophe to the vessel's power in an image that combines a reference to the iridescence of the *cauda pavonis* with one to *Hermes duplex*, the two-faced god of alchemy (Figure 7): "O glass subtle and cunning, O powdery gold! / O filaments of amber, two-faced iridescence!" (*Personae* 96). Three stanzas of this sequence became "A Song of the Degrees" in *Personae*. Akiko Miyake has shown that the title comes from John Heydon's alchemical work *Holy Guide* and means a "song of alchemical ascension, an uplifting of the material to the spiritual realm."[24] The explanation for Pound's ambiguous feelings about the alchemical process in the poem is found in the first line of the shortened *Personae* version: "Rest me with Chinese colours, / For I think the glass is evil" (*Personae* 95). The poem announces the poet's misgivings about his experiments with alchemy and magic amid his growing interest in Chinese art and Confucian ethics. Miyake suggests that Pound in this poem was questioning his desire to become a "great magician-artist"

(62). Pound was generally questioning his art and beliefs in 1913, and the outbreak of World War I brought him to a crisis.

The early versions of the Cantos during the war years reflect Pound's doubts not only about alchemy but also about the shadowy spiritual masters of his early poetry, who begin to fade from his poetic world. Although the seventeenth-century alchemist John Heydon is Pound's example of the visionary poet in the early Canto 3 (1917), he is described as a "half-cracked fellow." His methods are those of the "old way" of imaginary encounters and dreams, or of Wordsworthian "false-pastoral." Trying this "old way," Pound has John Heydon appear in a vision and declare that all minds are capable of taking on any shape—the essence of Pound's concept of reincarnation. But here the idea loses its mysterious, occult tone because it is expressed philosophically in decorous Latin: *"Omniformis omnis intellectus est."*[25] To assert that the intellect can take on any form it chooses suggests a general theory of the imagination rather than a specific belief in reincarnation.

By the time of the post–World War I Cantos, Heydon disappears from the poem, and personae such as Odysseus, Malatesta, and Confucius receive the hero worship once given to Prometheus and Paracelsus. (Plotinus, however, guides Pound's persona out of hell in Canto 16.) The appearance of Confucius is especially significant. Pound once wrote that, intellectually, he had "no satisfaction till I got to Kung."[26] Not only Pound's increasing social concerns, which developed after World War I, but also his interest in Chinese thought altered his understanding of spiritual mastery. The change was socially positive because the occultist tends to desire secret knowledge and power rather than practical virtue and ethical commitment. It is a genuine revolution in Pound's thought when he devotes Canto 13 to Confucius, who spoke of "'brotherly deference'" and "said nothing of the 'life after death'" (Cantos 59).

Although the reincarnation theme remains important to Pound, he uses it now in a subtler, Joycean manner. In Joyce's *Ulysses*, Stephen mocks Yeats's and Æ's belief in reincarnation. Yet Leopold Bloom is in a sense the reincarnation (in terms of Joyce's "metempsychosis" motif) of the Greek hero Ulysses; and as a Masonic inheritor of a secret tradition, Bloom is to some degree Stephen's spiritual master—indeed he is portrayed, after he rescues Stephen in Nightown, in a Masonic "attitude of secret master."[27] In *The Cantos*, the Ulysses of Canto 1 is incarnated throughout history and lives again in such Poundian heroes as Sigismundo Malatesta, Thomas Jefferson, John Q. Adams, Martin Van Buren, and of course Pound himself. In Canto 23 (which opens by stating the "omniformis" theme) through Canto 28, reincarnation is implied in the motifs of metamorphosis and the theme of the living presence of the pagan gods.[28]

Nevertheless, occult lore becomes less important as a poetic source. In his important essay "Pagan and Magic Elements in Ezra Pound's Works," Boris de Rachewiltz argues that in Pound's career "a leaning towards magic was already noticeable in his earliest poems and, while largely absent from the poetry of his middle years, reasserts itself more strongly than ever before in his old age" (177). Although this judgment has been challenged, Pound's interest in the occult certainly declines in the nineteen-thirties.[29] In his roles as a Confucian sage, economic reformer, and Italian Fascist, he was concerned with the social and not the spiritual realm. There were, though, signs that Pound's religious or mystical side was not entirely repressed. He published *Guide to Kulchur* in 1938, in which the spelling of "kulchur" indicated that he was not writing about a Western, Christian, mainstream tradition. His culturally significant figures could make up a reading list in occultism: Pythagoras, Plotinus, Iamblichus, Porphyry, Psellus, Plethon, Erigena, Heydon, and Swedenborg.[30] He admitted in October 1939 to Henry Swabey, an Anglican minister, that the study of Confucius cannot "satisfy *all* the real belief of Europe," although he maintained that Confucius was a sufficient guide to ethical behavior. Pound reveals what he means by "real belief" when he adds that the "mysteries are *not* revealed, and no guide book to them has been or will be written."[31] Thus Pound's *Guide to Kulchur* (1938) can refer to but not explicate the mysteries that "*can not* be revealed. Fools can only profane them (145). In November 1939 he advised Douglas Mc-Pherson, who was hoping to publish a journal entitled *Pan*, that he could not publicly discuss the mysteries: "The SECRETUM stays shut to the vulgo." Nevertheless, he tells McPherson that his economic work is largely completed and that he is now "definitely onto questions of BELIEF."[32] A passage in *Guide to Kulchur* suggests that belief can only be approached through poetry and not prose: "Prose is NOT education but the outer courts of the same. Beyond its door are the mysteries" (144–45). The mysteries are explored in the poetry of *The Pisan Cantos.*

The defeat of Italy in the war and Pound's imprisonment in 1945 on charges of treason inevitably turned his spirit inward to a personal world rather than outward to a social one. While a military prisoner in Pisa for six months, he wrote poetry about the ideal "city of Dioce,

whose terraces are the colour / of stars" (Cantos 425). This city, Ec-
batan, had appeared long before, in Canto 5, where it is the site for a
mystic marriage between Danae and Zeus who comes in the form of
a shower of gold. Although such mythological images are not absent
in the Cantos after *A Draft of XXX Cantos* (1930), they flood back into
Pound's poetry with *The Pisan Cantos,* along with his renewed interest
in mystical themes. As Leon Surette has shown, the opening of the
Pisan sequence, with its juxtaposition of Mussolini and Manes (the
founder of Manichaeism) appeals to a tradition of secret history.
Within occultism, Manichaeism is the prototype of all the heretical
movements, such as Albigensianism, persecuted because they challenged the established church.[33] According to Pound, Manes was
"tanned and stuffed" (Cantos 425), and so Pound compares him with
the allegedly victimized Mussolini and, of course, to himself as a political martyr. In the Pisan prison camp, Pound has become Odysseus
in the etymological sense of the name, "No Man." The "city of Dioce"
is compared with the fortress city of Montségur (as in Canto 80:510),
which was destroyed during the pope's crusade against the Albigenses: "and in Mt Segur there is wind space and rain space / no more
an altar to Mithras" (Canto 76:452). Although Pound's linking of Manichaeism, Albigensianism, and the Persian religion of Mithra is a historical fantasy, these religions are indeed merged in the underground
stream of occultism. The only note that relieves the despair of these
opening lines is that Pound hints that heroes such as Manes and Mussolini may be like Dionysius, "DIGENES," or twice born. Similarly,
there is hope for the rebirth of the Odyssean poet.

The poet is sustained by his visions of a spiritual world, which are
expressed through the kind of imagery of sphere, gyre, and crystal
examined in Chapter 1. Equally important are the sun and moon images, sometimes mythological and sometimes naturalistic, and also the
continuous references to the cloudscape around Pisa as it transforms
the poet's view of the mountain to which he gives the sacred Chinese
name of Mt. Taishan. These references culminate in the final Canto of
the Pisan sequence with the statement "Under white clouds, cielo di
Pisa / out of all this beauty something must come. . . ." (Cantos, 84:
539). As Leon Surette and Walter Baumann have shown, Pound's
Odysseus persona, the "brother of Circe" (Canto 17:79), is associated
with magic and ritual rebirth.[34] In the opening lines of *The Pisan Cantos,* the spiritual initiate is one who has "passed the pillars and outward from Herakles" (425); and the Canto's final line refers to the
initiate as among those "who have passed over Lethe" (449). The "pil-

lars of Herakles" are the Straits of Gibraltar through which Odysseus passed on his last adventure.[35] In the ritual of the Order of the Golden Dawn, which Yeats himself underwent, the initiate passes through such symbolic pillars into a new spiritual world.[36]

In Canto 82, the hope of rebirth accompanies the motif of the mystic marriage. The poet is married with the earth—"connubium terrae"—and drunk with the Dionysian power of the earth's ichor ("ICHOR of CHTHONIOS"):

> . . . I will come out of this knowing no one
> neither they me
>   connubium terrae.
>   (Cantos 526)

The most sustained passage devoted to this rebirth occurs earlier, in Canto 79 (488–92) and reprises the form and imagery of Pound's "The Alchemist." The alchemical elements of the later version, however, are not merely elements in the tour de force of the 1915 poem but are deeply a part of the poet's spiritual transmutation. The Canto opens with a stark reference to the night, "Moon, cloud" (484), but the scene soon changes to dawn, the moment of enlightenment: "the morning sun lit up the shelves and battalions / of the west, cloud over cloud" (488). Echoes of the lines "Remember this fire" and "Guard this alembic" from "The Alchemist" appear in the Canto's invocation of bacchanalian lynxes, which are asked to guard the divine "ichor" as the Provençal ladies were asked to guard the alchemical alembic: "O Lynx keep watch on my fire" and "O Lynx, keep the edge on my cider" (489, 491). The most crucial parallel of the two poems is in the metaphor of distilling an ichor (or wine, or cider) through a magical fire: "No glass is clearer than are the globes of this flame" (490), which recalls the "glass subtle and cunning" of "A Song of the Degrees" as well as "The Alchemist." The distillation of the ichor proceeds under the care of Aphrodite ('Αφρόδιτη), the moon goddess Delia (Δήλια), the male sun god Helios (Ηλιος), and the god who is the most crucial to the marriage of male and female elements, Hermes, the two-faced god of alchemy:

> O lynx, guard my vineyard
> As the grape swells under vine leaf

This Goddess was born of sea-foam
She is lighter than air under Hesperus

δεινὰ εἶ, Κύθηρα
terrible in resistance
Κόρη καὶ Δήλια καὶ Μαῖα
trine as praeludio
Κύπρις 'Αφρόδιτη
a petal lighter than sea-foam
Κύθηρα
>   aram
>   nemus
>   vult

O puma, sacred to Hermes, Cimbica servant of Helios.

(492)

Pound's echoes of his early poems in *The Pisan Cantos* are a natural product of his nostalgic memories of his pre–World War I life in London. This return to his early work continues during his imprisonment at St. Elizabeths Hospital, when he wrote the *Rock-Drill* (1955) and *Thrones* (1959) Cantos. The reissue of his collected early poems in the 1949 *Personae* revived his memory of his early poems and their mystical themes. The reissue of *The Spirit of Romance* (1953), moreover, reawakened his interest in the mysticism of medieval and Romance literature.[37] As he tried to finish *The Cantos*, Pound saw that echoing his early work might help give the poem a sense of completion. According to K. K. Ruthven, Pound's quotation in Canto 94 of the phrase "under the larches of paradise" from "The Alchemist" (1915) shows that he "entertained the idea of a circular form for the Cantos: he would end where he began, establishing the unity of his life's work by echoing some of his early poems in the last few pages of his epic."[38]

The most striking example of Pound's backward glances is that, while working on the *Rock-Drill* Cantos, he asked Mrs. Yeats to send him Yeats's own copy of John Heydon's alchemical tract *Holy Guide* so that he could draw on it for Canto 92.[39] In this Canto, alchemical imagery introduces the theme of spiritual transformation in the opening lines:

and as engraven on gold, to be unity
but duality, brass
and trine to mercurial

> shall a tetrad be silver ...
> and from this a sea-change?
>
> (Cantos 618)

This passage uses the traditional numerology of alchemy, in which the metals undergoing transformation are assigned mystical numbers. The four numbers that make up the tetrad represent the four elements, with the philosopher's stone representing the quintessence.[40] The poet, recalling the ambiguity expressed in "Xenia," seems doubtful, however, that a transformation will emerge from such a formula. Hence the questioning of the possibility of a "sea-change." Although the transformation does take place in this Canto, as indicated by the image of the "sphere of crystal," it happens only "For a flash, / for an hour. / Then agony" (Cantos 620). Alchemy nevertheless appears throughout Pound's late poetry to offer at least the hope of transformation.

Canto 92 is part of the *Rock-Drill* Cantos, where occultism recurs with renewed force and is now in harmony rather than opposition to Confucian thought. The late Cantos are Pound's *paradisio*, where the thinkers and rulers he admires appear like saints in a mosaic. His concern is political wisdom in the first two *Rock-Drill* Cantos; but in the third, Canto 87, the poet asserts the vitality of a secret "wisdom tradition" that stretches from ancient China ("from the San Ku") to Poictiers in the twelfth century. The "San Ku" was a secret advisory council that Pound read of in Séraphin Couvreur's *Chou King: Les annales de la Chine*.[41] The Canto associates these masters of Confucian wisdom with Jacques de Molay, the last grand master of the Knights Templar; with the architects of Poictiers, who understood the Pythagorean rule of the Golden Section; and with the "Selloi," yet another "secret society," which guarded the oracles of Zeus.[42]

Among the spiritual masters in this Canto, it is no surprise to find John Heydon, Mencius, Rémy de Gourmont, or even George Santayana. But two of Pound's personal friends, one from his early days in London and another from St. Elizabeths, may seem unexpected in this elite company. The London friend is B. Cyril Windeler, a London wool broker and author who once selected and read an individual letter from a visualized file of three hundred folios.[43] The new friend also had a visionary experience: "Monsieur F. saw his mentor / composed almost wholly of light" (Cantos 573). "Monsieur F." is not, as the *Companion to the Cantos* suggests, Gustave Flaubert. He is William French, a young friend of Pound who attended the "EZuversity" at St. Elizabeths in the early fifties. Pound was indeed French's mentor during their visits, but the vision of someone composed of light was of a Persian or Arabian figure who appeared to French in a vision (in 1954) to guide his search for spiritual understanding.[44] Such mentors are essential in the search for spiritual wisdom, which is paradoxically written on the face of nature and yet hidden. Using a phrase from John Heydon, Pound writes, in Canto 87, "In nature are signatures / needing no verbal tradition" (Cantos 573). In observing that Santayana held that there was a "tradition" that "was not mere epistemology" (573), the poet suggests that a "tradition" is not composed merely of philosophical discourse. The meaning of *tradition* is addressed in the two Cantos that form the heart of *Rock-Drill*, 90 and 91. These Cantos are Pound's demonstration that a secret tradition of magi transmits the "SECRETUM" through the centuries.

In Canto 90, Pound again takes the "San Ku" as his starting point and again mentions the architecture of Poictiers:

> That is Sagetrieb,
> that is tradition.
> Builders had kept the proportion,
> did Jacques de Molay
> know these proportions?
> And was Erigena ours?
> (Cantos 605)

"Sagetrieb" is Pound's own coinage to indicate something more intangible, informal, and oral than an established, documented tradition. The spiritual masters he cites can only be associated if the word *tradition* means something as vague, to use the phrase Graham Hough suggested, as "family resemblances." Neither the word *Neoplatonic* nor *Eleusinian* can describe under a single heading Confucian sages, Knights Templars, a Mason-like society of architects, and the medieval philosopher Johannes Scotus Erigena. The two rhetorical questions of course seek an affirmative answer. Jacques de Molay of the Knights Templar was burned at the stake in Paris as a heretic. Pound associates Erigena with the Albigensians here and in Canto 74 because his work *De divisione naturae* was condemned by the church in 1225 (after his death) during the Albigensian Crusade. In Pound's view, their persecution by the established Church is enough to link them as transmitters of secret wisdom.

Canto 91 develops Pound's conviction that there is an occult body of knowledge that has been nourished by spiritual masters. In a Yeatsian gesture, he invokes a spirit through alchemical imagery: "that the body of light come forth / from the body of fire" (Cantos 610). The figure is specified only as "Reina" (Queen) to suggest a number of women, such as Aphrodite, the Princess Ra-Set, Queen Elizabeth, and Empress Theodora of Byzantium. The "body of light" is what G. R. S. Mead called the "Subtle Body" or "Radiant Body" of "psychical alchemy."[45] If there is a central figure, however, it is Aphrodite, who appears at the Canto's end as "Queen Cytherea" (617). The poet refers to her in a passage that identifies his conception of the secret tradition:

> and the stone eyes again looking seaward
>   Thus Apollonius . . .
> & Helen of Tyre
>   by Pithagoras
>   by Ocellus
> (pilot-fish, et libidinis expers, of Tyre;
> Justinian, Theodora.
>   (Cantos 610–11)

Referring to this "role of honor," Donald Davie writes that Helen of Tyre is an "odd name out."[46] If the list is not an honor role, however, but a Yeatsian invocation of powerful spirits, the obscure figure of Helen of Tyre indeed belongs in this esoteric company. As we saw in discussing *The Spirit of Romance*, she is the spirit of beauty discovered by Simon Magus after Helen of Troy was metamorphosed into Helen of Tyre and lived in a brothel of that city. Mead claimed that Simon's "doctrine of the divine fire . . . [was] entirely in keeping with the subtle body theory of psychical alchemy."[47] Simon Magus invoked Helen as his muse as Pound invokes the spirit of his "Reina." To the spiritual figures already mentioned, the Canto adds Odysseus, John Heydon, and Porphyry (referring to the latter's symbolism of regeneration [Cantos 615–16]). Pound uses the word *arcanum* to refer to the hidden knowledge of the spiritually awakened. One of the metaphors in the passage recalls the name of the occult order to which Yeats belonged for some thirty years, the Order of the Golden Dawn:

> They who are skilled in fire
>   shall read 𝐇 tan, the dawn.
> Waiving no jot of the arcanum
>   (having his own mind to stand by him)
>   (615)

"Skilled in fire" describes the poet as an alchemist who invokes the alchemical "body of fire" and as an uncompromising master of the "arcanum." Although Pound believed that the "mysteries are *not* revealed," the poet can draw on their wisdom and express it symbolically.[48] The line in parentheses refers to Odysseus as spiritual adventurer with a steadfast mind, Pound's own persona.

This claim of access to an arcanum which permits one to "read" the dawn and acquire spiritual illumination is reaffirmed throughout *Rock-Drill*. This volume is the record of the knowledge and experience that allowed Pound to endure the humiliation of his imprisonment in St. Elizabeth's. His certainty about the arcanum helped him endure his imprisonment and gave him the courage for his defiant claim that he would "waiv[e] no jot" of his beliefs, depending on nothing but "his own mind." But Pound's defiant assertion of arcane values is of course not entirely a poetic strength. Even the most loyal of his readers find the obscurity of *Rock-Drill* and *Thrones* excessive. His conviction that certain matters must necessarily be obscure to all but initiates results in his gnomic listing of sacred names and glancing notations of sacred texts.

The obscurity of these late volumes is a natural development of Pound's conception of himself as a magus illuminated by the golden dawn of wisdom. Whether he considered himself an alchemist, a "master of the soul," or an economic savior, he spoke chiefly to initiates. Perhaps it is significant that Pound was introduced to economic theory by A. R. Orage, who was equally dedicated to the doctrines of social credit and occultism, eventually becoming a follower of Gurdjieff. Friends—T. S. Eliot, for instance—were puzzled by Pound's ability to make a difficult subject like economics still more difficult by assuming that his audience should already know certain alleged economic facts. But the habit of speaking like a magus was ingrained, whether the topic was mystical or economic. Equally dangerous was his belief that the avatar of both economic and mystical wisdom would necessarily live at odds with society, which made him seem to welcome opposition as proof of his wisdom.

This combination of obscurity and authoritative stance returns us to my earlier contrast of Pound and Yeats. The self-doubt of Yeats's Magi or Ribh, which is absent from Pound's mystical personae, moderates Yeats's tone. One sees the same balanced tone in Shakespeare's characterization of the magus in *The Tempest*. When Prospero boasts in Act 4 of his power over the elements and even over life and death, Shakespeare immediately reminds us of the weakness of an old man who must still his "beating mind." Yeats's claims to occult wisdom and magical power, even in *A Vision* or in a poem like "All Souls' Night," are never without such reminders of human limitations. Pound does express his own weaknesses, especially in the final *Drafts and Fragments* (1969) volume, when he admits, "I lost my center / fighting the world" (Cantos, "Notes for CXVII," 802). But such admissions are usually separate from the magisterial assertions of secret wisdom, and even this one suggests that the fault was as much the world's as Pound's. Unlike the passage from *The Tempest*, or those throughout Yeats's poetry, the assertions are rarely modulated with acknowledgments of Pound's own limitations. The one exception is in Canto 107, with its claim that the poet has "brought the great ball of crystal," followed by the admission that

> my errors and wrecks lie about me.
> And I am not a demigod.
> I cannot make it cohere.
>
> (796)

Yet even here, in a passage where Pound's persona appears genuinely humble, the humility is the peculiar one of admitting that one has failed at a task only a demigod could complete.

This general lack of modulation in Pound's poetry accounts in part for the frequent stridency of his tone and also contributes to the oracular note of his visionary passages. A magus risks sounding pretentious and merely oracular, and Pound's gnomic utterances in the late Cantos certainly run this risk. True occultists, such as Yeats and H.D., seem to avoid this portentousness through their evident sincerity. They reveal a reverence in the use of sacred images like the sphere which is missing in the brashness of Pound's poetry. Robert Duncan and James Merrill use occult themes with an ironic sophistication that eliminates or distances the oracular tone. But Ezra Pound and Ted Hughes often adopt the pose of the magus without the humility or reverence of Yeats and H.D. or the ironic perspective of Duncan and Merrill. Pound wrote magnificent poetry when he spoke as a magus. But his poetic career alerts us to the risk, run by all the poets of the occult, of sounding obscure rather than learned and portentous rather than profound.

T. S. Eliot:
Occultism as Heresy

[The poet may feel] haunted by a demon, a demon
against which he feels powerless, because in its first
manifestation it has no face, no name, nothing; and the
words, the poem he makes, are a kind of form of
exorcism of this demon.
                    —T. S. Eliot, "The Three Voices of Poetry"

3 "What does Mr. Pound believe?" T. S. Eliot once
asked at the end of a 1928 review of Pound's *Personae* collection. In what Eliot calls the "curious syncretism" of Pound's philosophy, he found only a "muddle." He criticized Pound's "medieval mysticism" (as seen in Pound's "Cavalcanti" essay) for being insincere because it is "without belief" in the religion from which it developed and because it is strangely "mixed up with Mr Yeats's spooks." Still worse in Eliot's view is that Pound's medievalism is just one ingredient in a mélange ("Mélange Adultère de Tout," as the title of Eliot's poem puts it) that includes 1890s aestheticism, Confucian ethics, and crackpot theories about hormones.[1]

In a direct reply, Pound said that he did not believe in "abstract and general statement" and could only answer Eliot's question by saying that he would replace the statue of Venus on the cliffs of Terracina and erect a temple to Artemis in London. Much earlier, however, in his 1921 "Axiomata" he had expressed in more general terms his belief in a "*Theos*" that transcends human consciousness. Although he wrote then that it was impossible to tell if the *theos* were one or many, he warned that the "greatest tyrannies" have arisen from monotheistic religions.[2] In 1928 he criticized Eliot for suggesting that Christianity or monotheism provided the only alternative to irreligion: "as if monism or monotheism were anything more than an hypothesis agreeable to certain types of very lazy mind too weak to bear an uncertainty or to remain in 'uncertainty'" (LE 394). The pagan and occult qualities of what Pound called his "Religio" came from his belief in the *theos* manifesting itself as many gods. If this situation leaves one in uncertainties, wondering which god to honor, it may make the believer more receptive to a variety of spiritual influences and more tolerant of other beliefs.

In Eliot's view, Pound is guilty of the prime heresy of denying the one true God. In his "Primer of Modern Heresy," *After Strange Gods* (1933), Eliot links Pound with Irving Babbitt as a thinker in whom the "width of his culture" suggests a belief in many things (or gods) but a deep and genuine belief in nothing (42). In the introduction to a book entitled *Revelation* (1937), Eliot criticized such writers as Irving Babbitt and D. H. Lawrence for believing in exotic or primitive systems that had been "made palatable for the intellectual and cultivated modern man" and "not only purified but *canned*; separated from all the traditional ways of behaving and feeling." He related such beliefs to a "psychological mysticism" typical of "cults whose aims are not far removed from those of magic." Unlike orthodox mysticism, the aim of magic is power rather than illumination. Eliot distrusts those who seek the "sources of supernatural power, divorced from religion and theology" (22–23).

This criticism was an extension of the argument, developed in *The Sacred Wood* (1920), that Dante was a greater poet than Blake in part because he drew naturally upon a system of belief that he, along with most of his contemporaries, could generally and quite naturally accept. Dante benefited from "a mythology and a theology which had undergone a more complete absorption into life," whereas Blake had to create a "framework" of his own (163). If Eliot had known how much Blake depended on occult sources for his framework, his criticism could only have been harsher.[3] Whether Blake was developing a personal mythology or drawing on occultism, he faced not only the challenge of expressing his thoughts poetically but also the additional burden (compared with Dante) of advocating a philosophy his own culture ignored or rejected. As a result, Eliot argues, the weakness of Blake's poems are that they "are too visionary, too remote from the world" (156). Eliot will make a similar criticism of Yeats; moreover, this criticism is applicable to all the poets surveyed in this book.

Eliot considered Pound's influence more dangerous than Babbitt's because he held that Pound was one of the two great poets of the age—the other being Yeats. Because the occult aspects of Yeats are so prominent, he became a major target in *After Strange Gods*. Eliot's obsession with Yeats reveals, however, not only his criticism of occultism but also the subtle attraction occultism had for Eliot himself. Even the occultism of later poets such as Robert Duncan and Sylvia Plath is strongly influenced by Yeats's works, but Eliot's interest may be understood to be almost entirely the result of Yeats's influence. Yeats haunts Eliot's poetry like a ghost—the ghost, specifically, of "Little Gidding"—who must be exorcised.

Eliot's criticism of Yeats's occultism began as early as 1919 when he wrote, with the kind of wit that imitates F. H. Bradley's treatment of spiritualism, that Yeats's mind was "in some way independent of experience" and that his poetic world of "sprites" and curious doctrines was "unknown and unknowable."[4] After Eliot's conversion in 1927, his criticism of Yeats became far stronger. In *After Strange Gods*, he scorned Yeats's "artificially induced poeticality," which was "stimulated by folklore, occultism, mythology and symbolism, crystal-gazing and hermetic writings." As an orthodox Christian, Eliot also made the more serious charge that Yeats's supernatural world was "the wrong supernatural world. It was not a world of real Good and Evil, of holiness or sin, but a highly sophisticated lower mythology" (48–49). In 1936, Eliot scorned Yeats's "wanderings among oriental philosophies and dubious mysticisms" as "journeys unsafe for any but the Christian, and which the Christian informed about the historic wealth of his Faith has least need to make."[5]

Eliot's self-canceling dictum, which allows only the orthodox to explore the heretical, reveals his postconversion disapproval of the occult. Yet such disapproval might well coexist with fascination. Indeed, his dictum gives him the license to journey into an occult world. In a psychological sense, *occult* means "repressed," or literally, "covered over." The appeal of occultism is that it makes available ideas and rituals, such as divination and direct communication with the dead, that mainstream religion has repressed. This appeal may be as strong to the traditional religionist as to the unorthodox. For example, Eliot's Anglican friend Charles Williams was a member of the revived Hermetic Order of the Golden Dawn. One might detect a taste for these repressed features in Eliot's rather bizarre remarks in the thirties about the "Evil One" and the influence of "daemonic powers."[6]

We have seen in the Introduction that Auden, like Eliot an Anglican, derided Yeats's occultism as "Southern Californian." Yet Auden too was drawn to magical practices, and not before but after his reconversion to Christianity. To gain control over personal enemies he practiced such rituals as the dismembering of portraits and the casting of

spells through Tarot cards. Igor Stravinsky was surprised to learn that
Auden believed in astrology and black magic as it appears in the
novels of Charles Williams.[7] (Both Auden and Eliot admired Williams's novels, in which wicked occultists are defeated by the forces
of good.) However seriously Auden took such practices, it is clear that
he derived great satisfaction from them. Richard Ellmann acknowledges Auden's personal attraction to the occult but concludes that in
his works he "includes the occult only to overcome it." For example,
although Auden models the medium in his play *Elegy for Young Lovers*
on Mrs. Yeats, his character is cured only when she stops seeing her
visions. In *The Ascent of F6*, the symbolic crystal of the play's conclusion is not a magical gem but a mirror that, as Ellmann writes, "lays
bare not secrets of the preternatural but traumas of childhood."[8]

Auden's mixed feelings about the occult may give us some perspective on Eliot's. As a Christian, Auden criticizes a Yeatsian view
of art and life in his religious sonnet sequence "The Quest." A Yeatsian tower is described as an "architecture for the odd," and the
"great magicians" who live in these towers are "caught in their own
spell." In another sonnet, a "gift for magic" is dangerous because the
control of "those boyish powers of the air" blinds one to simple truths
and leaves one clinging to an inauthentic "tall belief."[9] One of the
personae of Auden's sequence is on a Gnostic quest (as Harold Bloom
said that Yeats was), which implies an underlying despair about human fate. Auden's quester, "panting up the spiral stair," prays for
freedom from the "Uncreated Nothing"; but as Yeats wrote, "The last
kiss is given to the void," and Auden's quester plunges from the
tower to his death.[10] Whether a form of art or religion, "magic" con-
notes a diabolic will to control spiritual forces.[11] In his poetic commentary on Shakespeare's *The Tempest*, Auden celebrates Prospero's
rennunciation of magic and acceptance of human limitations.[12]

Auden's attitude toward occultism suggests that, although the
Christian poet, like any other, may be drawn to it, such an attraction
can only be seen as a temptation. One might speculate that the greater
the attraction, the stronger the Christian poet's denunciation. Thus
Auden ridicules occultism, but Eliot condemns it as a grave threat to
true spirituality. Eliot's interest developed far earlier than Auden's
and was so deeply ingrained that it became a major preoccupation of
his poetry. His sternness seems a reaction to his own interest in occultism during the period when he was writing *The Waste Land*. By
1935 he said he regarded his interests in such "dubious mysticisms"
with "the reformed drunkard's abhorrence of intemperance."[13] In the

early twenties, Eliot continued the study of Eastern and Western mysticism which he had pursued at Harvard, attended the "séances" of P. D. Ouspensky, and studied the tarot cards.[14] The tarot pack indeed provides a major structural device in *The Waste Land*. In the occult tradition, the Tarot is considered a book, or the fragments of one: the book of Hermes Trismegistus, the legendary Egyptian priest whose Hermetic lore is a major source of many forms of occultism.[15] The characters in *The Waste Land* are identified when the fortune teller, Madame Sosostris, lays out her "wicked pack of cards": the "man with three staves," or the wounded Fisher King who must be healed if the Waste Land is to revive; the Phoenician sailor, or the doomed quester who fails the king; the "Hanged Man," or the sacrificial victim whom Sosostris fails to elicit from the pack; and "Belladonna . . . the lady of situations," who may be any of the various women in the poem who fail the quester.

The occult tradition in *The Waste Land* is of course not used without reservations. Like Madame de Tornquist in "Gerontion," Madame Sosostris is a tawdry figure despite the wise instruction she gives unconsciously through the Tarot. Moreover, her role is negative because she can only identify the reason for spiritual failure in the absence of the redeeming "Hanged Man." Nevertheless, the Tarot is, like the other sacred texts cited in the poem, a medium of spiritual wisdom. Like the Grail legends as interpreted by Jessie Weston, the tarot cards are the disjecta membra of a once-vital spiritual tradition.[16] As Leon Surette has noted, Weston's study of the Grail tradition shares much with Ezra Pound's notion of a secret history of Provençal "fideles d'amour."[17] In a book that preceded *From Ritual to Romance*, she compared the hidden meaning of the quest stories to that of alchemy and Freemasonry and wrote, in a passage that recalls Ezra Pound's speculations on the continuity of Provençal poetry, "There is a stream of tradition, running as it were underground, which from time to time rises to the surface, only to be relentlessly suppressed. It may be the Troubadours, the symbolical language of whose love poems is held to convey another, and less innocent, meaning; or the Albigenses, whose destruction the Church holds for a sacred duty."[18] Weston is heavily indebted to W. B. Yeats, Arthur Waite, and G. R. S. Mead; and she believed, like them, that secret groups continued to keep the mysteries alive.[19] In *From Ritual to Romance* she wrote, of one Grail legend, that it is *"the story of an initiation . . . carried out on the astral plane"* [her italics] (182). In a vague reference to cults like the Golden Dawn, she writes in her concluding chapter that the Grail quest "is actually possible to-day, for the indication of two of our romances as the final location of the Grail is not imagination, but the record of actual fact" (205). Citing Weston's emphasis on initiatory rites, Leon Surette argues that *The Waste Land* makes more sense if a reader recognizes the pattern of an "initiation ritual" rather than a quest.[20] His interpretation of the poem as initiation rather than quest resembles Lyndall Gordon's, but Gordon's reading of the poem as a "spiritual journey from sin to salvation" seems less persuasive because Surette's more accurately emphasizes the occult rather than the Christian background of Eliot's thought in 1922.[21]

Although Eliot felt drawn to a traditional faith, he could not in 1922 decide whether an Eastern or a Western spirituality was more compelling. After he became an Anglican in 1928, the force of his conversion was reflected in his denunciation of unorthodox spirituality not only in a prose polemic like *After Strange Gods* but also in his poetry. He was virtually rejecting the influence of Jessie Weston when, in his church pageant *The Rock* (1934), he disdained the "affirmation of rites with forgotten meanings" as a pagan "dead end" (CPP 107). Such rites he relates to the traditional image of the world snake, the "polar dragon" of Yeats's verse, in a portentous warning not to be too curious about spiritual matters such as the "future waves of time" and the command to renounce "those who prize the serpent's golden eyes" (CPP 112). Eliot's magus in "The Journey of the Magi" (1927) discovers the wave of the future in the knowledge of Christ but is left uneasy with the old dispensation and an "alien people clutching their gods" (CPP 69). His experience is simply "satisfactory," in the strictly theological sense of "satisfaction" as Christ's sacrifice to atone for original sin. He has experienced a unique gnosis, but it is a privilege that burdens him, rather as Yeats's "Magi" (1919) are burdened by their continual quest. Eliot's magus might be described in the same terms in which Yeats describes his Magi: "the pale unsatisfied ones" (Poems 126). But Eliot's protagonist is ready for death, whether a despairing one clutching his old gods or a redemptive one into a new birth. Yeats's Magi, on the contrary, continue their Gnostic quest for direct mystical experience, hoping to find once again the "uncontrollable mystery" revealed at Bethlehem. The approach to spiritual experience of Yeats's Magi is utterly different from that of the protagonist of Eliot's companion poem to the "Journey of the Magi." In "A Song for Simeon," Simeon is content with the promise of redemption and modestly asserts, "Not for me the ultimate vision" (CPP 70).

Rather than the ultimate vision Yeats's Magi continually hope for, Eliot's personae have fitful and frightened glimpses of another world, particularly through visions of ghosts. If "nothing is more dramatic than a ghost," as Eliot wrote in 1928, no drama is so primal as a character's confrontation with the ghosts of his past.[22] Harry's vision of the "spectres" in *The Family Reunion* is the clearest example, but there are several more that, to borrow a phrase from "The Hollow Men," fall like a shadow over his protagonists' experiences. In *The Waste Land*, Eliot's quester sees the dead flowing over London Bridge as well as the Baudelairean *"spectre"* who *"en plein jour raccroche le passant"* (CPP 51n.60). The ghostly presences in the garden of "Burnt Norton" are related to these midday ghosts and anticipate Eliot's most dramatic specter, the "familiar compound ghost" of "Little Gidding": "I caught the sudden look of some dead master / Whom I had known, forgotten, half recalled" (CPP 140). Helen Gardner's *The Composition of Four Quartets* has confirmed earlier identifications—by Richard Ellmann and other critics[23]—of Eliot's ghost as W. B. Yeats, although, Gardner observes, "The drafts make it clear that he began with Yeats in mind and worked towards a greater generality" (67). In *Eliot's Compound Ghost*, Leonard Unger has cited the presence of Yeats as the "compound ghost" of "Little Gidding" to support his analysis of Yeatsian echoes in the opening scenes of "Burnt Norton" and "Little Gidding" (111–14).

The presence of the poet of occultism as a spirit haunting Eliot's poetry is fitting, but as a "compound ghost" Yeats is more than that—he is also Eliot's double, as his persona in "Little Gidding" acknowledges when he "assumed a double part" to greet the specter in the predawn twilight. (The ghost is also compound, of course, because he represents many of Eliot's precursors—Swift, Mallarmé, and especially Dante.) As ghost and double, Yeats resembles Harold Bloom's description of the poetic precursor: "The strong poet peers in the mirror of his fallen precursor and beholds neither the precursor nor himself but a Gnostic double"[24] Bloom's description applies, even in its reference to the Gnostic quality of the double, to Eliot's dramatic encounter with Yeats in *Four Quartets*. Few critics of *Four Quartets* have failed to comment on Yeats's presence in the poem; but they have assumed that he is simply present, to use Auden's phrase, as an "honored guest." Although Eliot indeed honors him, Yeats also represents a kind of poetry that Eliot was drawn to and yet rejected. The precursor poet has become a "Gnostic double" and is both honored and threatened by virtue of being repressed. Like a Freudian double, Yeats represents something out of Eliot's past, a repressed poetic quality that emerges to be confronted and judged. Within the spiritual world of *Four Quartets*, Yeats stands for an approach to what Eliot called "the religious sources of poetry," an approach that may be called occult or Gnostic.[25] This approach is motivated by what Eliot once called, in a criticism that recalls Auden's distaste for "magic," a "reckless desire for the absolute" which attempts to achieve an unmediated and virtually magical access to the supernatural.[26]

For Bloom, the term *Gnosticism* suggests a tradition counter to the Christian and always reflects its root meaning in gnosis, or the direct knowledge of spiritual truths. In his study of Yeats, Bloom places him in a Gnostic tradition (stressing its fascination with a shadowy world of evil and determinism) and is highly critical of its influence on him. Although he values Yeats's poetry far more than Eliot's, Bloom and Eliot agree in finding Yeats's spiritual quest deeply flawed by his occult researches.[27] In representing an aspect of poetry that was repressed in Eliot's own work, Yeats's double plays a role that the ghost customarily plays in Eliot's poetry: the symbol of a buried life. For example, Prufrock's double (perhaps indicated by the "you and I" of the opening lines) represents the repressed self—though only in the poem's manuscript version, as this double was itself repressed in Eliot's final revision. In the manuscript, Prufrock, after a sleepless night, sees from his window a man sitting on a curb and realizes it is his own double. When the man begins to sing, Prufrock realizes that the double embodies his own madness.[28]

The apparition Prufrock sees is as much a Freudian double as the "gnostic" one that Bloom describes. In "The Uncanny," Freud wrote that the "uncanny is in reality nothing new or foreign, but something which is familiar and old-established in the mind that has become estranged only through the process of repression" (148). A double appears "uncanny" because it triggers repressed fears of madness (Prufrock's dissociation from his self) or death (a person's soul is a double that appears at death). As Freud writes, neatly linking the personal to the mythical, the "'double' has become a vision of terror, just as after the fall of their religion the gods took on daemonic shapes" (143). In general, a double signifies some aspect of our life that is out of control and exists independently of our everyday consciousness. None of the ghostlike creatures of *The Waste Land* are as uncanny as the spirit "gliding wrapt in a brown mantle, hooded" of "What the Thunder Said"; for it represents just this sense of something familiar but alien: "—But who is that on the other side of you?" (CPP

48). This double is related to Christ after his death on the journey to Emmaus, when his followers cannot recognize him because, though he may seem familiar, their weak faith makes him unrecognizable. Like Madame Sosostris, the disciples cannot recognize, or are "forbidden to see," the figure that represents salvation. Yet the familiar spirit somehow appears on the margins of consciousness, which produces the uncanny effect.

Eliot's ghosts in his play *The Family Reunion* also represent this doubling process. But unfortunately the ghosts (or furies) that haunt his character Harry, Lord Monchensey, lack a disquieting or uncanny quality. As Eliot himself complained, there is no theatrically viable way to stage the scenes in which they appear. When concealed by gauze, they "suggested a still out of a Walt Disney film," and when they were dimmer they looked like "shrubbery just outside the window."[29] Eliot concluded that they should not appear at all on the stage but only in the protagonist's mind, as of course the ghostly double appears in the journey to Emmaus in *The Waste Land*. The ultimate source of the ghosts is suggested by Harry's servant, who says that Lord Monchensey suffers from a "kind of repression" and a sensitivity the servant describes as "rather psychic" (CPP 240–41). The furies are symbols of the repressed past of Harry and his dead wife, whom he hated with what he fears became a murderous rage.

Harry's "psychic" quality is indicated in the scene of reminiscence with the family friend Mary, who recalls their childhood meetings in the moonlight to "raise the evil spirits" (CPP 248). Although this necromancy is obviously childish, it indicates a nature receptive to spiritual experience. The specters themselves reinforce this point at the play's conclusion:

> We know various spells and enchantments,
> And minor forms of sorcery,
> Divination and chiromancy.
>
> (291)

By revealing that Harry's spiritual life has been limited to these "minor forms" of religious experience, the ghosts play the role of a Yeatsian double in disclosing spiritual truths. A speech by the sibyl-like Agatha links the specters to the double through an allusion to Henry James's story of a man's confrontation with his double in the labyrinthian rooms of an empty house. In James's "The Jolly Corner," the double represents the more crude and American aspect of the prota-

gonist's nature. Like James's character, Harry has returned to his past
home to confront his past and present selves. The encounter will be
similarly traumatic because in the "jolly corner" where he glimpses
his past self, the "hidden is revealed, and the spectres show themselves" (229). If Harry, like Eliot's Simeon, has the humility to recognize his spiritual weakness, he may still work out his redemption—
as Harry's servant confidently expects that he will (288–89).

Harry's ultimate redemption is only hinted at in *The Family Reunion*,
but the parallel character in *The Cocktail Party* is clearly redeemed—
and a ghostly double is the early sign that her fate is to be a Christian
martyr and saint. Sir Henry Harcourt-Reilly, a psychotherapist, tells
us that when he first saw Celia Coplestone he saw her image standing
behind her revealing the astonishment of "the first five minutes after
a violent death" (CPP 384). Harcourt-Reilly explains that the image
merely signifies the way "certain minds" express themselves. But the
specificity of seeing her "five minutes" after death suggests that he
has occult knowledge of the afterlife, like that Yeats claims to have in
Book 3 of *A Vision*. Indeed Celia's state is parallel to that of Yeats's
Cuchulain, who experiences such astonishment in "Cuchulain Comforted." Critics of Eliot's play immediately noticed that Reilly was
Eliot's own persona, disguised as a psychotherapist. He is not only a
persona but also Eliot disguised as a Yeatsian magus (or the one-eyed
shaman of Celtic folklore), complete with second sight and virtually
magical powers.[30] *The Cocktail Party* shows us Eliot the "reformed
drunkard" again indulging his taste for the occult.

The passage in which Reilly speaks of seeing Celia's double, although it fits the Freudian view of the double as a harbinger of death,
is introduced by Reilly's quotation of Shelley's *Prometheus Unbound*,
in which the double has a different significance. In this passage, Earth,
the mother of Prometheus, is telling her son that there is a duplicate
world beyond death which his own double may disclose:

> The Magus Zoroaster, my dead child,
> Met his own image walking in the garden.
> That apparition, sole of men, he saw.
> For know there are two worlds of life and death.
> (1. 192–95)

The ghostly double discloses preknowledge of Celia's death to Harcourt-Reilly, which signifies its Yeatsian significance; for example,
Yeats's "Ille" in "Ego Dominus Tuus" hopes his double will disclose

occult wisdom. Reilly's perceptiveness leads some of the play's characters to compare him to the Devil, but he is instead someone who helps initiate suitable candidates for sainthood and helps Celia to fulfill her fate.

In terms of the classical background of the play, Reilly recalls Heracles in Euripides' *Alcestis*. The Greek hero rescues Alcestis from death by a descent into the underworld after the pattern of the rituals in Greek mystery cults.[31] This action is parallel to Reilly taking charge of reconciling Edward Chamberlayne and his estranged wife Lavinia, whom he brings back (Heracles-like) from spiritual death. In this rescue, Reilly is helped by his "Guardians," a term that signifies the two characters (Julia and Alex) who customarily assist him in moving candidates like Celia toward enlightenment. The term *guardian* is also used by Edward to signify the "tougher self" that one discovers through enlightenment. In an earlier draft of the play, Edward used the more charged and Yeatsian term *daemon* rather than "tougher self" (210). Either term signifies another form of the double; in Celia's case, her inner "daemon" has brought her to salvation.

Eliot's quotation from Shelley, a writer he little admired, comes secondhand from one he did admire, Charles Williams, a friend who was a member of the Hermetic Order of the Golden Dawn. The opening of Williams's novel *Descent into Hell* (1937) is entitled "The Magus Zoroaster" and cites the same Shelleyan passage.[32] The novel's setting is a London where the barrier between this life and the next often collapses so that characters may enter a timeless world. One of the major characters has seen her double and is terrified of meeting it. As she becomes more enlightened, however, she realizes that the double is her true self—or Eliot's "tougher self"—and instead welcomes its appearance. A haunted London is also the scene of a Williams novel for which Eliot wrote an introduction, *All Hallows' Eve* (1945). In this work, a sinister Jewish magus sends out his doubles to help him in his plan to enslave the world spiritually and is frustrated by a spirit who, like Celia Coplestone, is struggling to overcome her astonishment at her violent death. Through her devotion to the living, she exerts herself to help foil the necromantic plot. In Williams's novels, as in *The Cocktail Party*, one finds a fascination with occult trappings and power combined with a conclusion that reaffirms the power of Christian orthodoxy.

Although the London of Eliot's "Little Gidding" resembles the wartime London of *All Hallows' Eve*, the rural scenes of *Four Quartets* are also haunted. The culminating encounter of Eliot's persona with the ghost of "Little Gidding" is presaged by less dramatic encounters in the earlier quartets. In "Burnt Norton," the ghosts of the past hover around a ruined country house in a scene that again recalls James's "Jolly Corner." As these uncanny "guests" fade into the sunlight, the encounter is introduced by a passage of concentrated symbolism which begins: "Garlic and sapphires in the mud / Clot the bedded axel-tree" (CPP 118). The tree is the mythical world tree, or cabalistic tree, so familiar in Yeats's poetry. The Hermetic principle—as above, so below—means, as Paul Murray writes of this passage, that "natural substances such as herbs, plants, and precious stones have stars or planets corresponding to them in the heavens."[33] They are thus "figured in the drift of stars," as our fates are "reconciled among the stars" (CPP 119) in a Yeatsian ascent of the cabalistic tree. The passage thus invites us to "ascend to summer in the tree" and move in concert with the "moving tree" (118).

This passage parallels the opening lyric of Part 2 of "East Coker," which also follows a ghostly encounter when the spirits "long since under earth" appear in the light of a summer midnight. The spirits are announced, as they once were for Yeats (Vision 17), by faint pipe music and appear only "if you do not come too close" (CPP 123–24). The lyric also uses occult astrological imagery to reprise the Hermetic theme that the world above is like the one below:

> Scorpion fights against the Sun
> Until the Sun and Moon go down
> Comets weep and Leonids fly.
> (125)

In "Burnt Norton," the image of the "axel-tree" supports Eliot's assertion that we need to find the still point of the turning world. (Eliot said that his image of a dance around a still center was suggested by a Williams novel in which the greater trumps of the Tarot dance around the Fool.[34]) The "vortex" imagery also implies a still point at a turning center, but the imagery is called into question by the prose-like passage that immediately follows it, which claims that this style of poetry is "not very satisfactory: / A periphrastic study in a worn-out poetical fashion" (CPP 125).

As Eliot moves into a meditation on the "wisdom of age," the ensuing references to the "folly" of old men and their "fear of fear and frenzy" echo Yeats's "The Spur," "An Acre of Grass," and "Vacillation." Both Richard Ellmann and Helen Gardner read these echoes in terms of Eliot's late essay "Yeats" (1940), which contains little but high praise for Yeats's "moral, as well as intellectual, excellence" and for his treatment of the "feelings of age."[35] As a result, Ellmann and Gardner find nothing but praise of Yeats in "East Coker." Yet the late essay on Yeats still contains traces of Eliot's disquiet about Yeats's achievement. In his comment on the lines about "lust and rage" in "The Spur" and Yeats's play "Purgatory," Eliot allows himself to say of both that they are "not very pleasant." He questions the orthodoxy of the play's conception of purgation even though it is perfectly plain that Yeats wishes to be highly unorthodox. In "East Coker," Eliot prefers frenzy and folly to "deliberate hebetude," but scorns as well the attempt to acquire the "knowledge of dead secrets" (CPP 125), recommending instead the acquiring of the "wisdom of humility" (126).

A word even more Yeatsian than "folly" or "frenzy" is "daemonic," which Yeats uses for the poet who seeks fulfillment by seeking his double or anti-self. Indeed, in *A Vision* his term for the poet of Phase 17 who achieves this fulfillment is "The *Daimonic* Man" (Vision 140–41). Eliot's critique of occultism in "The Dry Salvages" is openly stated as he dismisses those who seem driven by "daemonic, chthonic Powers" and study the omens released: "By sortilege, or tea leaves, riddle the inevitable / With playing cards, fiddle with pentagrams" (CPP 135). In this passage, he is still attacking the tradition of poets like Yeats rather than affirming a tradition of his own. But in the final section of the poem, "Little Gidding," which is named for a seventeenth-century Anglican religious community, he imagines a spiritual experience that is communal and open rather than private and occult. As he visits the church at Little Gidding, he feels "suspended in time" during the shortest day of the year, when "the brief sun flames the ice, on pond and ditches" (CPP 138). The experience is mystical but also natural—it is not a daemonic revelation but a "hint" that must be developed by orthodox religious practice and social commitment. Thus the visitor to this Anglo-Catholic shrine is told, "You are not here to verify, / Instruct yourself, or inform curiosity," but instead, "You are here to kneel / Where prayer has been valid" (139). There are no Gnostic revelations or "dead secrets" to be found at "Little Gidding." The pilgrim is offered only the "wisdom of humility."

In *After Strange Gods*, Eliot quoted approvingly I. A. Richards's opinion that Yeats's trancelike states were "insufficiently connected with normal experience" (49).[36] In "Little Gidding," Eliot attempts to avoid Yeatsian flaws in the treatment of spiritual experience. The timeless "midwinter spring" is trancelike but not disconnected from a "normal" feeling of natural beauty as a hedgerow is "blanched for an hour with transitory blossom / Of snow" (CPP 138). The day is suspended "between pole and tropic," but there is no "worn-out" imagery in which "comets weep and Leonids fly" (125) to mark its otherworldly quality. Moreover, the ghost of "Little Gidding" is not invoked like a Yeatsian anti-self who comes to fulfill the quester's self.

The "ghost" is carefully presented as a hallucinatory experience, the perception of a man under stress after a bombing raid, and is more like a ghost out of Henry James than W. B. Yeats. But the ghost comes to give the great lesson about old age which Eliot finds in Yeats's late poetry. In Harold Bloom's phrase, Eliot confronts his "fallen precursor." But Yeats is no longer the poet of occultism Eliot had earlier deprecated and had so steadily ignored in his 1940 essay. His treatment in the late essay virtually makes Yeats into a compound poet, and so he has to apologize in the essay for seeming to give "the impression that I regard his earlier and his later work almost as if they had been written by two different men" (298). He gives this impression not only by praising the later poetry at the expense of the earlier but also by ignoring the later poems that still draw on Yeats's occultism, such as "Byzantium," "Supernatural Songs," and "Cuchulain Comforted." Instead, he stresses the personal lyrics that make Yeats "pre-eminently the poet of middle age" (301).[37] Thus the "dead master" of "Little Gidding" is a Yeats refashioned in Eliot's own image who returns only to enforce a lesson in humility. In Yeats's "Ego Dominus Tuus," Ille's hope is that the ghostly double will "disclose / All that I seek" (Poems 162). But in Eliot the ghost ironically says, "'Let me disclose the gifts reserved for age,'" which include the "cold friction of expiring sense" and the "rending pain" of remorse (CPP 141–42).

In the ghost's final advice, to accept pain and suffering and to "move in measure, like a dancer" amid the purgatorial flames, Richard Ellmann sees a reference to Yeats's "Byzantium."[38] The dance in Yeats's poem, however, is agonized rather than measured, and the poem ends with "spirit after spirit!" breaking into Byzantium from the "gong-tormented sea." The imagery of Eliot's lines is inspired more by Dante than Yeats, and the sentiment represents Christian resignation rather than the spirit of the author of "The Magi" or "Byzantium." Ellmann entitles his study of Yeats and Eliot "Possum's Conversion" and claims that "Little Gidding" marks the "reconciliation of their lifelong differences."[39] There is a reconciliation, but only because Eliot controls his dead rival. It is not Eliot who is converted but Yeats—into a poet who has renounced, as Eliot did, his preoccupations with "dubious mysticisms" and who has become a poet of Christian humility and resignation. Although his inclusion in the poem honors him, Yeats's role in *Four Quartets* is to help further Eliot's critique of the occult.

In a deeper sense, Yeats's role in Eliot's work is to serve, in Bloom's phrase, as his Gnostic double. Eliot's Christianity seems all the more orthodox when defined against Yeats's heresies. Yeats, however, made his own penetrating criticism of Eliot's religious poetry, commenting on its relative lack of "strong emotion; a New England Protestant by descent, there is little self-surrender in his personal relation to God and the soul."[40] Yeats based this criticism on an analysis of *Murder in the Cathedral*. Perhaps he would have revised his opinion if he had lived to read *Four Quartets*. In the second movement of "Little Gidding," the alchemical death of the elements of air, earth, water, and fire denotes the self-surrender that prepares for the ghost's visit. Only ash remains, but it is the ash left by burned roses.[41] Eliot rejects the Yeatsian Rosicrucian flower and recreates his own symbolic rose, with its roots in medieval Catholicism and Tudor and Stuart history. Yeats appeared as both a dangerous heretic and a humble quester in Eliot's distorting mirror. The image altered with Eliot's need to measure his own poetic achievement against that of Yeats.

Eliot's misreading of Yeats as a poet of quasi-Christian humility suggests that his criticism of Yeats's "artifically induced poeticality" is also mistaken. There is nothing artifical about Yeats's occult world in poems like "Byzantium" or "Supernatural Songs," and Eliot's silence about such poems seems to concede the point. When Eliot wrote that Pound was too influenced by Yeats's "spooks," he allowed that these spirits were "excellent creatures in their native bogs."[42] However condescending the remark, it makes the essential point that if a poet vividly believes in a subject, the writing will be not be artificial but genuinely "native" to the poet. Eliot's ghosts are quite different from Yeats's, but the shades of "Byzantium" or the shroud-sewers of "Cuchulain Comforted" seem no less convincing than the ghost of "Little Gidding"; and from Eliot's own testimony, we can conclude that the ghosts of *The Family Reunion* are far more artificial than Yeats's.

Despite Auden's criticism of Yeats's occultism, he is not so quick as Eliot to conclude that it is artifical or insincere: "he really went to seances, he seriously studied all those absurd books." Auden maintains that the major concern for a poet is whether a particular dogma "involves your emotions profoundly," as it clearly did for Yeats.[43] Of course there is a point where a poet's statements will seem too artificial or inflated to engage the reader's emotions. As I suggested in Chapter 2, Pound reaches it at times when he adopts his pose as a magus. But there is no way to specify this point, as Eliot tries to do in *After Strange Gods*, by determining what is orthodox or heretical in a particular culture—much less decide what is "normal" or "abnormal" about spiritual experiences. Auden is far wiser than Eliot when he maintains that an awareness that modern poets lack a tradition to help them interpret their experience should make us more, not less, tolerant of the variety and strangeness of their doctrines. In particular, Auden holds that the "polemical situation" resulting from the challenges of scientific rationality should help us understand the irrational qualities of Yeats's cosmology, which expressed the poet's defiance of this rationalism.[44] Perhaps Auden could be more sympathetic toward Yeats's occultism than Eliot because he seemed less important as a rival to the younger poet. To Eliot, Yeats the occultist (in the words from Baudelaire quoted in *The Waste Land*) was "mon semblable,—mon frère!"

H.D.'s Hermeticism:
Between Jung and Freud

Every act of [Hermes] is marked by this unstable
ambivalence. This god of calculation, arithmetic, and
rational science also presides over the occult sciences
astrology and alchemy.

—Jacques Derrida, *Dissemination*

4 We have already seen how occultism shaped
Pound's conception of the poet, and Chapter 5
shows how important occult lore was to Robert
Duncan. These poets, however, did not seriously
pursue occultism outside of their poetry. Pound be-
lieved in the importance of mystery cults but did not, like Yeats, join
one himself. Of the poets examined in this book, only Yeats and H.D.
were practicing occultists. Although Sylvia Plath and Ted Hughes
used astrology, the Tarot, and the Ouija board, they did not demonstrate the obsession with them that marks the true occultist. Neither
was as persistent as Yeats or H.D. in their attempts to contact the
dead. James Merrill's use of a Ouija board (1955–95), which rivals the
endurance of Yeats's preoccupation with contacting the dead, suggests
a true occult obsessiveness. Unlike Yeats, however, Merrill neither
joined a cult nor expanded his interest in the Ouija board to exploring
other forms of occultism.

Similar as Yeats and H.D. appear as occult poets, there is a major
difference: H.D. did not weave doubts about the validity of the
"dreaming wisdom" or "daemonic images" into the fabric of her poetry. Of all the poets of the occult, and despite her psychoanalytic
insights into it, H.D. seems the least self-conscious about occultism.
She discriminated less than Pound among its various strands, embracing equally the knowledge from classic Greek texts and from ta-
ble-tipping sèances. The countertradition represented by occultism

seemed to her a native heritage she need never doubt. Indeed she wrote her unpublished novel, *The Mystery* (1950–51), to link the Moravian faith of her childhood with occult sources. Her protagonist, Louis Saint-Germain, who is inspired by an eighteenth-century magus described in Eliphas Lévi's *History of Magic*, experiences a "visitation" from the founder of the Moravian Church, Count Zinzendorf, which confirms his powers and mission. Saint-Germain is thus initiated into Zinzendorf's secret plan to redeem the world.[1] Similarly, Hilda in H.D.'s novel *The Gift* (1941–43) learns, Susan Stanford Friedman says, that the gift itself is "her legacy from the Hidden Church" of the Moravians.[2] The notion of a "Hidden Church" is what Dianne Chisholm refers to as one of H.D.'s "autobiographical fantasies"—in this case a "myth of a visionary tradition."[3]

The conjunction of H.D.'s passionate interest in both occultism and psychoanalysis is not surprising given that Freud himself saw (and worried about) the relationship between the two. Both explore the "hidden." According to Friedman, the difference between occultism and psychoanalysis was that the latter "found the locus of meaning in the individual unconscious, while the occult located the center of significance in a universal spirit."[4] Because most forms of occultism, including H.D.'s, assume a universal spirit or Yeatsian anima mundi as the repository of archetypes and images, Jung's psychoanalysis has always seemed more attractive to occultists than Freud's.[5] H.D.'s reference to a "universal spirit" is clearly Jungian, and she makes Freud seem Jungian in her memoir of her 1933–34 psychoanalysis, *Tribute to Freud*. Apparently with *Totem and Taboo* in mind, she writes that Freud's exploration of the unconscious proved that "the shape and substance of the rituals of vanished civilizations ... were still inherent in the human mind—the human psyche, if you will" (Tribute 13). H.D. also says, however, that Freud "shut the door on transcendental speculations" and that he believed that the "soul" manifested itself only through individual minds and bodies. He had no theory of an oversoul or collective unconscious and, most disturbing to H.D., no belief in individual survival after death (Tribute 102, 43).

Despite the Jungian spirit of her occultism, H.D. showed little interest in Jung, although her doctor Erich Heydt thought she became more Jungian later in her life.[6] Friedman has criticized Norman Holmes Pearson for referring to H.D. as a "quasi-Jungian," but Pearson's comment did not imply that she was not essentially Freudian. He does suggest that a Freudian can nevertheless embrace Jungian concepts: "like many Freudians, she became quasi-Jungian and could bring the cabala, astrology, magic, Christianity, classical and Egyptian mythology, and personal experience into a joint sense of Ancient Wisdom."[7] This emphasis on the Jungian turn H.D. gave to essentially Freudian insights seems correct to me and characteristic of many modern writers. In his book *Joyce between Freud and Jung*, Sheldon Brivic argues that Freudian and Jungian approaches can be complimentary in literary studies because Freud "deals with causes, while Jung, in describing eternal symbolic patterns of value, deals with goals (6)." My analysis of the occultism in H.D.'s poetry takes both approaches but without losing sight of her basically Freudian understanding of both the occult and literary arts.

H.D.'s approach to a "joint sense of Ancient Wisdom" is seen in her conception of a secret, syncretic wisdom best described as Hermeticism. Although the Hermetic tradition is ancient, H.D.'s poetry has given it a unique twentieth-century meaning. As she found her own voice as a poet, Hermeticism became her intellectual and poetic inspiration. She identified with the tradition so closely that she associated her "writing signet," "H.D.," with it as if one led inevitably to the other: "H.D.—Hermes—Hermeticism" (Tribute 66). In "Hermes of the Ways," the Greek messenger of the gods is the subject of H.D.'s first poem as "H.D. Imagiste." He symbolizes poetic vision throughout her poetry, particularly in *Trilogy*.

H.D.'s critics refer to Hermes as an exclusively male figure. For example, Norman Holland describes H.D.'s identification with Hermes as a "fusion with a man" in order to escape emotional chaos. Deborah Kloepfer disagrees, asserting that H.D. must evade "thralldom" to Hermes. Yet they agree that she regards Hermes, in Kloepfer's phrase, as a "male patron."[8] My impression is that Hermes is too mercurial a figure to be considered specifically male or female. An understanding of the Hermetic tradition will demonstrate the full significance of Hermes' sexual nature and the way H.D.'s occultism sustains her challenge to sexual and religious orthodoxies.

The philosophical tradition known as "Hermeticism" arose early in the Christian era. It expressed Hellenistic mistrust of traditional Greek rationalism and attempted to fuse Eastern thought with Western Platonic and stoic philosophy. The *corpus hermeticum*, attributed to the legendary Hermes Trismegistus, was composed by Alexandrian scholars in the first two centuries A.D. as a series of texts that dealt with subjects such as alchemy, astrology, and magic. After Marsilio Ficino translated the Hermetic texts into Latin (1463), Hermeticism influenced and even challenged traditional Christianity and influenced English writers from the Renaissance down through the Romantic poets and Yeats (who belonged to Hermetic societies in both Dublin and London).[9] Works that deeply influenced H.D.'s poetry were explicitly Hermetic. For example, Robert Ambelain in *Dans l'ombre des cathédrales* (1939), which was a major influence upon her poem *Hermetic Definition*, said his work was written for modern "disciples of Hermes" and for the purpose of transmitting "the general principles of an esoteric tradition (9)." H.D. also admired and drew upon Jean Chaboseau's *Le tarot*, which defined Hermeticism as "the more subtle side of philosophy, the more mysterious if you wish. It incorporates the totality of 'secret' spoken knowledge—Kabbalah or the science of letters and numbers, astrology, alchemy (19)."[10]

H.D. goes beyond her sources by identifying Hermeticism with the Greek god Hermes as well as with Hermes Trismegistus. Hermes is clearly the Greek god rather than the Egyptian magus in her early poetry. *Tribute to Freud* shows how she later conflated the two figures, and their single identity is crucial to the theme of *Trilogy*. In the early poem "Hermes of the Ways," the Greek god appears in his roles both as messenger of the other gods and as the guide of souls (Hermes Psychopompous). He is placed against a background of natural forces both creative and destructive. Part 1 describes the wind and waves playing over a vast seascape, but Hermes in his sheltered "sea-orchard" welcomes and protects the wayfarer. Part 2 presents a landscape with a chthonic stream, "flowing below ground," in which trees and their fruit struggle for existence. Hermes again appears, at the margin of land and sea, as a protector and guide. A finely musical stanza states the essential theme:

> But more than the many-foamed ways
> of the sea,
> I know him
> of the triple path-ways,
> Hermes,
> who awaits.

> (CP 37)

As a guide to the poet or wayfarer, Hermes offers not merely an alternative path but a choice of three: "Dubious, / facing three ways, / welcoming wayfarers" (38). (The triad also suggests the epithet for the other Hermes, Trismegistus ("Thrice Great.") In its separate line, the word *dubious* seems to apply better to the wayfarers than to Hermes. Unlike Janus, Hermes does not insist on one path or another but points three ways in an implied dialectical movement that may lead one, in the face of challenge, away from doubt and timidity.

As Friedman observes, the triads that pervade H. D.'s poetry also appear in the vision she experienced in her Corfu hotel in 1920.[11] The first of the images she saw, as if projected on a wall, was a head of Mercury (as she later realized), the second a cup or "mystic chalice," and the third a form like the "tripod of classic Delphi" (Tribute 45–46, 100). In *Tribute to Freud*, she related this vision (or hallucination as Freud considered it) to the need for a modern synthesis: "Religion, art, and medicine, through the latter ages, became separated; they grow further apart from day to day. These three working together, to form a new vehicle of expression or a new form of thinking or of living, might be symbolized by the tripod, the third of the images on the wall before me.... The tripod, we know, was the symbol of prophecy, prophetic utterance or occult or hidden knowledge" (50–51). These three separated arts are paralleled by the three pathways of Hermetic thought, which point toward the achieved synthesis. H.D. describes them in the long poem that best demonstrates the importance of Hermeticism in her poetic career. Her posthumous poem *Hermetic Definition* (1972), might be described as her definition of herself as a Hermeticist. Rachel Blau Duplessis has shown that the poem's structure is "based on the nine-month gestation period with its three trimesters" and represents a "thesis, antithesis and abrupt synthesis" of conflicting emotions.[12]

Ambelain's *Dans l'ombre des cathédrales* prepares us to understand H.D.'s alchemical imagery. The Cathedral of Notre Dame in Paris is rich in medieval symbolism, which one could imagine Yeats searching out—as in Pound's Cantos 83 and 113—"over that portico" of the richly carved cathedral doors. Ambelain claims that Notre Dame was constructed on the site of an ancient temple to Isis, worshiped by the early settlers, known as the Parisi, and constructed on an alchemical formula for the control of natural forces. H.D. contributes to the argument with some characteristic wordplay: "Isis, Iris, / fleur-de-lis ... Bar-Isis is Par-Isis" (HD 5), which leads her to "Paris" as the word to indicate the site for Isis's worship. She acknowledges Ambelain's alchemical interpretation when she writes:

the stones hold secrets;
they tell us vibration was brought over
by ancient alchemists.

(HD 8)

Not only alchemy, however, but all three (astrology and magic too)
of the specifically Hermetic arts are invoked. (In terms of the "separate
arts" of *Tribute*, alchemy corresponds to medicine, astrology to religion, and magic to art.)

The three hermetic arts are symbolized by the three doors of Notre
Dame. The first door H.D. names is sacred to Our Lady, "*Astrologie*";
she next names the last door, sacred to Saint Anne or her pagan equivalent Cybele, "*Magie*" (for some reason, not italicized); and the
"middle door is Judgment, (*Alchimie*)" (HD 8–11). She walks through
the middle door to an "implacable" judgment on her hopeless passion
for a much younger man, Lionel Durand, the Haitian journalist; but
she triumphs over it as she defines herself as a poet who shares in the
creative force of Isis/Cybele/Notre Dame:

I did not cheat
nor fake inspiration . . .
auguries, hermetic definition . . .
my hand worn with endeavour,
our curious pre-occupation with stylus and pencil,
was re-born at your touch.

(HD 26)

Her love is justified because it led to the birth of the poem. Part 3
("*Star of Day*") draws upon the Hermetic science of astrology to signify this birth. The poet prays to one of the "*génies zodiacaux*" and
discovers the symbol of her creativity in an Egyptian goddess. Although it is Christmas time, the star of birth is of course not the star
of Bethlehem ("my Christmas candles had burnt out" [47]) but the
star sacred to a goddess whom H.D. finds in Plutarch, an equivalent
to Isis, Cybele, or Notre Dame:

they say, Saïs brought forth the Star of Day,
at midnight when the shadows are most dense,
the nights longest and most desperate.

(HD 45)

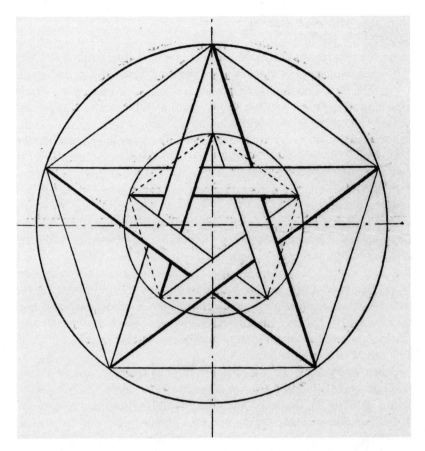

Figure 8. Pentagram, from Robert Ambelain, *Dans l'ombre des cathédrales,* 1939.

In struggling toward the birth signified by the star, the poet has been sustained by the Hermetic tradition:

> The five-petalled *rose sauvage*
> (pentagram of the alchemists)
> sustains me.
>
> (HD 33)

Traditionally, the pentagram is not an alchemical sign, but Ambelain interprets it as such by ingeniously seeing in it a diagram of the Pythagorean "golden section" (Figure 8). Like Ezra Pound in Canto 90, Ambelain finds, in the proportions of the golden section, an architectural principle transmitted within the esoteric tradition. In his description of the magical powers of the pentagram, he cites the most famous of the medieval alchemists, Paracelsus (63). In a passage particularly important to H.D., he sees the "pentagramme d'harmonie" in the rose symbols of Notre Dame, which signify "l'aspect féminin de Dieu." The "rose sauvage" on one of the cathedral's portals is called "l'emblème par excellence de l'Adeptat," or initiate into occult learning (12). The "feminine aspect of God" is crucial to H.D.'s interpretation of the Hermetic tradition and is related to the importance of Hermes in her poetry. After noting that in H.D.'s horoscope Mercury was the ruler of H.D.'s sun sign, Friedman shows how her astrological studies encouraged her to associate Mercury "with the Greek Hermes, the Egyptian Thoth, Hermes Psychopompous, Hermes Trismegistus, and the Christian 'Word.' As Thoth, he invented writing; as Psychopompous, his magic wand Caduceus led the dead souls to a new life in the underworld; as Trismegistus, he was the patron of alchemy and hermetic wisdom.... The central role Hermes plays in the *Trilogy* emerges partially, I would argue, from the sense of personal initiation H.D. found in her horoscope."[13]

Alchemy as well as astrology is essential to Hermes' role in *Trilogy* and thus to the role Hermeticism plays in H.D.'s poetry. Carolyn Merchant argues in *The Death of Nature* that an anti-Aristotelian conception of the "equal importance [of] male and female principles in generation, permeated many alchemical treatises" (17). She would agree with Jung that alchemy kept alive Gnostic conceptions of a female or androgynous deity. *Trilogy* shows how deeply H.D. appreciated the underground power of this medieval art. The alchemical imagery appears early in Part 1 ("The Walls Do Not Fall") when the poet laments that in wartime the poet's "stylus is dipped in corrosive sublimate" (CP 512). The reference to the "corrosive" background of her art is superficially negative. But the process of sublimation is basic to the alchemical transformation, and a "corrosive" stage must be endured to reach it. The poet speaks of her heart as a "dead canker" (511), of the difficulty of raising herself from "snuffling the ground" (527), and of transforming "fixed indigestible matter" (534). The very reconciliation of opposites that is supposed to occur in both alchemy and poetry seems unattainable: "juxtaposition of words for words' sake, / without meaning, undefined ... clash of opposites, fight of emotion / and sterile invention" (535). And yet the poet dreams of disclosing the "alchemist's secret" (526) and moves at least "a step further / toward fine distillation of emotion":

the elixir of life, the philosopher's stone
is yours if you surrender

sterile logic, trivial reason.

(CP 533)

The importance of the feminine aspect of Hermes emerges as *Trilogy* unfolds the alchemical process in more detail. The goal of alchemy was not always or even usually considered to be the creation of gold from base metals. Its goal could also be an elixir that granted eternal life (*aqua vitae*), a stone that would give one magical powers over matter (*lapis philosophorum*), or even the creation of human life itself (*filius philosophorum*). The basic elements of the alchemist's art were sulphur and mercury. Sulphur represented combustibility, mercury liquidity; sulphur was masculine and solar, mercury feminine and lunar. Both elements, however, represented the spiritual qualities of the psyche. To represent the body, the sulphur/mercury duality became the "alchemical triad" with the addition of salt to represent the body. The merging of these contraries is what Carl Jung, the chief historian of alchemy, calls the *mysterium coniunctionis*, or alchemical marriage. Jung cites an alchemical work attributed to Hermes Trismegistus himself on this sacred marriage: "When we marry the crowned king with the red daughter, she will conceive a son in the gentle fire."[14]

In alchemical texts, Mercury was conceived in sexual terms that implicitly challenged the dominant masculinity of the Christian deity, which naturally was, for H.D., a crucial feature of the tradition. This belief in androgyny, which Jung says was far too radical for the alchemists to admit consciously, was central to their conception of Mercury. As the tradition develops, Mercury is regarded as a hermaphroditic figure (Figure 7). (In Greek legend, Hermaphroditus is the son of Hermes and Venus.) Jung believes that the sexual implications of alchemy were even more central to its cultural importance than its preservation of pagan mythology and that Mercury was the key figure in this revaluation of sexuality: "Hermes or Mercurius possessed a double nature, being a chthonic god of revelation and also the spirit of quicksilver, for which reason he was represented as a hermaphrodite."[15]

Part 2 of *Trilogy* ("Tribute to the Angels") opens with an alchemical theme that governs the development of this part of the poem according to the traditional alchemical patterns. H.D. begins by invoking the legendary Hermes:

> Hermes Trismegistus
> is patron of alchemists;
>
> his province is thought,
> inventive, artful and curious;
>
> his metal is quicksilver,
> his clients, orators, thieves and poets.
>   (CP 547)

The naming of seven angels from the Judeo-Christian and Muslim traditions is the major structural device of the poem. Yet Hermes is the first spiritual entity that H.D. honors through naming, and because his "metal is quicksilver" (or mercury), he is also conflated with the Roman god Mercury. (Mercury in turn enters the Christian tradition as Saint Michael the Archangel, which H.D. reflects upon in sections 33 and 34 of "Tribute to the Angels.") Mercury is prefigured in Part 1 (521) by his caduceus and in the lines "Mercury, Hermes, Thoth / invented the script, letters, palette" (519). In this brilliantly condensed juxtaposition, she relates the middle figure, Hermes, to Mercury as the Greek god Hermes and to Thoth as the magus Hermes Trismegistus.

This elaborate syncretism is the essence of H.D.'s poetry, even though (perhaps thinking of Jungian studies) she feels that

> This search for historical parallels,
> research into psychic affinities,
> has been done to death before.
>   (CP 539)

Despite the breaking of the "vessel of integrity" (526) that faces the modern poet, H.D. proposes to "collect the fragments of splintered glass ... melt down and integrate" them (547), and attempt a new distillation. The alchemical tradition, in its enormous complexity and obscurity, gives her the room to follow her own direction: "as the vein-paths on any leaf / differ from those of every other leaf" (540). In Friedman's reading of the alchemical theme of *Trilogy*, however, H.D. is practicing "revisionist alchemy" because "centuries of religious tradition have so systematically repressed or denigrated the female form in which the 'One' has manifested." Friedman discovers this revisionism at the conclusion of the alchemical process because the "living jewel distilled in the crucible of words is not gold, not a traditional version of the long-sought philosopher's stone."[16] In fact,

H.D. is quite traditional in making the jewel living or organic. Friedman's phrase "revisionist alchemy" is redundant because alchemy itself, as Jung has maintained, is a criticism and revision of some major assumptions of Western culture. Although I disagree with Friedman that H.D. rejects the traditional conception of the stone, it is true that the poet does not at first understand the nature of "this bitter jewel" (CP 552).[17]

There is an inexhaustible series of names to describe the goal of alchemy, whether symbolized as the philosopher's stone or the offspring of the alchemical marriage. The names include "pelican's milk," "*aqua divina*," "pearl of great price," "four-in-one," and "*lapis angularis*." "Gold" is merely one of them. One name or another is never quite right; the goal is always something a little different, the meaning deferred from term to term. Thus the poet in section 9 of "Tribute" puzzles over the "bitter jewel": "what is your colour? / what do you offer?" (CP 552). The fires of inspiration burn with the varying colors associated with alchemical change—known as the *cauda pavonis*, or "peacock's tail" (Figure 6). The colors include "green-white, opalescent," "white agate," and "rose vein"; and, as the distillation moves toward completion, it develops "a pulse uncooled that beats yet, / faint blue violet" (554). Because H.D. begins with the *prima materia*, transformation is slow; and the flame under the crucible must be protected from uninitiated "knaves and fools" and at times relit—as it is from sections 8 through 14. But it develops an organic form as H.D. introduces the imagery, familiar from the poetry of Yeats and Pound, of a mystical marriage. In the final section of the poem (section 43), the "rainbow feathers" of the *cauda pavonis* signal the approach of the marriage at "the point in the spectrum / where all lights become white:

> and white is not no-colour,
> as we were told as children,
>
> but all-colour;
> where the flames mingle . . .
>
> to rainbow feathers, to the span of heaven.
> (573)

H.D. might have been looking at the following passage from Jung's *Psychology and Alchemy*, so closely does it describe not only the above lines from *Trilogy* but also the culminating ones that follow it. Jung is explaining the signs that precede the transmutation of alchemy:

The "many colours" (*omnes colores*) or "peacock's tail" (*cauda pavonis*), lead to the one white colour that contains all colours. At this point the first main goal of the process is reached, namely the *albedo* [whitening]. . . . It is the silver or moon condition, which still has to be raised to the sun condition. The *albedo* is, so to speak, the daybreak. . . . The *rubedo* then follows direct from the *albedo*, as the result of raising the heat of the fire to its highest intensity. The red and white are King and Queen, who may also celebrate their "chymical wedding" at this stage (231–32).

The "chymical wedding" is exactly what takes place as the heat increases and the bitter jewel "melts in the crucible." In the passage attributed to Hermes Trismegistus quoted above, the marriage of the "crowned king" with the "red daughter" proceeds "in the gentle fire" so that the child may be born. The birth of human life, as it occurs, for example, in Goethe's *Faust*, Part 2 (2.2), is as traditional an end to the process as the production of the *lapis*, or stone. In H.D.'s poem, the king is Hermes and the goddess is Venus, who is praised throughout the trilogy. H.D. relates both Venus and Mary to the greek goddess Maia, the mother by Zeus of Hermes. Venus, Mary, or Maia have as many names as the alchemical jewel, which the poet shows by listing some of the more recondite, such as "Our Lady of the Goldfinch, / Our Lady of the Candelabra":

> and we have seen her
> with a single flower
>
> or a cluster of garden-pinks
> in a glass beside her.
> (CP 564)

Tribute concludes with the birth of a child, which would exactly fit the pattern described in Jung's quotation from Hermes Trismegistus. Janice Robinson writes, "The birth of the child with 'a face like a Christmas rose' brings the final affirmation of the passion which creates life. The god is the jewel; the lady is the crucible; from their union is born a child."[18] The transformation is described thus:

> but when the jewel
> melts in the crucible,

we find not ashes, not ash-of-rose,
not a tall vase and a staff of lilies,

not *vas spirituale*,
not *rosa mystica* even,

but a cluster of garden-pinks
or a face like a Christmas-rose.

(CP 574)

The product resulting from the melting of the jewel is defined in four negative phases that shows how deeply H.D. absorbed an alchemical process of thought. First, ash is not found because it has been consumed in the transformation (like sulphur, which some alchemists refered to as "ash" because of the chthonic qualities of both substances). The lines themselves are a variation on another great poem written in wartime London, "Little Gidding": "Ash on an old man's sleeve / Is all the ash the burnt roses leave" (CPP 139). Both poets are concerned with moving away from the ashes into a healing and purifying fire.[19] Second, the result is not a vase or a staff of lilies (imagery developed in "The Flowering of the Rod") because the vase and staff symbolize the male/female qualities that have produced the alchemical result and cannot be the result itself. From the word *vase* the poem moves through etymological play to the Latin phrase *"vas spirituale,"* which means a "spiritual vessel" in reference to Mary's womb as the vessel that carried the Christ child. Finally, the product is not, as in Eliot's *Four Quartets*, the *rosa mystica*. Although it is mystical, the product is also human—not the mystical rose itself, but a human face "like a Christmas-rose."

The reference to the "cluster of garden-pinks" takes us back to the fleeting appearance of the Venus or Mary figure in section 29, where she is seen with the "cluster of garden-pinks / in a glass beside her" (CP 564), where the glass or vase prefigures the mother's womb and the flowers the child. The conclusion to Part 2 of *Trilogy* thus parallels the conclusion of the entire poem in Part 3 ("The Flowering of the Rod"), when we see Mary holding the Christ child. Part 3 also parallels the conclusion of *Hermetic Definition* (Part 2, "Star of Day"). In both poems, a star signifies the birth of a child. At the conclusion of *Trilogy*, the three astrologers known as the Magi place their gifts before Mary and her child. Whether Venus, Mary, or Maia, she is the feminine archetype who signifies the perfection of love and creativity.

The language of images is universal, but it is no more fixed for H.D. than the identity of Thoth/Hermes/Mercury. This universal language was preserved not only by poets but also by alchemists and astrologers. Alchemy offered H.D. a tradition that did not exclude the kind of symbols "the new-church spat upon" (CP 547) and thus provided a way of absorbing pagan and occult elements purged from orthodox Christianity, including an understanding of the "feminine aspect of God." H.D. is drawn to the Hermetic disciplines of alchemy and astrology for the very reasons Jung gives for their importance in *Psychology and Alchemy*, where he deplores much as H.D. does the damage done when the pagan images were shattered: "Whereas in the Church the increasing differentiation of ritual and dogma alienated consciousness from its natural roots in the unconscious, alchemy and astrology were ceaselessly engaged in preserving the bridge to nature, *i.e.* the unconscious psyche, from decay." Like H.D., Jung laments the loss to the individual who has "never experienced the sacred images as his inmost possession and has never realized their kinship with his own psychic structure" (16). To help remedy this loss, H.D. renews the occult arts and writes poetry in which her readers may experience its sacred images.

H.D.'s revival of Hermetic tradition seems Jungian both in its interest in a countertradition and in its goal of discerning a feminine archetype. But their very similarity of approaches may account for her greater interest in Freud. She wrote that Jung "left as they say, medicine for mysticism and as I have said, I studied my mysticism or magic from the French writers Ambelain and Chaboseau."[20] This statement seems consistent with the Freudian criticism of Jung as someone who confused his psychoanalytic philosophy with unverifiable hypotheses and diluted his research by drawing on obscure texts to substantiate his theory of a collective unconscious. If one desires a mystical philosophy, one might as well go directly to the mystical writers.

Even though Jung wrote three brilliant scholarly volumes on alchemy, it is Freud whom H.D. refers to as the *"alchemist si remarkable."*[21] The alchemical themes and motifs that Jung described in his research on the tradition were relatively superficial aspects of alchemy for H.D. True alchemy for her was the Rimbaudian alchemy of the word, and it was Freud's approach to the unconscious that discovered such verbal alchemy. H.D. believed that alchemy would help her to "find new words as the Professor found or coined new words to explain certain as yet unrecorded states of mind or being. . . . We retreat from the so-called sciences and go backward or go forward into alchemy" (Tribute 145). Her conception of finding new words, as Freud did, is related to the wordplay one finds throughout her work. For example, we have noted her multiple names for the alchemical jewel, her verbal juxtapositions such as Isis/Paris and Maia/Mary, and the way her wordplay with her "writing signet," "H.D.," suggests the word association: "H.D.—Hermes—Hermeticism." The Freudian understanding of the unconscious deals with words in individual minds rather than symbols and archetypes in a collective unconscious.

In early works such as *The Interpretation of Dreams* and *Totem and Taboo*, Freud too speculated that dreams and primitive rituals could imply some kind of innate archaic knowledge in the human psyche. But Jung's example showed him that such speculations led to making psychoanalysis a kind of mysticism rather than a kind of science. Jacques Lacan asserted that Freud, unlike Jung, turned away from the "romantic unconscious." Freud's unconscious "is not the locus of the divinities of night. This locus is no doubt not entirely unrelated to the locus towards which Freud turns his gaze—but the fact that Jung, who provides a link with the terms of the romantic unconscious, should have been repudiated by Freud, is sufficient indication that psychoanalysis is introducing something other."[22] The "something other" is related to what H.D. sees as Freud's significance as a literary Hermes. Freud showed that the way to explore the psyche was through relaxing conscious control and allowing, as Lacan puts it, "the play of the signifer." The locus of the unconscious is not some mysterious archaic realm: "In the dream, in parapraxis, in the flash of wit—what is it that strikes one first? . . . In a spoken or written sentence something stumbles. Freud is attracted by these phenomena, and it is there that he seeks the unconscious" (25). In her poem about Freud, "The Master," H.D. reveals her similarly linguistic understanding of Freud's route to the unconscious or unknown. Although each word is separate, and "each word led to another word,":

> . . . the whole made a rhythm . . .
> till now unguessed at,
> unknown.[23]

The link between H.D.'s "play of the signifier" and the process of alchemy is seen in the most explicitly alchemical section of *Trilogy*:

now polish the crucible
and in the bowl distill

a word most bitter, *marah,*
a word bitterer still, *mar,*

sea, brine, breaker, seducer,
giver of life, giver of tears;

now polish the crucible
and set the jet of flame

under, till *marah-mar*
are melted, fuse and join

and change and alter,
mer, mere, mère, mater, Maia, Mary,

Star of the Sea,
Mother.

(CP 552)

As the poet notes in Part 3 of *Trilogy,* "*marah-mar*" (masculine and feminine forms) means "bitter" in Hebrew. Part 3 also links the word to "Mary" as well as to the medicinal and aromatic spice "myrrh" (590). The salt ("sea, brine") bitterness of the liquid is distilled or sublimated into the sweetness of the names Maia (the mother of Hermes by Zeus) and Mary. So also the still bitterer word meaning "to break or damage," *mar* ("breaker, seducer"), is restored in a "vessel of integrity" as the first syllable of "Mary" in the alchemical melting and rejoining. Mary is a Jungian archetype, but *Mary* is also a word with, like all words, a unique history and special associations that the poet exploits.

This alchemy of the word opens up, as she said in *Tribute to Freud,* "an unusual dimension, an unusual way to *think*" (47). As they were for the alchemist, words for H.D. were "anagrams, cryptograms" (CP 540):

the ancient rubrics reveal that
we are back at the beginning:

> ... and idols and their secret is stored
> in man's very speech.
>
> (517)

As the god of alchemy and linguistic play, Hermes is again an inspiration for H.D.'s poetry. Writing of the Egyptian God Thoth, Jacques Derrida notes his identification with Hermes and describes him as "sly, slippery, and masked, an intriguer and a card, like Hermes, he is neither king nor jack, but rather a sort of *joker*, a floating signifier, a wild card, one who puts play into play."[24] This "play" is the essence of H.D.'s "unusual way to think." In *Trilogy* (CP 568) her play on *mar*, *myrrh*, *mère*, and *Mary* is an example of this technique, as is her use of the initials "SS" to identify and thus merge both the feminine *Santa Sophia* (Holy Wisdom) with the masculine aspect of the Trinity, *Sanctus Spiritus* (the Holy Ghost).

We see the same kind of linguistic play in her memoir of Freud: "SIGNET—as from sign, a mark, token, proof; signet—the privy seal, a seal; signet-ring—a ring with a signet or private seal; sign-manual—the royal signature.... (I have used my initials H.D. consistently as my writing signet or sign-manual" (Tribute 66). Dwelling on the various concepts signified by the very word *signet* increases her sense of the power of words: "all from the French, *signe*, and Latin, *signum*. And as I write that last word, there flashes into my mind the associated *in hoc signum* or rather, it must be *in hoc signo* and *vinces*" (Tribute 66). This sense that the poet will conquer experience through words (adapting the Christian motto for the cross *in hoc signo vinces*) is summed up in a statement in *Tribute to Freud* that is as Jungian as it is Freudian. She writes that Freud showed that the language and imagery of the dream was meaningful and could be interpreted: "The picture-writing, the hieroglyph of the dream, was the common property of the whole race; in the dream, man, as at the beginning of time, spoke a universal language, and man, meeting in the universal understanding of the unconscious or the subconscious, would forgo barriers of time and space, and man, understanding man, would save mankind" (Tribute 71).

By speaking of a "universal language" to help "save mankind," H.D. may seem open to the kind of criticism Norman Holland has made of her poetry. Holland thinks that the precision in her poetry arises from an "over-concern for boundaries and discrete units... choppy stanza forms." He argues that such precision is related to "her insistence on treating symbols as having fixed meanings and the dream as 'a universal language,' despite Freud's cautions to the contrary."[25] My experience of H.D.'s poetry reverses everything Holland says here. To use Pound's term, her poetry is a "phantastikon" in which one mythical figure or image merges into another, in a manner that defies "fixed meanings," and in a process that her ply-over-ply stanza forms re-enforces. Her "choppy" stanzas lend themselves to the verbal juxtapositions and play that express her careful exploration of an experience or vision. Yeats's bravado in "The Second Coming" ("Now I know!") is alien to her style of visionary poetry. The brief and "discrete units" of her verse are quite unlike the strong rhythms and run-on lines of Yeats or Pound when expressing their visions of a rough beast or Dionysian leopard. Her stanza forms have a tentative quality that allows her to avoid (at least in *Trilogy*) the rhetorical inflation of many passages in *The Cantos*.

H.D.'s synthesis of Freudian and Jungian approaches shows that she drew on pyschoanalysis as creatively as she drew on occultism. For someone who was analyzed by Freud himself, she was also remarkably independent. Although her poem about him was called "The Master," the poem itself tells of her anger at being treated like a child and by his talk of "the man-strength" (CP 455). She not only countered his disbelief in the afterlife but also pitied him for it: "It worried me to feel that he had no idea—it seemed impossible—really no idea that he would 'wake up' when he shed the frail locust-husk of his years, and find himself alive" (Tribute 43). Although it was Freud who "had dared to say that the dream-symbol could be interpreted," she felt equal to Freud as a reader of "picture-writing, the hieroglyph of the dream" (71). Freud's interpretation of the hieroglyph was narrower than H.D.'s because his was directed at therapy for a patient. Like W.B. Yeats, he knew the danger for someone on "Hodos Chameliontos," or "The Path of the Chameleon," where one is obsessed by daemonic images (see Chapter 1). Unlike Yeats or H.D., however, he could not approve the poet's determination to follow the stream of images wherever it led, even when it led as Yeats feared in "Coole Parke and Ballylee" into a "darkening flood" (Poems 245). Thus Freud considered the vision H.D. had of the "writing on the wall" at Corfu, like her feeling of being enclosed in a bell jar, a "dangerous symptom" (Tribute 51). Both Freud and H.D. considered the vision—the goblet, the spirit lamp, the head of Mercury—a language to be deciphered. But if the vision is merely a symptom, the therapy if successful will end the play of images. No poet would desire that but would instead, in Yeats's phrase, ask that the images endlessly beget fresh images.

H.D. writes, in *Tribute to Freud*, "Symptom or inspiration, the writing continues to write itself or be written" (51). Her memoir of Freud shows how tolerant she could be of his analysis of the source of her "symptoms." Freud duly analyzed her bisexuality, fixation on her mother, rivalry with her brothers, emotional distance from her father (a professor of astronomy), and "suppressed desire to be a Prophetess . . . megalomania they call it" (51). The analysis or critique did not threaten her as long as Freud acknowledged her as a poet. In "The Master," she is thankful that Freud did not speak to her as a student or disciple but told her simply: "you are a poet" (CP 458). H.D. was ready to risk madness rather than let her inspiration be reduced to a mere symptom. As she wrote in *Tribute*, "I know that I must drown, as it were, completely in order to come out on the other side of things" (54). Sylvia Plath willingly ran the same risk.

Robert Duncan is a poet whose work not only reveals affinities with H.D.'s but is also directly inspired by it. He is the first of the poets in this book whose occult themes and motifs were as much influenced by H.D. and Ezra Pound as by Yeats. In assimilating these influences, Duncan reveals a new level of sophistication in the use of occultism, which reaches a peak in James Merrill.

Robert Duncan and
the Mercurial Self

But the essential difference is that Jung thinks
theosophically, where Freud thinks mythologically.
—Duncan, "The Truth and Life of Myth"

5 We have seen that W. B. Yeats in "Rosa Alchemica"
wrote that the alchemists considered their art "no
merely chemical phantasy" and "sought to fashion
gold out of common metals merely as part of an
universal transmutation of all things into some di-
vine and imperishable substance."[1] The grandest goal of such an alchemy was the transmutation of the self—from a wretched scarecrow,
for example, in Yeats's "Sailing to Byzantium" into a magical golden
bird.[2] The use of alchemical imagery and occult sources was as natural
to Robert Duncan as to W. B. Yeats. Duncan, unlike the other poets
discussed so far (including H.D., who exaggerated the occult elements
of her Moravian heritage), knew occultism as part of his family background rather than as exotic countertradition.[3] He tells us that his
grandmother was an elder in a Hermetic Brotherhood "similar to and
contemporaneous with the Order of the Golden Dawn to which Yeats
belonged," and his parents adhered to a Hermetic and Rosicrucian
tradition developed from the "orientalizing Theosophy of Blavatsky
and the Hermetic Brotherhood out of the texts translated by G. R. S.
Mead" (FC 3, 224). In Blavatsky, Duncan writes, one finds a "mess of
astrology, alchemy, numerology, magic orders, neo-Platonic, kabbalistic and Vedic systems combined, confused, and explained." Despite
a confusion that would scandalize a rationalist, as would the alchemical tradition itself, Duncan says, of Blavatsky, "Her sense binds: that
until man lives once more in these awes and consecrations, these obe-

diences to what he does not know but feels . . . he will not understand what he is."[4]

This analysis of Blavatsky occurs in Duncan's "H.D. Book," a "work-in-progress" he wrote from 1966 to 1981. As noted in the Introduction, Duncan related the imagist movement of 1912–14 to a rebirth of interest in occultism in which "the germ-idea of the 'image'" in the early twentieth century arose from a theosophical renaissance that "brought back the matter of old mystery cults."[5] Duncan discovered the material of this "renaissance" particularly in H.D.'s *Trilogy* and in the "estatic voice" of *The Cantos*: "In his affinity for Plotinus, Proclus, Iamblichus, or the 9th century Erigena, in his poetic cult of the sublime Aphrodite ('crystal body of air') and of Helios, not without Hellenistic hermetic overtones, in his fascination with form in nature ('Germinal') having signature, Pound, as does H.D. in her later work, revives in poetry a tradition or kabbalah . . . which came to the Rosicrucian John Heydon on Bulverton Hill."[6]

To Duncan, occultism is not only a fertile source of poetic images but also a source of knowledge about the world which a rationalistic age has unfortunately scorned. Although his adoption of such beliefs could not be a sign of rebellion against his family, as it was for Yeats, Duncan was pleased that his heritage challenged the tenets of conventional religion. He noted that Yeats's reputation as a poet was "tarnished by the disreputability of his 'beliefs,'" and so "the cult of my grandmother and of my parents where Bucke was read seriously and messages were taken from Atlantis and Masters in the Astral realm, was . . . a disgrace indeed" (FC 128–29). This was a "disgrace" he was glad to share in his rebellion against conventional beliefs. Although he did not literally believe in occult doctrines, they were so natural to him that he has employed them with complete assurance. In this confidence he resembles many intellectual Christians and Jews in mainstream culture who are imbued with the spirit rather than the letter of their religions.

Although alchemy is among the most scientifically discredited of occult doctrines,[7] Duncan believed its conception of the human soul was still relevant and valuable. As Yeats and Duncan knew well, distinguished English poets have drawn upon this ancient system of thought since the medieval age. Chaucer in *The Canon's Yeoman's Tale* and Ben Jonson in *The Alchemist*, even though they satirized the alchemist, used the imagery of this art to brilliant effect. The poets of the seventeenth century also ridicule alchemy, but Henry Vaughan, George Herbert, and John Donne—poets Duncan loves and imitates—

do employ its concepts positively. In Donne's *VIIIth Elegy*, for example, he compares making gold to making love:

> Then like the Chymicks masculine equall fire,
> Which in the Lymbecks warme wombe doeth inspire
> Into th'earthe's worthless durt a soule of gold,
> Such cherishing heat her best lov'd part doth hold.[8]

By the time Donne wrote these lines, alchemy was engaged in its losing battle against the scientific world view. Duncan writes, "Since the seventeenth century . . . men have boldly striven to put away as irrational not only the enthusiasms of contending churches but myth and revelation itself" (FC 5). The Cartesian split between the mental or spiritual world and the material world was denied by the kind of alchemy Donne called the "true religious Alchimy," which was concerned with purifying the self and seeking the divine spirit in material things within the tradition Duncan describes as "the great tradition of hermetic poetry from the Renaissance" (FC 228–29).

In the modern age, alchemy continues to stand for a world view in which the material world is not dissociated from the spiritual. The definition of *spiritual*, however, has changed from the religious seventeenth-century sense to a modern psychological one. This shift in meaning appears in the writing of Jung, who is the great scholar of alchemy as well as its major interpreter. These two aspects—scholarship and interpretation—should be kept separate when discussing Jung's enormous influence on contemporary poets. He collected the rare and scattered texts of the alchemists and quoted extensively from them in *Psychology and Alchemy*, *Alchemical Studies*, and *Mysterium Coniunctionis*. In interpreting the alchemical philosophy as a confirmation of his own theory of archetypes and an enactment of his theory of individuation, Jung opens up a line of interpretation that is also influential. Duncan is well aware of this interpretation and critical of it.

Jung and Duncan agree, however, on alchemy's importance in keeping alive ways of perceiving that are virtually lost in the modern age. Like H.D., they saw alchemy as a fresh and different mode of thought. Jung believed that the medieval alchemists kept alive psychological truths that Christianity (what H.D. in *Trilogy* called the "old church") was trying to bury: "Whereas in the Church the increasing differentiation of ritual and dogma alienated consciousness from its natural roots in the unconscious, alchemy and astrology were ceaselessly engaged in preserving the bridge to nature, i.e., to the unconscious psyche, from decay."[9] For Duncan, the preservation of this bridge is more truly the work of the poet: "It is the work of creation then. It is Poetry, the Making. It is also the *opus alchymicum* of Hermetic and Rosicrucian alchemy." The poet's mission is "to arouse in a contemporary consciousness reverberations of old myth, to prepare the ground so that when we return to read we will see our modern texts charged with a plot that had already begun before the first signs and signatures we have found worked upon the walls of Altamira or Pech-Merle."[10]

The "plot" is of course no simple narrative; it is the "groundwork" of all of Duncan's poetry. A major strand of the work is vitally linked to his use of alchemy: the recovery of Eros in the modern world. Duncan describes the results of the church's suppression of Eros as a Jungian/Freudian return of the repressed:

The *vis imaginativa* in which the things of men's souls and the things of the actual universe dance together . . . is disowned. And what appears is dogma and heresy. The primal Eros rages in the division: sex witches brew their ointments in Thessaly, devils and lamiae swarm about the bodies of saints, familiar animals that were once dear to the household come now as familiars with messages from beastly hell. The old reverences die out or are scattered out from their centers to flare up in new woods and fountains, in the hearts of guilty lovers or upon pagan hearths. (74–75)

Whether Eros is known as Osiris, Lucifer, or Mercury, he is "scattered in sparks throughout the darkness of what is matter," and the poet must find him: "We are drawn to Him, but we must also gather Him to be" (69).

Eros lived on as Mercury in alchemical texts in which he was a chemical element as well as a god. Moreover, alchemy was conceived of in sexual terms that implicitly challenged the dominant masculinity of the Christian deity. The two key elements of the alchemical equation were mercury and sulphur—the latter, in Ben Jonson's words, "supplying the place of male, / The other of the female, in all metals." The implied equality of male and female is further asserted, as we can infer from Jonson's alchemist, because "some do believe hermaphrodeity, / That both do act, and suffer."[11] This belief in hermaphrodeity, or androgyny, which was far too radical for the alchemists to admit consciously, was central to their conception of Mercury; as the tradition develops, he is invariably understood as a hermaphroditic figure (Figure 7). According to Jung, the sexual implications were even more central to the cultural importance of alchemy than its preservation of pagan mythology. Thus he writes that the "moral task of alchemy was to bring the feminine, maternal background of the masculine psyche, seething with passion, into harmony with the principle of spirit." This unity of the Jungian "mother-world" with the "father-world" is grasped through the alchemist's imagery, which over the centuries built up (as with Yeats's *spiritus mundi*) a "treasure-house of symbols."[12] As the hermaphroditic Mercury suggests, the symbols expressed paradoxical truths—not male and/or female, but somehow both female and male in a paradoxical unity: "The tremendous role which the opposites and their union play in alchemy helps us to understand why the alchemists were so fond of paradoxes. In order to attain this union, they tried not only to visualize the opposites together but to express them in the same breath."[13] The alchemists thus recovered the paradoxical vision of the pagan world where, as Duncan writes, "if God was man, He was also beast and sun, wind and tree; where before there was man, there was Beauty, Eros and Himeros."[14]

In his first major volume, *The Opening of the Field* (1960), Duncan explores the theme of the self through the alchemical process of the creation of the *filius philosophorum* (human life itself), which is as traditional a goal of the alchemical process as the creation of gold. Before one reaches this magical human figure in the concluding poem of *Opening of the Field*, the poem "The Question" introduces the alchemical theme into the volume:

> Does the old alchemist
> speak in metaphor
> of a spiritual splendor?
>   (Field 54)

Even for a rhetorical question, the answer seems too obvious in that the occult interest in alchemy is precisely that it described spiritual realities. Duncan laments that in the contemporary age the "color of gold, feel of gold, / weight of gold" has merely a usurious meaning (Ezra Pound on true wealth as productivity is cited in the ninth stanza) as opposed to the mythical value it once had. Another question asks how our culture uses its wealth:

> in Cuzco llamas of solid gold in the *Inti Pampa*
> the Sun's field with Stars, Lightning, Rainbow, Moon
> round it? or impounded at Fort Knox?
>   (54)

Gold used for a religious purpose, like the art of the Inca capital of Cuzco, or for a secular but public one ("gold leaf to the house roof") has a value that is not encompassed by the value of Fort Knox. The Peruvian gold is enriched by the surrounding alchemical symbols of transformation: the sun and moon, corresponding to the sulphur/mercury, male/female dualities; the rainbow symbolizing the completion of the process; and lightning symbolizing the transformation itself. Duncan stresses the importance of drawing on such a Jungian "treasure trove" of symbols:

> Work the old images from the hoard,
> *el trabajo en oro* that gives wealth semblance
> and furnishes ground for the gods to flourish.
>
> (55)

Mercury enters this book not only because he is the god of alchemy but also, as Duncan writes in "After Reading Barely and Widely," because he is "a cheat and thief, so it is said" (Field 91). In a submerged alchemical drama, Hermes

> spited out with Aphrodite, shows
> the soul through dark ways indeed,
> an école des Sages ou Mages.
>
> (91)

As the god of thieves, he is also the patron of the artist as fabulator because "the poet's art is one of tact and guile" (91). As Duncan notes, Hermes is also "psychopompos, undertaker" of the dead and thus our link to the underworld of the unconscious. A final and perhaps most important of Mercury's qualities is his "hermaphrodeity":

Mercury, the *Liber de arte chymica* says
"is all metals, male and female" . . .
"an hermaphroditic monster even in the marriage of soul and body."

(Field 91)

Mercury is the prime symbol of what Jung described as alchemy's ability "not only to visualize the opposites together but to express them in the same breath."[15] To be poetry, words must be "mercurial," obedient to the laws of verse making but also able to rise above the law:

seeming almost to flounder
helpless into meaning, by rime
restricted.

(91)

The experience within the poem must also be mercurial, rising from the depths to the height of emotion. As Jung writes, "Hermes or Mercurius possessed a double nature, being a chthonic god of revelation and also the spirit of quicksilver. As the planet Mercury, he is nearest to the sun, hence he is pre-eminently related to gold. But, as quicksilver, he dissolves the gold and extinguishes its sunlike brilliance . . . [He] had many of his attributes in common with the devil."[16] In Duncan's "Out of the Black," Mercury appears under his diabolic aspect as Lucifer, "Lord of the cold shade" who represents the "teeth of despair" (Field 76). Like Hermes in "After Reading," he is the father of fiction as well as lies, or as Duncan wittily puts it, "the Great Father of Likelihood." He is thus a "fiery essence, the black desolation / ascending thru the created hierarchies" and so represents the poetic "I" of "Out of the Black": "for I went down into the end of all things / to bring up the spirit of Man before me" (76).

It is this "spirit of Man" that burns in the final poem of *The Opening of the Field*. In "Food for Fire, Food for Thought," the poet speaks of seeing faces in the shapes of clouds and of Leonardo seeing figures in the stains on a wall. Figures are also seen in the "red glow, that might-be-magical blood" of the fire of "good wood / that all fiery youth burst forth" (Field 95). The "fiery youth" suggests the *filius philosophorum*, which, as in Goethe's *Faust* (2.2), can lead one to spiritual insight. Duncan quotes an unidentified alchemical text to indicate the progress toward this transformation: "'If you look you will see the salamander,' to the very elements that attend us" (95). The salamander (Figure 9) is traditionally considered "an immature, transitional form of the philosopher's son. It dwells in the 'hellish fire' as the mercurial animal the fire does not consume."[17] The *filius* may be conceived as the hermaphrodite Mercury or as newborn child. (He appears as a "burning babe" in Duncan's 1984 *Groundwork*). The alchemical *anthropos* (like the Cabalistic Adam Kadmon, whom he resembles) represents his ideal of a complete human being, the product of the poetic imagination (Figure 10):

Figure 9. The alchemical salamander, from Michael Maier, *Scrutinium chymicum*, 1687.

> —Did I stare
> into the heart of desire burning
> and see a radiant man?
> (Field 96)

This final question of *The Opening of the Field* need not be answered. The poet has indeed had the vision of the fiery man, and the last lines of the collection show the "unlikely" vision itself, and not its plausibility, is what matters: "Flickers of unlikely heat / at the edge of our belief bud forth" (96). The "radiant man," whether we take him as a type of the poet or simply the object of the poet's love, reconciles life's opposites in his nature—particularly the male/female duality. In one of his essays on Whitman, Duncan says that he sensed, even before puberty, that "the inner longing and promise of love was hidden for me in the finding of another man; from the first I have had this bond with Whitman in this pathos that was not to be justified by the dom-

Figure 10. Mercury in the alchemical fire, from Johann Conrad Barchusen, *Elementa chemiae*, 1718.

inant conventions of society"(FC 194). This search for his identity and the gradual recognition of his unconventional sexuality was conducted under the aegis of Mercury. Contrary to Duncan's claim that he had not yet stated the "theme of the self" in *The Opening of the Field*, his alchemical imagery states it powerfully in this book. The later books certainly explore the theme in greater detail, but he never expressed his burning desire for a self that could reconcile the opposites of his experience more eloquently than in "Food for Fire, Food for Thought."

When Duncan explains that the theme of self began in *Roots and Branches* (1964), he specifically refers to "A Sequence of Poems for H.D.'s 73rd Birthday." Throughout *Roots*, H.D. serves as Duncan's muse, the "Mother of mouthings" as he calls her in "Doves," which he wrote when he heard of the stroke she suffered in 1961.[18] H.D.'s influence is seen in the way Duncan uses the figure of Hermes/Mercury, just as H.D. does, to explore bisexuality. In the birthday poem for H.D., "the Prince in his laboratory, assisted by the boy" (Roots 10), performs alchemical experiments in search of the self. (The alchemist is a "Prince" because Duncan is alluding to Gérard de Nerval's "prince d'Aquitaine" in Nerval's alchemical poem "El Desdichado.")[19] The sexual implications are clear; as the Prince and the boy "experimented in sensations. . . . they referred to / tanks or cribs in each which male torsos" (Roots 10–11). The results of these experiments, however, may be "deformd? mutilated?" because "Without love" they are "dead in being alive, / alive-dead" (11).

The poem entitled "Returning to the Rhetoric of an Earlier Mode" beautifully describes the "radiant man" of his poetic vision. In this case, however, "if I think of my element, it is not of fire, / of ember and ash, but of earth." The move from fire to earth suggests Duncan's growing sense of being rooted in a self, but the self is as mercurial as ever:

> I found the form of a man in his redundance,
> sun-dancer, many-brancht in repeating,
> many-rooted in one thing.
>
> (Roots 90)

This "sun-dancer" becomes the Adam Kadmon figure in what Duncan calls his "theosophical" play, "Adam's Way," in *Roots and Branches*. Early in the play, Hermes learns that his supernatural race (like the one described in Blavatsky's *Secret Doctrine*) is destined to be replaced by mankind. During this transformation, Adam must listen to theosophical advice ("When from your self you are undone / What thou truly art will be begun") in his search for the "fullness of your self . . . but not in yourself" (Roots 144, 156). This play does not successfully order the "mess of astrology, alchemy . . . kabbalistic and Vedic systems" that was Duncan's early heritage. His occultism seems artistically successful only when it is a source of selected, and indeed refined, images. This play was nevertheless important to Duncan because "Adam's Way" showed him that poetry may be a communication between 'You,' first person, and 'yourself.' . . . The Erdgeist stirs the thoughts of men 'until they are like / whirlpools in the water and no longer / resemble themselves.' One's self, it appears, may be a reflection in the water" (FC 221). Duncan is treating "Adam's Way" as if he were merely its reader rather than its author, listening to what it says about human identity as the expression of the "Erdgeist," or Yeatsian spirits. He thus becomes like "The Great Writers" as his parents thought of them, inspired by dead masters: "They lost themselves, theirselves, in their work. Here 'self' disappears and 'work' appears" (225).

In his third major volume, *Bending the Bow* (1968), Duncan's poetic sequence "Passages" explores this theme of finding and losing the self. The sequence is called "Passages" because it is "a work in which I seek to lose myself in the hearing of the voice of the work itself, a work not of personality or oneself but of structures and passages" (FC 227). In "Tribal Memories" ("Passages 1"), Duncan restates the theme of the "Erdgeist" of "Adam's Way" by invoking "Her-Without-Bounds" as the muse of his poetry and the guardian of the "company of the living." She may also be called "Mnemosyne" and "Memory":

> the great speckled bird who broods over the
>   nest of souls, and her egg,
>   the dream in which all things are living,
> I return to, leaving my self.
>
> I am beside myself with this
>   thought of the One in the World-Egg
> enclosed,   under a shell of murmurings.
>   (Bow 9–10)

The "self," which he is illogically but colloquially "beside," is lost within the spirit of the tribe. In what seems a virtual gloss on this passage, Duncan comments on the centrality of language to tribal experience and suggests what he means by a "shell of murmurings." He explains he is searching for a "poetics in which the poem is thought of as a process of participation in a reality larger than my own—the reality of man's experience in terms of language and literature—a community of meanings and forms in which my work would be at once derivative and creative."[20] As with T. S. Eliot's sense of tradition, the "community of meaning" overwhelms the self.

In "At the Loom" ("Passages 2"), Duncan calls his mind "a shuttle among / set strings of the music" (Bow 11). The theme of self is perhaps most lyrically expressed in "Where It Appears" ("Passages 4"), where the poet's mind is again a shuttle weaving an airy web in a

Yeatsian process: "let image perish in image" (15). Within the play of images in the poet's mind, the poet's self seems (in an appropriately prosaic line) "statistically insignificant as a locus of creation." Witnessing "an iridescence," "an ocean of experience," he doubts his ability to "cast a shadow" (15). This iridescent, changing world of experience is symbolized in the poem's conclusion as "this pearl":

> as if I could handle • this pearl • that touches
>   upon every imagination of what
>   I am •
>   wrong about the web,   the
>   reflection,   the lure of the world
>   I love.
>
> (16)

Duncan subtly balances the "I am," which is consumed by the world's vastness, with the "I love" that nevertheless asserts its presence. (The • mark in this context reminds one of the • on the final page of Joyce's *Ulysses*, the black dot representing the sleeping self of Leopold Bloom.) This poem and others in the "Passages" sequence address what Duncan calls in Whitman "the tension between speaking oneself and the utter commonality of the language that must be the medium of that self" (FC 200). In his study of "Passages," Thomas Gardner says that Duncan never resolves the tension of "using a medium to speak for an inaccessible self . . . medium remains medium, never becoming transparent and providing full access."[21] This theme of the limitations of using the medium of language for reaching the self is developed in the two *Ground Work* volumes that follow *Bending the Bow*.

The essay that concludes Duncan's *Fictive Certainties*, "The Self in Postmodern Poetry," prepares us for the approach to the self he developed in the years that separate *Bending the Bow* (1968) from his next complete volume, *Ground Work: Before the War* (1984). Duncan approaches the concept of the self as we perceive it through the language we use—specifically, personal pronouns—as he brilliantly combines childhood memories with linguistic insights:

How vividly I can remember my parents' voices: "They don't know yet"—that "they" was "us," my sister and me, in our third person present company subjectivity. "'We' are going to have a good time." "Is that you?" "No, it's not 'you,' it's 'I.'" This change and interchange of persons was so actively set at play that the basic structures underlying the mind's architecture arise along lines that provide for shifting and multiple roles.[22]

From his earliest memories—through the children's stories he was read to his readings in Emerson, Whitman, Freud and Jung—Duncan traces the multiplicity of selves until he defines the importance of this linguistic experience in his work: "What I would point out in my work as one of its underlying currents is the weaving of a figure unweaving, an art of unsaying what it says, of saying what it would not say. . . . Back of the 'Self' . . . I want to see the mercurial genius of language . . ." (FC 231–32). The weaving and the unweaving of the self, as in "Passages 4," corresponds to that of the body itself, "and back of it hovers the dissolution of the physical chemical universe which I take to be the very spiritual ground and body of our being." For Duncan, it is a blessing if, as he says in the concluding sentence of his essay, "the Me-Myself-and-I trinity is dissolved" (234).

This play with pronouns appears more frequently in *Ground Work II: In the Dark* (1987) than in the first *Ground Work* (1984). In one of the "Passages" poems, "ENTHRALLD," the treatment is rather didactic: "notes of Who 'I' is   sounded / thruout we search   to be   'He', 'She', and 'It'" (GWII 65). A less awkward use of this "interchange of pronouns" occurs in "An Alternative Life," in which Duncan reflects on the lives he did not live but might have. The following lines use his familiar image of a gem that reflects the bewildering nature of the self:

> And 'I" come forward to gaze into the downpouring glass,
> the black crystal in which I find the world
> looking for "me."   I hide in my looking.
>
> (GWII 3–4)

The "me" must remain hidden because it is constituted by language and therefore cannot be discovered through it. As in *Bending the Bow*, however, the "I" (whatever it may be) is sustained by its power to love:

> "He," "She"   are mysteries for Love I've drawn upon
> . . . . The Good remains.   I cannot dispose of it—

> the good of living, the good of aging, the good of the
> [alchemical changes
> I love in loving
>
> (GWII 59)

In *Ground Work II*, Duncan expresses the theme of the self in a tentative and exploratory manner; it is expressed more eloquently in two of the *Ground Work: Before the War* poems. Appropriately, the first one appears in a sequence of variations on seventeenth-century themes. The ponderous title of the sequence is "A Seventeenth Century Suite in Homage to the Metaphysical Genius in English Poetry (1590–1690): Being Imitations, Derivations & Variations upon Certain Conceits and Findings Made among Strong Lines." Duncan includes the texts of entire poems by Sir Walter Raleigh, George Herbert, and the Jesuit poet Robert Southwell. In Southwell's "The Burning Babe," as a Renaissance scholar explains, "the infant Christ announces Himself as an entire alchemical process of redemption."[23] The image of a burning babe in an alchemical furnace encompasses for Duncan the opposites of experience that must somehow be reconciled and understood. Such an aesthetic experience may not always be possible, however; and indeed the second part of the poem makes this point; for Duncan can find nothing in himself to correspond to Southwell's image: "He's Art's epiphany of Art new born, / A Christ of poetry, the burning spirit's show" (GWBW 75). The reason is that the burning child reminds him of pictures he has seen of the victims of Vietnam atrocities. He turns from such images in "self-loathing."

> to ease the knowledge of what no man
> can compensate.   I think I could bear it.
>
> I cannot think I could bear it.
>
> (76)

Without the need for quotation marks around the "I," Duncan shows how fragile this entity is as it faces emotions it cannot reconcile.

When he turns from the historical world of the newspaper photographs to the aesthetic one of art, the alchemical resolution is possible. Quoting a passage from Southwell's poem (*"scorcht with excessive heat"*), he admits that Southwell's fiery metaphor "is no more than an image in Poetry." But for the period of time in which we read the poem, the opposites are indeed reconciled. The fire reaches

the bitter core of me,
the clinker soul, the stubborn residue
that needed the fire and refused to burn.
(GWBW 74)

The first section of this two-part variation concludes:

I an undone from what I am,   and in Imagination's alchemy
the watery Moon and fiery Sun   are wed.

The burning Babe, the Rose,
the Wedding of the Moon and Sun,
wherever in the World I read
such Mysteries come to haunt the Mind,
the Language of What Is   and I
are one.

(74–75)

In Duncan's view, all one can ask of Southwell's poem, or of his own, is an aesthetic experience, a sense of the dissolving of the barriers between the self and the world which takes place only within the poem.

This significance of the aesthetic experience distinguishes Duncan's sense of self-individuation from Jung's. The resolution in his poem (when it is possible) is aesthetic rather than religious or psychological: the alchemy of the self only within the alchemy of the word. For Duncan, alchemy is a means of approaching the sacred images through language. The traditional title of the alchemist was *artifex*, a maker or artist, which suggests that the medium of the alchemist may be words rather than material elements or chemicals. As Jung himself observes, the alchemist's difficulty in expressing the concept of the *lapis philosophorum* leads to verbal analogies and rhetorical *amplificatio*: "Treatises were even written for the purpose of supplying the artist with analogy-making material. The method of alchemy, psychologically speaking, is one of boundless amplification."[24]

To view alchemy as verbal art rather than psychological or religious insight is natural to Duncan. To mix the psychological with the artistic, as Jungian critics of poetry tend to do, confuses the issue. Indeed, Duncan's use of alchemy suggests an interpretation of this medieval art quite different from Jung's. In discussing the Jungian poetic theory of Charles Olson, Duncan told an interviewer: "Well, I wonder how any poet could be attracted to Jungianism. To me poets use symbols to be initial and in the universe. Jung uses them to be in a psyche and around a center."[25] Although Duncan admires Jung's insights into the psyche, he is skeptical of the Jungian system: "Everything we see is posited in the material world. So that an archetype doesn't get to be very arche. Instead of an archetype, we'd better look at a tree or a particular individual" (72). Duncan's attitude toward the "unconscious" not only is truer to its Freudian conception but also leaves more room for creativity: "The unconscious must mean a sense of void or blankness or unavailable information or otherness. And this the consciousness doesn't dream about. But the conscious mind imagines what is in it, and fills it with imaginings and in that, it is creating"(73). Duncan would perhaps agree with Jacques Lacan that "it is only in so far as interpretation culminates in the here and now of this play [of signifiers] that it will be distinguished from the reading of the *signatura rerum* in which Jung tries to outdo Boehme."[26] For both Lacan and Duncan, the unconscious does not represent some mysterious primordial realm. They both approach the unconscious through close attention to linguistic structures. Here again Duncan is a disciple of H.D. in his understanding of verbal alchemy.

In Duncan's view of alchemy, the *ars chemica* becomes an end in itself, like literary art. Jung maintains that the alchemists were not truly looking for a material goal but for psychic integration and that "they themselves did not know what they were talking about."[27] But who can really say? Jung has simply substituted a different goal for the stated one on the paradoxical grounds that the alchemists did not really understand their own quest. This criticism does not deny the profundity of Jung's interpretation of the alchemical search, which is highly relevant to Duncan's long search for his identity both as a man and as a writer. Yet it is also possible to see that the alchemists were just as caught up in the richness of their imagery as a poet (or an artist like Leonardo) would be; one sees such involvement, for example, in a sixteenth-century treatise Jung cites: "They say also that different names are given to the stone on account of the wonderful variety of figures that appear in the course of the work, inasmuch as colours often come forth at the same time, just as we sometimes imagine in the clouds or in the fire strange shapes of animals, reptiles, or trees" (248). This alchemist seems unable to give a name to the stone because he is so absorbed by what Yeats would call "phantasmagoria" or Pound the "phantastikon" of his art.

The sense of the weaving and unweaving of the self, the experience of losing it in the play of the alchemical process, is the experience expressed in Duncan's finest poetry. When he writes, as in "Passages 4," "let image perish in image," Duncan's alchemy of the word seems very close to Yeats's. But he is actually closer, as the title of *Fictive Certainties* suggests, to the poet of supreme fictions, Wallace Stevens. One sees the affinity between the two poets' aesthetics, for example, when Duncan writes of the poet's ambition to create an inclusive but ever-changing poetic fiction: "furnishing forth each time a life of the book. . . . A fiction of the existence of the whole, a fictional ensemble in which we become aware of the ensemble" (FC 181).

This affinity extends even to the two poets' use of alchemical metaphors. No one has expressed the glamour of the alchemical search better than Wallace Stevens. Although he does not use its imagery as frequently as Duncan, his poetry reveals a continuing fascination with it. For Stevens, the poetic stanza itself was his philosopher's stone or *lapis* ("*stanza my stone*" he wrote in "The Man on the Dump"). In *Notes toward a Supreme Fiction*, the imagination of a "gold centre, the golden destiny . . . the lapis-haunted air" involves "One of the vast repetitions final in / Themselves and, therefore, good" (WS 404–5).[28] The appeal of these "vast repetitions" is a subject of the final poem of *Ground Work: Before the War*, "Circulations of the Song." Like the concluding poem of *The Opening of the Field*, "Circulations" is a love poem in which alchemy provides the imagery to describe the new self found through love. But in the later poem the emphasis is as much on losing the self as on finding it in the alchemical process:

> Were you talking?   Were we discoursing
>   upon the mercurial Hermes?
>
> The mysteries of quick-silver and the
>   alchemical gold,
> the transports of Beauty,   dissolve themselves
>   and are nothing,
> —are resolved again,   everything—
>   a wave of my own seeing you
> in the rapture of this reading.
>   (GWBW 173)

Duncan immerses himself not in the *spiritus mundi* or collective unconscious but in the flow of language. He anticipates James Merrill in his understanding of the links among the occult motifs, the unconscious motives, and the play of language in the poetic work. Although he draws upon occultism as naturally as does H.D., he believes in it not literally but as a fiction. Nevertheless, he does not use occult images with Wallace Stevens's detachment. They have more than aesthetic value for him. His absorption of occult rituals and doctrines from childhood on gives them so natural a place in his poetry that one can scarcely distinguish his sympathy for them from belief. Duncan's skeptical yet affirmative openness to occult experience makes a stark contrast with Sylvia Plath's dread certainty about its reality.

Sylvia Plath:
Occultism as
Source and Symptom

My writing is a species of mediumship. I become the person.

—Virginia Woolf, *Diary* (5:101)

Sylvia Plath resembles W. B. Yeats and H.D. in using occultism to signify a break with traditional culture and religion. Her husband, Ted Hughes, seems to describe her when he comments on contemporary writers who have gone beyond the modernist "state of belonging spiritually to the last phase of Christian civilization." The postmodern phase is pre-Christian in spirit: "It is the world of the little pagan religions and cults, the primitive religions from which of course Christianity itself grew."[1] Plath shares with Hughes an attempt to find a new ground for writers beyond the traditions represented by Oedipus and Christ. ("O Oedipus. O Christ. You use me ill," she complains in the concluding lines of "The Ravaged Face" [SP 116].) Hughes also discovers this ambition in East European writers like Vasko Popa who "have in a way cut their losses and cut the hopelessness of that civilization off." At its most profound, such an attitude is "a shifting of your foundation to completely new Holy Ground, a new divinity, one that won't be under the rubble when the churches collapse (207)." Ezra Pound's praise of mystery cults and the "light from Eleusis" expresses a similar attitude.

In her earliest work, Plath directly attacks Christianity but soon goes beyond this mere negativity in her search for a religious position of her own, a search that does indeed take her into the world of "cults," or rather of the occult. Her occultism may be taken either as a sign of an attempt to find "new Holy Ground" or as a symptom of mental disturbance. Although Anne Stevenson's biography of Plath, *Bitter Fame*, documents the poet's occult interests, the biography's negative tone makes the occultism seem a mere symptom of psychological instability. As I suggest later, Plath's occultism was indeed a symptom that may be interpreted psychoanalytically. But one should first understand it, as Paul Alexander has in his Plath biography *Rough Magic*, as a stage in her poetic development and a source of her mature symbolism.[2]

A study of Plath's occultism reveals the kind of patterns one finds in mythical interpretations of her poetry. One of the first treatments of Plath as a major imaginative artist rather than an extremist "confessional" poet was Judith Kroll's *Chapters in a Mythology*. Drawing on Robert Graves's *The White Goddess*, Kroll shows how Plath's use of the symbol of the moon as both creator and destroyer, and also her use of the rituals of marriage and rebirth, unify her poetry. Kroll's book has been criticized because it makes Plath's poetry seem too systematic a development of a personal mythology and because her major symbols were in fact developed before she read Graves in 1959.[3] It is true that Plath's career did not and, given its tragic briefness, could not reveal the kind of development one sees in the careers of William Blake or W. B. Yeats. Nevertheless, Kroll's admittedly exaggerated sense of the unity of Plath's work helps one appreciate the Yeatsian power of her major symbols. To say that Plath's symbols antedated her reading of Graves, moreover, is no criticism of Kroll's thesis because to Plath *The White Goddess* was an inspiration and an encouragement to develop her symbolism rather than a handbook of mythology. Her ability to alchemize a poetic vision from occult sources indeed rivals Yeats's.

An important early poem (c. 1952–56), "Sonnet to Satan," shows the effort it took for Plath to avoid the mere negativity of the "last phase of Christian civilization." A dramatic means of rejecting the Christian God is to praise his adversary Satan, as Baudelaire did in "Litany to Satan." Such a stance came naturally to the young Plath, who said at age eight when her father died, "'I'll never speak to God again.'"[4] In her correspondence with her friend Robert Cohen, she was openly hostile to religion: "'Those who believe in God are mental cowards; those who devote their lives to his service are physical cowards as well.'"[5] The poetic result of this hostility appears in "Sonnet to Satan." The first stanza describes the "black out" of "bright angels" that represent conventional belief. The phases of the creative mind are described as "moonly": "In the darkroom of your eye the moonly mind

/ somersaults to counterfeit eclipse" (SP 323). In this Yeatsian eclipse of daylight and reason, Plath celebrates Satan's power. Through a reference to ink and white paper, this power is identified with that of the creative mind. Satan commands that a "corkscrew comet jet forth ink" and flood the white world of a sheet of paper, overcasting and turning "god's radiant photograph to shade" (SP 323). Although comets are the traditional signifiers of portentous events, the comet in this stanza writes revelations not across the heaven but across writing or photographic paper. This creative flood is a reimagining of the world as the daylight is "overcast." Compared to this heroic re-creation of the world, God's photograph is a timidly mimetic work of art.

In its final quatrain, the spiral movement of the comet gives way to that of a "steepling snake" that is also an agent of revelation and of course traditionally associated with Satan. A still more significant association is with the world-snake Ouroboros in the opening of Plath's "Snakecharmer" (1957): "As the gods began one world, and man another / So the snakecharmer begins a snaky sphere" (SP 79). In "Sonnet to Satan," the snake creates a world in the sense of printing it. The snake replaces God's photograph with a "flaming image" in "contrary light" which

> invades the dilate lens of genesis
> to print your flaming image in birthspot
> with characters no cockcrow can deface.
> (SP 323)

To borrow Wordsworth's phrase, these are "characters of the great Apocalypse," but they reveal the satanic rather than the divine.[6] This praise of Satan may be intended to shock. The rhetorical problem, however, with preferring Satan to God is that it is shocking only if one assumes belief in the traditional God; otherwise there would be no shock in attacking him or calling upon the Adversary. Thus the poem unfortunately leaves Plath in "the last phase of Christianity," which she hoped to escape. As a means of beginning a new spiritual phase, "Sonnet to Satan" is ineffectual. But it adumbrates, in black and white, the dualistic mythology behind her mature work.

For much of her adult life, Plath was not ready to cut her ties to religion. Her mother was raised as a Catholic and her father as a Lutheran; after her father's death, she was reared by her mother as a Unitarian. At Smith College, she wrote a term paper on Unitarianism in which she praised a Unitarian congregation she had joined the year before.[7] Plath may eventually have thought, as T. S. Eliot did, that Unitarianism is rather a code of ethics than a religion and that it could not offer the symbols and rituals (confession, communion, even exorcism) that she craved. She introduced her own children to traditional religious services. In 1961 she wrote to her mother about attending the Anglican church in her village and sending her daughter to Sunday school. Although she expected her daughter eventually to drift away from religion, Plath wanted her to experience it as she had: "I know how incredibly powerful the words of that little Christian prayer, 'God is my help in every need,' which you taught us have been at odd moments of my life." (LH 280).

Plath was not of course, like Eliot, on a track from Unitarianism to Anglo-Catholicism. Her religious development was more like Yeats's. Occultism provided both Yeats and Plath with a system of symbols and ritual that did not demand intellectual assent to a traditional religion. It also populated the afterlife with spirits that may have been frightening but less so than a world utterly without them. Plath feared more than anything a spiritual void. When her persona faces the spiritual desolation of Brontë country in "Hardcastle Crags," she turns back from a landscape that contains "no family-featured ghost" (SP 63). Plath fears the "vacuous black" (255) and the "immortal blankness between stars" (164). Of the Hardyesque "big God" of "Lyonnesse," she writes that the "white gape of his mind was the real Tabula Rasa" (234).

Consequently, Plath was prepared to appreciate the occult doctrines and practices to which Ted Hughes introduced her. (Alexander's biography describes the occultism of Hughes's Yorkshire family.[8]) As he shows in "Craig Jack's Apostasy," Hughes, like Plath, rejected "all the dark churches," instead calling upon the god who comes from the "world under the world."[9] Hughes particularly encouraged Plath's interest in the tarot deck, which later provided the imagery for many poems—for example, "The Hanging Man"—and even an organizing principle for her novel *The Bell Jar*.[10] A letter she wrote just before her marriage in 1956 shows how central occultism was in her relationship to Hughes: "When Ted and I begin living together we shall become a team better than Mr. and Mrs. Yeats—he being a competent astrologist, reading horoscopes, and me being a tarot-pack reader, and, when we have enough money, a crystal-gazer" (280). One recalls the frontispiece of *Letters Home*, showing Plath gazing over a transparent globe.

In 1959 at Yaddo, to help her over a block in her writing, Hughes

introduced her to meditation exercises based on handbooks of cabalistic and Hermetic magic.[11] A poem of 1956, "Crystal Gazer," shows
Plath and Hughes exploring the dangerous world of the occult. The
poem is based on their visit to a crystal gazer (called "Gerd" in the
poem) near Hughes's home in Yorkshire to ask about the future of
their married life. The prediction is banal: despite some harm to
"tender limb," the marriage will thrive and produce "crop's increase,
and harvest fruit" (SP 55). When the newlyweds leave the crystal
gazer to her own thoughts, the tone changes drastically. We're told
that, braving "Church curse," Gerd began her fortune telling with a
"crooked oath / Whereby one hires a demon." Like Plath's Satan, the
crystal gazer is a kind of poet, or at least a muse, "with power to
strike to stone / Hearts of those who pierced time's core" (55). But
the price she pays for her vision is the knowledge of the skull grinning
in its "crystal center": "Earth's ever-green death's head" (56).

In addition to crystal gazing and tarot divination, Hughes and Plath
manipulated a Ouija board together. In her poem "Ouija," as in "Crystal Gazer," they find death at the core of this occult practice. The
satanic figure in this poem, still associated with the "shade" of "Sonnet to Satan," is now the spirit of the Ouija board: "It is a chilly god,
a god of shades, / Rises to the glass from his black fathoms" (SP 77).
He is a god not only of darkness but also of the spirits (in the Greek
sense of "shades") whom he can summon as he rises from the wine
glass used to point at the board's letters. Like Virginia Woolf, Plath
conceives of art as mediumship, which allows the dead to speak
through her. They come swarming to her glass as the shades in
Pound's Canto 1 gather around the blood Odysseus brings them. The
dead and the unborn assemble like pale moths: "Imagine their deep
hunger, deep as the dark / For the blood-heat that would ruddle or
reclaim" (77).

These shades must be ignored to hear the voice of her "control" in
the spirit world, and it requires a sacrifice from the medium or poet
to hear this spirit: "The glass mouth sucks blood-heat from my fore-
finger. / The old god dribbles, in return, his words." More clearly
than Plath's Satan, this god is a muse for her poetry because this old
god "writes aureate poetry / In tarnished modes . . . ." He is like Satan
in the way he darkens the "blue, divine hauteur" of the heavens,
which under his influence "mistily descend, / Thickening with motes,
to a marriage with the mire" (77). But he is hardly a satisfactory muse.
Devoted to the "queen of death" (one aspect of the "White Goddess"
of the later poems), his work may be aureate but only in "tarnished

modes" that express his "nostalgias," as the poem says in its conclusion:

> He, godly, doddering, spells
> No succinct Gabriel from the letters here
> But floridly, his amorous nostalgias.
>
> (78)

The reference to "Gabriel" leaves the reader with a puzzle. As a Christian angel, the one who will play the last trump, one would expect him to be contrasted with, or opposed to, the "old god" of pagan expression. But this allusion is undeveloped and indeed makes the poem seem "occult" or "obscure" not only in its subject matter but also in its expression. The ambiguity of the poem's conclusion is appropriate to a work in which Plath is trying to find her own untarnished mode. An analysis of her intense interest in the occult can, however, answer some of the questions "Ouija" raises.

A poem crucial to Plath's exploration of the occult world, and to a full understanding of her poetic development, is one that Hughes prints in *The Collected Poems* as a note to "Ouija": "Dialogue over a Ouija Board" (1957–58). She first mentions the Ouija sessions in 1957 when she tells her mother about "Pan (our Ouija imp)," who has been providing tips on betting the football pools: "We keep telling Pan we want it so we can have leisure to write and have lots of children" (LH 294). In his note, Hughes writes that they came near to winning, though the credit probably goes less to their clairvoyance than to Hughes's knowledge of football (SP 276). A deeper significance of the Ouija experience emerges when Plath tells her mother that she is writing her first poem in six months: "a short verse dialogue which is supposed to sound just like conversation. . . . It frees me from my writer's cramp and is at least a good subject—a dialogue over a Ouija board, which is both dramatic and philosophical" (LH 324). "Writer's cramp" hardly seems an adequate term for a six-month lapse in poetry writing when we know how depressed Plath became during fallow periods. Considering the centrality of this dialogue to her subsequent published work, it seems more adequate to describe it as a breakthrough to the subjects that truly inspired her imagination.

In the note to "Dialogue," Hughes explains that "she never showed the poem" (SP 276), which suggests that it does not belong in the official body of her work. Plath's critics neglect the poem even though the quality of its verse and its dramatic form make it one of her most important works. For example, Steven Axelrod writes that Plath's dramatic poem "Three Women" (1962) was a "major departure." Yet "Dialogue" preceded it by some four years as a dramatic poem for voices, and it is equally long and even written in the same stanza form.[12] If the "Dialogue" is so important, then, why did Plath not "show" it? To give a brief answer, one could echo Ezra Pound when Eliot showed him an autobiographical section of *The Waste Land*, which struck Pound as too photographic. Pound thought that the section of "The Game of Chess" in which a man and wife demonstrate the tension between them reflected Tom and Vivien Eliot's life too graphically.[13] So too the husband and wife of "Dialogue" are transparently Ted and Sylvia revealing not only their occult interests but their desire for a child and the competitiveness of their lives together as poets. Plath did publish, in 1957, a story that reflected their creative rivalry, "The Wishing Box," but the story is not so densely biographical as the poem.[14]

The control spirit of the Ouija board is the child the couple have not yet had, and they argue about its puzzling behavior like "rival parents over a precocious / Child" (SP 284). (We find a similar motif in James Merrill's *Changing Light at Sandover*, where the Ouija spirit is interpreted as the child that Merrill's and David Jackson's love for one another cannot produce.) When the spirit disappoints her, the wife calls him a "psychic bastard / Sprung to being on our wedding night / Nine months too soon for comfort" (280). An argument about whom the Ouija spirit takes after, husband or wife, develops into an argument about who is the more creative. If one assumes that the spirit is actually a product of poetic imagination, whose imagination is creating it? Is one partner's imagination stronger than the other, or is the spirit the result of a true poetic collaboration? The issue is highly sensitive because it goes to the root of Plath's concern that her husband's imagination is overpowering hers.

As in Merrill's *Changing Light at Sandover*, the alphabet of the Ouija board is a metaphor for language itself, and the stylus used as a pointer (a wine glass in Plath's case) is a metaphor for the poet's manipulation of it. Selected one at a time, the letters seem "jabberwocky" and "a balderdash / Of half-hints," but the Ouija players struggle to make sense of the mysterious letters. The two experimenters also scrutinize the metaphors that emerge for whether they are characteristic of one or the other, and it seems that the major one is the husband's: "one of my similes / For rot" (SP 283). At its starkest, the question that arises is whether two poets can live creatively in the same house. ("Such duels infect best friendships.") The answer appears positive because the last lines of the poem are spoken in unison: "When lights go out / May two real people breathe in a real room" (286). Despite the unity of the voices, however, the statement itself does not resolve the issue; for that hinges on the ambiguous word *real*. Are "real" people, for example, ordinary ones rather than highly self-conscious poets? Must one or both yield to the other to have a successful marriage?

The poem need not resolve these issues because its major subject is the reality of the afterlife and the occult world, a subject she explores in a dramatic form that is truly a breakthrough for her in 1957. The handling of speaking parts, moreover, is superior in one way to that of "Three Women": instead of voices speaking in a set order, the poem's two voices interweave and break up the stanza forms; and Pan's voice (speaking through capital letters) adds further variety and dramatic tension. The stanzas, despite the breaks within then as the voices speak, are unified by a recurrence of slant rhymes that never affect the naturalness of the dialogue. The second stanza is a good example of the pattern (*ababcbc*) that Plath will ring variations on throughout the poem. After a first stanza in which the two main characters, who are named Sibyl and Leroy, sit down before a coffee table with an inverted wine glass, the second stanza describes the spirits, imagined as "marble statues" or "heirloom furniture":

> Moving, being moved. And we'll imagine
> A great frieze, Egyptian, perhaps, or Greek
> And their eyes looking out of it: keen,
> With the cold burn dry ice has.
>
> (SP 276)

Sibyl is speaking, and she is reluctant to begin; but Leroy insists that they have the session. ("Leo" is Hughes's astrological sign, and the derivation from *le roi* is appropriate to Leroy's dominating personality.)

Their earlier sessions brought them a group of "minor imps" who wasted their time. Two are mentioned by name, Gabriel and Beelzebub, which explains the reference to "succinct Gabriel" in "Ouija." In this dualistic pair, it seems evident that Gabriel would be the "succinct" one and Beelzebub, like the "old god," would be a "talking whirlwind." The stage now belongs entirely to Pan, although Sibyl is discouraged by his poor performance with the football pools. A more serious reason for her reluctance is that, like a true medium, she is exhausted by the sessions. Pressing her, Leroy builds up the fire and brings Sibyl a brandy so that the session will not chill her heart and fill her body with "winter as you claim it does" (SP 277). Despite the strains and dangers of the experiment, they begin the session as they at length fix on a first question to ask Pan.

The poem expands around the replies to this question and two additional ones. The first question goes right to the heart of Plath's obsession: *"Do you know how my father is?"* (SP 278). The answer demonstrates both the unreliablity and the creativity of the Ouija board. Sibyl and Leroy are sitting at a coffee table ringed with the letters of the alphabet (apparently on heavy paper) and the words *Yes* and *No*. The pressure of their index fingers on the inverted wine glass moves it over the smooth surface. The poets provide the subject (the father) and manipulate the writing implement (the glass), and Pan inspires the words that are spelled out. The problem, however, is that Pan appears no more successful as a muse than as a predictor of the football pools. His answer to the question about Sibyl's father is that he is "I-N-P-L-U-M-A-G-E" ("in plumage"), which initially strikes Sibyl as an authentic message from beyond because she says the angelic metaphor would never have occurred to her. But Pan goes on to spell: "O-F-R-A-W-W-O-R-M-S" ("of raw worms"), which is the kind of metaphor both Sibyl and Leroy might typically use in their poetry: "That's what we'd say. About rot / Feeding at the root of things" (279). Responding to Sibyl's disappointment, Leroy criticizes her for expecting too much:

> The Faith-Maker, fisted in his cloud, or the chorus
> Of mandatory voices you half expect
> To fracture these four walls.
>
> (279)

The imagery of Leroy's speech recalls Wallace Stevens, as do the ideas in its conclusion: "we face / Obliteration hourly unless our eye / Can whipcrack the tables into tigers" (279). In other words, Pan's importance is that he is a poetic fiction that can be listened to *as if* he were true inasmuch as all "spiritual" experiences are poetic creations.

Sibyl's reply to this argument reveals the ambition of Plath's work. She dismisses Leroy with "All this I know." Because the fist does not in fact appear, she says, "I shrink . . . the size of my demand to magic," which explains why her interest in the occult is so much deeper than Leroy's. In occultism she seeks transcendental experience and not merely, as Leroy does, ideas or metaphors for poetry. Leroy is content with a psychoanalytic interpretation of occult experience as being of the unconscious mind. Sibyl violently rejects the interpretation of their experience as either the projection of the unconscious mind or the reflection of Jungian archetypes. She says she would rather be burned at the stake as a witch

> than meet a poor upstart of our nether
> Selves posing as prophet and slyly poaching
> Pebbles . . . to build his canting towers.
>
> (SP 280)

The difference between their two views of occultism heightens the poem's dramatic quality. Tension between the two players begins to rise as Sibyl scorns the notion that Pan is "a sort of psychic bastard" that substitutes for a real child. Leroy hopes to continue the session by putting a second question: *"Pan, tell us now: Where do you live?"* (SP 281) After a false start, he replies that he lives "I-N-G-O-D-H-E-A-D." Sibyl is encouraged by the answer to believe that Pan might be the source of genuine visions. If the imagination is a screen that "once in a blue moon" can reflect a vision of reality, "who knows what belief / Might work on this glass medium" (282).

The debate reaches its crisis as Leroy maintains that, no matter what Pan tells them, "the fight is ours, / And tongue, and thought." To settle what Leroy calls their "duel," they ask him once again, *"Where do you live?"* The answer spells defeat for Sibyl: "I-N-C-O-R-E-O-F-N-E-R-V-E" (SP 283). If Pan lives in the core of their nerves, he is nothing but a projection of their psyches. Sibyl observes bitterly: "My will has evidently / Curtseyed to yours" (284). Unfortunately, the board has become their "battlefield" as they argue over Pan like "rival parents." But they both are insulted when they feel the glass move once more, and Pan "romps round" to spell out "A-P-E-S." With Leroy's approval, Sibyl smashes the wine glass in the fireplace, and their supernatural revels are ended. (We find a similar ritual at the end of Merrill's *Changing Light*.)

The broken glass, with its symbolism of fragility and destruction, is the culminating symbol of the poem. Although Pan's name suggests a natural force, a friendly imp or psychic child, his name also suggests the name for primal fear as the root of the word *panic*. In the brilliant story inspired by her employment at a Boston psychiatric clinic in 1958, "Johnny Panic and the Bible of Dreams," Plath reveals the same ambivalence toward "Johnny Panic" as she does toward Pan. The clinic's patients, who have various amusing and disturbing phobias, are under the influence of Johnny; and the narrator is disappointed when one of his "converts" is cured: "Johnny Panic injects a poetic element in this business you don't often find elsewhere. And for that he has my eternal gratitude."[15]

More than a poetic "element," Johnny is a Hermetic figure who can conduct one to the source of dreams and poetry: "To be a true member of Johnny Panic's congregation one must forget the dreamer and remember the dream: the dreamer is merely a flimsy vehicle for the great Dream-Maker himself" (32). Although the narrator disapproves of casting out Johnny Panic by "spiritual stomach pumps," he is not a benign figure in her own life. In a scene reminiscent of Plath's poem "The Bee Meeting," the clinic doctors bring the narrator to a room for what is obviously electroshock treatment after they discover her reading confidential case histories. As she feels the electroshock, she sees Johnny's face as a Christian martyr might see Christ's: "At the moment I am most lost the face of Johnny Panic appears in a nimbus of arc lights on the ceiling overhead." But Johnny is also the panic fear of the shock itself ("I am shaken like a leaf in the teeth of glory"), and the religious language of the story's conclusion is sardonic: "His love is the twenty-storey leap, the rope at the throat, the knife at the heart. He forgets not his own" (39).

The terror inspired by Pan, or by what he represents, is revealed in "Dialogue over a Ouija Board" by the smashing of the glass. Sibyl destroys the link to the other world, but even the fragments seem to have symbolic power. The symbolism of the act is emphasized by Sibyl's comment that she once smashed a glass in a dream, and "ever since that dream / I've dreamed of doing it again" (SP 285). Although this leaves the glass's destruction no more specific symbolically, it emphasizes the importance Sibyl places on the action—as if it were the fated violation of a taboo. The moment of the smashing brings visions to both Sibyl and Leroy. His vision is so powerful that he now questions his own psychoanalytic interpretation of Pan as an expression of their combined consciousness:

> Those glass bits in the grate strike me chill:
> As if I'd half-believed in him, and he,

Being not you, nor I, nor us at all,
Must have been wholly someone else.

(285)

This fear develops into a vison of a threat to Sibyl in which cracks
appear in their living room:"And you, shackled ashen across the
rift, a specter / Of one I loved" (285). Leroy's vision of Sibyl is
matched by her's of him: "transfixed by roots, wax-pale, / Under a
stone" (285). The spiritual reality of their session seems authenti-
cated by these two visions ("Death's two dreams"). Sibyl has undergone a ritualized death and rebirth, with Leroy as her Orpheus. Her
hand is deathly cold, and she asks him to "chafe the cold / Out of
it. There. The room returns / To normal." Although she has escaped her danger, she can never really return to a "normal" state.
Outside, in the November evening, the "blown leaves make bat-
shapes, / Web-winged and furious," and the full moon makes the
"neighbors' gable-tops / Blue as lizard-scales." Leroy proposed to
"shut the door / And bolt it" by breaking off the sessions. Sibyl resolves that they must promise "to forget / The labyrinth and ignore
what manner of beast / Might range in it" (286). The dialogue concludes with both Sibyl and Leroy hoping that, when the session
ends, they will return to their everyday life as "two real people . . .
in a real room" (286).

In a journal entry of 1958, Plath speculated about how much the
Ouija sessions involved "our own intuitions working, and how much
queer accident, and how much 'my father's spirit.'"[16] As she continued
using the board, she gave more credence to the theory that the spirits
were driven, "being moved," by her father's spirit—as, in the allusion she makes in her journal, Hamlet was by his father's spirit. The
vision of death seems to come not from their psychic child Pan (although he is the medium for it) but from the spirit asked about in the
first question, Sibyl's father. Ted Hughes has said that Plath would
refer to her 1953 suicide attempt as a "bid to get back to her father"
and that some of "the implications might be divined from her occasional dealings with the Ouija board." Her father's name was Otto,
and Ouija spirits would arrive with "instructions for her from one
Prince Otto, who was said to be a great power in the underworld."
According to Hughes, when Plath tried to speak to Prince Otto directly, "the Colossus" forbade it, and the Colossus himself was inaccessible. Hughes thinks that "her effort to come to terms with the
meaning this Colossus held for her, in her poetry, became more and

more central as the years passed.[17] In his opinion, Plath's attempt to "get back" to her father through suicide seems "a routine reconstruction from a psychoanalytical point of view." But one could as justly use the word *classic* as "routine." The interpretation is routine only because the attempt to return to the father through suicide conforms so closely to a Freudian paradigm. Plath's understanding of psychoanalytic thought through her reading and especially her psychoanalysis in 1958–59 meant that she herself saw her symptoms in Freudian terms. For example, she found in Freud's "Mourning and Melancholia" an account of her motives for suicide as well as the "vampire" metaphor she used in "Daddy."[18]

A Freudian reconstruction provides insight into Plath's fascination with the occult. As Philip Rieff observes, the "unknown" is a closely related term for the phenomenon which is referred to as the "unconscious."[19] Both psychoanalysis and the occult deal with the "unknown." For example, both deal with "ghosts," although their appearance is treated as factual truth by occultism and as symptoms of mental disturbance by psychoanalysis. To Freud's displeasure, the apparent similarities between the two studies meant that they could be bracketed together intellectually. We saw in the Introduction that Freud associated the influence of occultism with the "loss of value" resulting from World War I and the "great revolution towards which we are heading and of whose extent we can form no estimate."[20] We are still living through this revolution in values, and here Freud's analysis resembles Umberto Eco's in *Foucault's Pendulum* that occultism flourishes in an "age of confusion" (261). According to Freud, occultism fills the place of no longer established religions by taking over religion's "attempt at compensation, at making up in another, a supermundane, sphere for the attractions which have been lost by life on this earth."[21]

Should Plath's occultism be considered a form of "compensation"? No one has suggested that Ted Hughes's interest in the occult is a psychologically significant symptom. Why should Plath's interest seem any more significant? One reason is that Hughes, on the evidence of "Dialogue over a Ouija Board" itself, regarded techniques like fortune-telling either as a game or as a way of exploring one's own psyche. In Plath's case, "Dialogue" suggests that her belief in occultism was an attempt to experience a spiritual world directly—as she put it in "Mystic," to be "seized up / Without a part left over" (SP 268). Such an experience, which reportedly obsessed her in the last few days of her life, was dangerous because, as she put it in

"Mystic," "Once one has seen God, what is the remedy?" (268).[22] The experience of this spiritual world makes the ordinary world somehow unreal, as Yeats shows in poems from "The Stolen Child" to "Sailing to Byzantium."

If one does consider Plath's occultism a symptom or a compensation for some loss, a Freudian interpretation of her Ouija experiments would of course center on her attempt to reach her father. Her admiration for Freud's "Mourning and Melancholia" is significant because in that essay suicide is not simply an attempt to "get back" to the dead but to revenge oneself on them. Freud notes that the ambivalent feelings of hate as well as love one may feel for someone close may cause intense guilt if that person dies, which may in turn lead to a self-torment that exacerbates negative feelings toward the dead. In Merrill's *Changing Light at Sandover*, for example, the poet admits that his fascination with the spirit world is related to his guilty feelings toward his dead father.[23] Freud's complicated explanation of the way this emotional syndrome may lead to suicide involves what he calls "emotional ambivalence in the proper sense of the term—that is, the simultaneous existence of love and hate toward the same objects [which] lies at the root of many important cultural institutions."[24]

Freud relates this ambivalence to religious feelings in his essay "A Neurosis of Demoniacal Possession." From his own patients, he knew that the attitude toward a father is "not merely one of fondness and submission but another of hostility and defiance." The same ambivalence is felt toward the divine: "From this unresolved conflict, on the one hand of longing for the father and on the other of dread and defiance, we have explained some of the important characteristics and most epoch-making vicissitudes of religion." Freud concludes that "it requires no great analytic insight to divine that God and the Devil were originally one and the same, a single figure which was later split into two beings of opposed characteristics."[25] In his essay "The Uncanny," Freud further relates this religious duality to the theme of the double: "The quality of uncanniness can only come from the circumstance of the 'double' being a creation dating back to a very early mental stage . . . . The 'double' has become a vision of terror, just as after the fall of their religion the gods took on daemonic shapes."[26] It is the kind of vision that Plath expresses in "Death & Co."

In deriving the origins of religion from ambivalence toward the father, Freud in effect identifies the patterns in Plath's work that stem from her love/hate feelings toward her own father: the communication with him in the quasi-religious afterlife of occultism; her ambivalence toward figures like Johnny Panic, Pan, and the "old god" of "Ouija"; the theme of the double that obsessed her from the time of her Smith College thesis to the writing of poems like "Death & Co."; and finally, the dualistic mythology of her mature poetry. In other words, considering Plath's occultism as a symptom, or as a compensation for the loss of a father, leads directly to a source for what Hughes called her "chapters in a mythology."

By using the terms Hughes employs, we may understand Plath's occultism as a creative element in her search for "new Holy Ground, a new divinity" and not only as a psychological symptom. Although her "new divinity" was no less threatening than the Christian God, it inspired rather than oppressed her imagination. In a discussion of the chronology and unity of her work, Hughes wrote that Plath could access "depths" that formerly only shamans and holy men could: "Her poetry escapes ordinary analysis in the way clairvoyance and mediumship do: her psychic gifts, at almost any time, were strong enough to make her frequently wish to be rid of them."[27] Just as Hughes says that her psychic gifts tend to escape analysis, he says of her "mythology" that "the origins of it and the *dramatis personae*, are at bottom enigmatic" (81). No one can fully account for the symbolic power of her terrible and beautiful moon goddess, her dying and rising god, or her ritual exorcisms. Nevertheless, one can conclude that Plath's occultism helped to liberate her creative energies. When Pan spoke to her from the ring of letters, she heard the true voice of her inspiration.

She also heard the voice of her "father's spirit." Plath resembles Yeats and H.D. in the subterranean links of her occultism with the dominance of her father's authority. Yeats's occultism expressed his rebellion against his father's rationalism. H.D.'s reaction to her formal and distant father is found (at least as Freud saw it) in her devotion to occult sciences like astrology rather than to her father's science of astronomy. But Plath's obsessive search for her father through the occult means of the Ouija board is unique. (The brief, comical Ouija message that James Merrill's father sends his son just after his death is a single communication and does not resemble the father's constant haunting in Plath.) In no other poet, despite Yeats's theory of "daemonic man," have we seen this sense of being possessed by a spirit rather than simply contacting one. Plath was taken up by the spirit of "The Collosus." As in "Ariel," "Something else / Hauls me through air——" (SP 239).

The title *Ariel* refers to the horse Plath rode in 1956 and alludes to the Hebrew name from which Plath derives the phrase "God's lioness" (Isaiah 29:7). But it is of course also a literary allusion to Shakespeare's *The Tempest* and to the theme of the father that pervaded her poetry. (Paul Alexander tells of the impact *The Tempest* had on Plath when at the age of twelve she was spellbound by a performance in Boston.)[28] Before deciding on *The Collosus* as the name for her first volume of poetry, she considered a title taken from *The Tempest*, "Full Fathom Five." In a journal entry she writes that the title relates "richly to my life and imagery" because it "has the background of *The Tempest*, the association of the sea . . . of the father image—relating to my own father, the buried male muse and god-creator risen to be my mate in Ted, to the sea-father Neptune."[29] The "rough magic" of Miranda's father Prospero, which liberated Ariel, was the power she desired in her own work. When she was ready to leave her exhausting teaching job at Smith to write full time, she speaks of her Ouija spirits ("my prophetic Pans and Devas") as if they were liberated Ariels. They seem "free already" and excite her with "their impatient tugs toward writing" (221). The poem "Ariel" celebrates, among other things, such a liberation. Yet "Ariel" also carries the association with Ariel's song of the dead father, the Collosus whom she describes as the "Mouthpiece of the dead" (SP 129–30). This sense of possession by the dead father's power gives a dramatic edge to her occultism no other poet has matched. Her deadly earnestness in the use of occult themes is particularly vivid against the background of Ted Hughes's poetry.

Ted Hughes's
Alchemical Quest

I am now like an Alchemist, delighted with discoveries
by the way, though I attain not my end.
—Letter of John Donne, August 10, 1614

7 If Sylvia Plath's fascination with the occult reached
the level of a neurotic obsession, Ted Hughes's
seems in contrast detached and intellectual. He regarded the occult practices he introduced to Plath
as poetic exercises, but she treated them with grim
seriousness as spiritual rituals and used them with the greater conviction and daring. A will to believe is a poet's gift, but that gift may
lead to imaginative assertions that seem too naïve or fantastic to win
a reader's interest or sympathy. For example, Eliot disapproved of
Yeats's occultism as a confused mélange of beliefs and disliked or
ignored Yeats's explicitly occult poems. Auden's reaction to Yeats was
not so strong. Although he considered Yeats's occultism silly and
rather embarrassing in a major poet, Auden was more sympathetic
than Eliot, considering the occultism a minor flaw; and he thought its
expression in the poetry carried conviction because it so profoundly
engaged Yeats's emotions. H.D. is an even better example than Yeats
of an occultist whose belief is so strong and unqualified that one never
questions its sincerity.

Eloquent and moving as it can be, Ted Hughes's poetry does not
seem to possess the same degree of conviction as the work of Plath,
Yeats, or H.D. Although he has claimed that certain occult phenomena
have been proved genuine, Hughes is not an occultist like H.D. or
Yeats.[1] He does not have their utter conviction when using occult motifs; nor does he have Duncan's restraint and sophistication or Mer-

rill's saving humor and irony. When I say, however, that his occult work does not convey the same conviction, I am of course making a highly subjective judgment. There is no way to demonstrate, as Eliot tried to do in his criticism of Yeats and Pound, that there is something inherently unbelievable or insincere in a poet's work. A reader's judgment may, as so often it does in Pound's *Cantos*, hinge on entirely subjective feelings about whether the poet's tone is uncertain or strident. The issue of "poetry and belief" arose in the Introduction and the chapter on T. S. Eliot and is also an issue in responding to Hughes. At the same time, what I see as the flaws in Hughes's work do not spoil its poetic achievement. Compared with Yeats, Hughes is an unsuccessful alchemist of the word; like John Donne's alchemist, however, he delights himself and his readers in "discoveries by the way."

Alchemy may particularly have intrigued Hughes because it provided the terms in which he thought about his relationship with Plath after her death. He described his wife's poetic development as "a process of alchemy" and said that her early writings were "like impurities thrown off from the various stages of the inner transformation, by-products of the internal work." Writing of the "unity of her opus," he said that its language "is the product of an alchemy on the noblest scale."[2] Some lines in Plath's "Lady Lazarus" read like a reply to this interpretation of her work as an *opus alchemicum*. Addressing "Herr Lucifer," Plath's persona reacts scornfully to the notion that "I am your opus. . . . The pure gold baby" (SP 246).

Alchemy is in fact central to Hughes's poetry rather than Plath's. He resembles H.D. not only in using its motifs, as do Yeats and Duncan, but also (as in H.D.'s *Trilogy*) using alchemy as a structural device for a series of lyrics. Alchemical references are found from Hughes's *Crow* (1970) through *River* (1983). Of *Moortown* (1979), he said that "the whole drift is an alchemising of a phoenix out of a serpent,"[3] and *Cave Birds* (1978) is subtitled "An Alchemical Cave Drama." As in the poetry of Robert Duncan, the alchemical imagery is used to describe the rebirth of the self; but the theme is not so deftly handled as in Duncan because Hughes in some crucial passages adopts the oracular tone of the magus; and unlike Yeats, Hughes then sounds more pretentious than magisterial.[4] The problem of the tone in *Cave Birds* may be traced to Hughes's difficulty in using its alchemical motifs to express his feelings about Plath—particularly, of course, her suicide while they were estranged.[5]

Although Hughes has read widely in the alchemical texts, not only much of his knowledge but also his interpretation of alchemy derive from Carl Jung, about whom Hughes said, "I met Jung early, and . . . have read all the translated volumes."[6] For example, Hughes wrote in 1976 that the failure of the Christian religion left nothing to humanize "the archaic energies of instinct and feeling," with the result that the "whole inner world has become elemental, chaotic, continually more primitive and beyond our control."[7] This is but a slightly more forceful version of what Jung wrote in *Psychology and Alchemy* of the decline of religion and the rise of rationalism:

Things have gone rapidly down hill since the Age of the Enlightenment. . . . We simply do not understand any more what is meant by the paradoxes contained in dogma; and the more external our understanding of them becomes the more we are affronted by their irrationality, until finally they become completely obsolete, curious relics of the past. The man who is stricken in this way cannot estimate the extent of his spiritual loss, because he has never experienced the sacred images as his inmost possession and has never realized their kinship with his own psychic structure. (16)

Jung considered alchemy a "treasure-house" of these sacred images and interpreted the alchemists not as precursors of modern chemistry but as thinkers trying to retain links to religious reality, which included pagan as well as Christian insights. The imagery of alchemy was so important because "concepts are coined and negotiable values; images are life."[8]

In the "Alchemical Cave Drama" of *Cave Birds*, Hughes employs not only alchemical images but also Jungian personae such as the "shadow" and "anima" to develop the drama. This development is complicated by a second structural device, a trial of the personae by anthropomorphic birds, which are inspired by the accompanying Leonard Baskin bird drawings. Yet a third element is the rather "confessional" poems about his grief over the suicide of Plath. Although these three separate elements do not work together harmoniously, one senses in the breaks among them Hughes's struggle to express perceptions virtually lost in his culture. His ambition in *Cave Birds* is to write a mythopoetic fable, and this ambition raises a problem faced by all writers who draw on occult lore. Poets draw upon occultism because it represents habits of mind, and a kind of sensibility, that seem lost to modern culture; and they hope to revive such feelings through their art. Yet no artist, nor even a group of artists, can replace what a civilization once provided. Even if contemporary poetry had a more general role in our lives, it could not compensate for the loss of beliefs, rituals, and everyday social practices characteristic of a vital culture.

Hughes is well aware of the challenge faced by a poet who feels at odds with his culture. We noted in Chapter 6 his warning that artists who portray "the state of belonging spiritually to the last phase of Christian civilization" inevitably "suffer its disintegration." He hopes the contemporary artist will realize that the Christian world is dead and build a new one that "is a continuation or a re-emergence of the pre-Christian world . . . the world of the little pagan religions and cults, the primitive religions from which of course Christianity itself grew."[9] In works such as *Crow*, *Cave Birds*, and *Gaudete*, Hughes attempts to alchemize a modern mythical fable out of such pagan elements as Dionysian orgies, underworld journeys inspired by the Tibetan Book of the Dead, shamanistic flights into the souls of animals, Mithraic rites (the bull sacrifice of *Gaudete*), and Eleusinian mysteries (the "cave" of *Cave Birds*). In such elements he hopes to discover a "completely new Holy Ground, a new divinity, one that won't be under the rubble when the churches collapse" (207).

A further difficulty is that Hughes's real concerns in the poem are more personal than cultural. One could imagine him saying of *Cave Birds*, as T. S. Eliot said of *The Waste Land*, that it was not a "criticism of the contemporary world" but instead a "grouse against life."[10] Hughes's fascination with alchemy increased after Plath's suicide in 1963. He then worked for over a year on a verse drama adaptation of a seventeenth-century German romance that is a basic text of the Rosicrucians, *The Chemical Wedding of Christian Rosencreutz*. Rosencreutz was a Lutheran minister who used alchemical imagery to describe the mystical unity of male and female qualities, which he symbolized through a series of such paired opposites as mercury/sulfur, bride/groom, and king/queen. Like Hughes, Jung considered the *Chemical Wedding* the most profound of the alchemical treatises and emphasized its concern with tracing the individuation of the quester. Hughes himself described it in 1977 as a "crucial seminal work—like *Parzifal* or *The Tempest*—a tribal dream."[11]

Although Hughes never finished his adaptation of *The Chemical Wedding*, he wrote two plays inspired by it: *Difficulties of a Bridegroom* (performed in 1963 by the BBC but never published) and *The Wound* (published in *Wodwo* in 1967). In the first play, the male protagonist accidentally runs down a hare on the road as he is driving to meet a

woman in London. Strangely disturbed by the incident, the protagonist dreams of marriage with a figure who resembles Robert Graves's
White Goddess, a creative/destructive woman or muse.[12] When he
emerges from his waking dream, he goes on to meet the woman in
London, who is referred to (like the woman in the dream) only as
"She." She is also disturbed by the accident until he sells the hare and
buys two roses for her; thus the atonement, in a dreamlike displace-
ment, is offered to the woman. The play ends with the possibility that
the man and woman may become lovers. In *The Wound*, Hughes dramatizes the hallucinations of a wounded soldier (named Ripley after a
Renaissance English alchemist) who believes that he and his commanding officer are trapped in a chateau, where a group of women,
like the Greek Bacchae, dismember his commanding officer. He is
spared because of the help of a woman whom he asks to marry him.
When the play ends, we do not know if he will live or die; but his
love for the mysterious woman has transformed him.

A third treatment of the alchemical marriage theme reads like a self-
parody of one of Hughes's violent narratives such as *Crow*. *Gaudete*
(1977) is a mixed volume of poetic prose and poetry that began as a
film scenario. Hughes's "argument" to *Gaudete* explains that a provin-
cial minister is captured by supernatural beings and, in a ritual in
which he is tortured and a bull is sacrificed, a double is conjured up
and sent to earth as the minister. This Jungian shadow organizes the
women in his flock into a witches' coven and impregnates them in
the hope of producing a messiah. He finally chooses just one woman
for his bride, but he makes this relatively positive choice on the day
he is beaten to death by the men of the village. The real minister then
reappears mysteriously "in the West of Ireland, where he roams about
composing hymns and psalms to a nameless female deity."[13] These
hymns appear in *Gaudete's* "Epilogue." Although most of them are
addressed to a symbolic White Goddess, one is an elegy for Sylvia
Plath. The memory of her waving goodbye from a hospital bed gives
way to the memory of her in the morgue as he kissed the graveyard
marble of her head, "lips queasy, heart non-existent" (186). The minister of *Gaudete*, the fictional author of this lyric, has been transformed
by his horrific experiences; but he is no closer to possessing the inte-
grated self symbolized by the marriage imagery.

In *Cave Birds*, as in *Crow*, there is a pre-text for the drama which
the poet himself has provided: In a symbolic trial of the persona by
birds, he is found guilty and subsequently punished for betraying or

"desecrating" a female persona; but he is ultimately redeemed through an alchemical marriage. The reliance of critics of *Cave Birds* on this narrative underpinning recalls early criticism of *The Waste Land*. Eliot's comment that Jessie Weston's *From Ritual to Romance* could help "elucidate the difficulties of the poem" led Cleanth Brooks and others to impose on *The Waste Land* a narrative unity, or what Brooks called a "scaffolding," that it did not have or need. Such interpretations were misleading because they treated *The Waste Land*, in Brooks's phrase, as a "unified whole."[14] (Eliot was indeed even less capable than he said Blake was of constructing a traditional long poem.) Eliot himself wrote in 1956 that he regretted "having sent so many enquirers off on a wild goose chase after Tarot cards and the Holy Grail."[15] Hughes's remarks about a new "Holy Ground" have had a similar effect on his critics.

Despite their power, his images in *Cave Birds* do not delineate what Leonard Scigaj calls an "alchemical journey to psychic wholeness."[16] Like Eliot's poem, *Cave Birds* is a brilliant "heap of broken images." Hughes's interpretation of his own poem has encouraged Scigaj, one of Hughes's best critics and the best scholar, to argue that the poem contains a narrative of a successful alchemical quest. An analysis of the alchemical images in their context, however, shows how little they support such an interpretation. Scigaj finds "the initial phase [of the] transformation process" in one of the most programmatic of Hughes' poems, "The Knight" (215). The persona "has surrendered everything" and experiences the disintegration of his personality, or alchemical *mortificatio*, when he is reduced "to the small madness of roots, to the mineral stasis / And to rain" (CB 28). Most of the explicitly alchemical references are to the process of dissolution: "A condensation, a gleam simplification" ("A Flayed Crow," 34); "You dissolve, in the cool wholesome salts" ("The Baptist," 36); "Sun, moon, stars, he fills them up / With his hemlock—They darken" ("The Executioner," 22). The positive elements are in relatively undeveloped allusions to the sun or to the solar hawk, with the possible exception of the transformation described in "The Accused," where the atoms of the quester are "annealed" and his body transformed "like an ore, / To rainbowed clinker and a beatitude" (24). In terms of the trial, the accused (like the quester) is punished for his sins, which are sins committed against women; and in this poem his despotic heart, "hard brain," and "hard life-lust" are assailed. In alchemy, the ore is transformed when the colors of the fire resemble a rainbow (*cauda pavonis*). The accused is thus "annealed" into a state of "beatitude." Even so, the transformation seems qualified because a "rainbowed clinker" is still a burned-out clinker, even though such an "annealed" state is presumably better than the hero's former one. In other words, Hughes communicates the pain of fragmentation and dissolution far better than the joy of transformation. In "A Flayed Crow" (the "crow's head" is an alchemical term for dissolved matter), the "condensation" and "simplification" that makes an "egg" of darkness (as in the "philosopher's egg" of the alchemical vessel) leaves the "I" of the poem "soul skinned. . . . A mat for my judges" (34). In "The Owl Flower," which precedes the last poem in the sequence, "big terror descends" in a "flickering face of flames" (58), and "in these fading moments" the persona is "char[red]to the spine" (20).

The trial and alchemical metaphors are abandoned in a passage of "In These Fading Moments" that is unusually confessional for Hughes. His persona hears a female voice murmuring "Right from the start, my life / Has been a cold business of mountains and their snow" (CB 20). The syntax allows an ambiguity; although the "my" refers back to the "female," the context suggests it is the male persona who is really the cold one. The recurrent theme of the quester having offended some female persona or force (or "anima") seems related to Hughes's reaction to Plath's suicide. The "I" of this particular poem, however, is not the knightly quester but an ordinary man who reads the newspaper and smells "stale refuse." The poem's setting is contemporary and realistic rather than timeless and mythical. One additional poem in *Cave Birds* also has a more personal, confessional quality; it too departs from the mythological quest pattern and seems to be about Sylvia Plath. Entitled "Something Was Happening," it begins as the "I" is strolling in the rain before he returns home for dinner and hears some terrible news that is never fully explained: "Her sister got the call from the hospital / And gasped out the screech" (CB 30). (When Plath died, Hughes informed not Sylvia's mother but her aunt, Mrs. Plath's sister.[17]) The poem contrasts the coldness of the reaction of the poem's "I" to the death by fire of a "she." In a variation on James Joyce's characterization of the artist indifferently paring his fingernails, the persona explains, "I was scrubbing at my nails" while "She was burning." The narrator explains that some, who were close to her, walked away from her suffering "because it was beyond help now. / They did not stay to watch" (CB 30).

The obsessive recurring immolation of the *Cave Birds'* male quester, which mirrors the death of the persona, is perhaps Hughes's way of admitting that he "walked away"; that it was "beyond help" does not seem to mitigate the guilt. The fire imagery itself relates the female persona to Plath. As we have seen, her persona in "Lady Lazarus" is an alchemical "pure gold baby" who is refined by fire: "I turn and burn" (SP 244). In "Ariel," she rides into the "red / Eye, the cauldron of morning" (SP 192). As Anne Stevenson tells us, Plath's imagination was haunted by the image of "Jeanne d'Arc's death by fire, which she alludes to in her poem 'Witch Burning.'"[18] In Plath's "Elm," the persona identifies with a tree that is "scorched to the root / My red filaments burn and stand, a hand of wires" (SP 192). The suffering of the persona of Hughes's "The Owl Flower" is described in similar terms. In the "flickering face of flames" that terrifies the quester, "something separates into a signal, / Plaintive, a filament of incandescence. . . . In the cauldron of tongues" (CB 58).

Freud found in a dream about a burning boy a father's obsessive guilt toward his dead son.[19] The fiery images of *Cave Birds* have a similar burden. Burning with his guilt, Hughes's persona in "Something Was Happening" sees the burgeoning of new life "in April / And cried in dismay: 'Here it comes again!'" (CB 30). His persona is as disturbed as Eliot's in *The Waste Land*, and if we read the poems biographically, in each a failed marriage has motivated the characterization. But Hughes is not as ready as Eliot to admit the failure of the persona's quest. In the final lines of "Something Was Happening," he shifts the focus from the contemporary world to the mythical and imagines an "eagle-hunter" in a primitive wilderness who "bowing towards his trap / Started singing." Although the song is "Two, three, four thousand years off key" (30), Hughes suggests the possibility that the quester of *Cave Birds* might recover the hunter's mythical consciousness.

Nevertheless, there is no hope for the woman consumed by fire. The alchemical process seems more destructive than restorative even in the concluding poems of the sequence: "Walking Bare," "Bride and Groom," "The Owl Flower," and "The Risen." "What is left" of the hero in "Walking Bare" is the Jungian

> gem of myself
> A bare certainty. . . .
> Through this blowtorch light little enough
> But enough.
>
> (CB 54)

In "Bride and Groom Lie Hidden for Three Days," the marriage of *sponsus* and *sponsa* is finally consummated, which Scigaj believes marks "the arrival of psychic reintegration."[20] But the marriage is described in mechanistic terms that paradoxically develop the imagery of fragmentation:

> She stitches his body here and there
> > with steely purple silk
> He oils the delicate cogs of her mouth.
> > > (56)

In "The Owl Flower" (a mandala-like solar bird in Baskin's drawing), the alchemical process is described in condensed images. An "egg-stone" bursts

> And a staggering thing
> Fired with rainbows, raw with cringing heat,
>
> Blinks at the source.
> > > (58)

Throughout the poem, the "source" is related to the sun, as are both the "owl flower" and the falcon of the final poem. The falcon of "The Risen" is a "cross, eaten by light, / On the Creator's face" (60). (In Jung's *Symbols of Transformation*, the cross symbolizes the human/divine wholeness of the self.)[21] This bird is the liberated "gem" of the self, a "burning unconsumed" and the completed symbol of the alchemical transformation:

> On his lens
> Each atom engraves with a diamond.
>
> In the wind-fondled crucible of his splendour
> The dirt becomes God.
> > > (60)

The transformation could not be more complete than for the self to become "God." Such a god is the one Jung describes as "a manifestation of the ground of the psyche" in which the "unavoidable internal contradictions in the image of a Creator-god can be reconciled in the unity and wholeness of the self as the *coniunctio oppositorum* of the alchemists or as an *unio mystica*."[22] As the "dirt becomes God" in the alchemical crucible, the falcon symbolically reconciles the opposites.

And yet these lines, which complete the imagist patterns of *Cave Birds*, are not the final lines of the volume. The poet undercuts his own carefully constructed image in the last lines of the final poem by asking, "But when will he land / On a man's wrist" (CB 60). Like the comment that the eagle is singing but singing off key, this question (or statement—for there is no question mark) challenges the authority of the image. The challenge is driven home by the two-line "Finale" (following page sixty) that Hughes adds next to Baskin's tiny drawing of a "goblin" emerging from the white of the page: "At the end of the ritual / up comes a goblin." The goblin in fact seems to be beyond Hughes's control.

The way the goblin and the recalcitrant hawk undercut the grandiloquence of the image of transformation poses a difficult problem for Hughes's critics. Only Keith Sagar dislikes the reference to the real falcon, which he says "makes nonsense of the whole conception of the symbolic falcon."[23] Graham Bradshaw directly contradicts Sagar: "Far from making 'nonsense of the whole conception', this return to the human protagonist is an integral part of the 'drama' as Hughes finally conceived it."[24] Terry Gifford and Neil Roberts acknowledge that the reference to the falcon landing on a man's hand "must come as a shock" because it challenges the view of the falcon as "an apotheosis of the transformed hero." But because they nevertheless believe the quest is successful, they attempt to nullify the shock: "It is encouraging and awe-inspiring that a writer should feel like that about a work as complete and ambitious as *Cave Birds*."[25] Similarly, Scigaj says, "The final lines of 'The risen' and those of the closing 'Finale' indicate that this new self is no guarantee of permanent well-being and perpetual self-control; the process of personality growth will recur when needed in the mutable world."[26] Craig Robinson also interprets this passage as "an acknowledgement of the unending dynamism of the psyche" and takes a general tendency among Hughes's critics to an implausible extreme by concluding: "Optimism is the most striking quality of *Cave Birds*."[27]

Despite these attempts to read the passage affirmatively, the falcon that will not land on a man's hand not only indicates that the quest is difficult and perpetual but also questions whether it can be achieved at all. Sagar is right that Hughes cannot have the falcon image both ways—as a symbol of the resurrected self and of an untamed, natural creature that does not relate to human consciousness. There is not so much an ambiguity here, as most of Hughes's critics seem to think, as a confusion. Such a contradiction would not appear in Robert Dun-

can because he avoids Hughes's style of oracular overstatement. Although Merrill does not avoid the oracular style in *Changing Light*, his
irony modulates both the occult assertions and the humble admissions
of spiritual ignorance and defeat, so that neither are jarring. One
should acknowledge Hughes's honesty in admitting that the goblin
can or will always spoil the desired transformation. But this contradictory admission points to a serious problem in the poem's Jungian
and alchemical development.

Hughes has developed a sense of "self" that little resembles the
results of a Jungian individuation drama. His poetry does not dram-
atize a self that reconciles the opposites of experience, or comes to
terms with its shadow or anima, or a self that has gone through (in
Scigaj's words) "a process of self-examination and final resolution."[28]
The dramatis personae of the Jungian unconscious, such as the
shadow of "The Summoner" and the anima in "Bride and Groom,"
play their archetypal roles; but they seem mere variations on a Jungian
theme, the results of literary influence, compared with images like that
of the fiery woman of "Something Was Happening" or the burning
figure of "In These Fading Moments." The very passage that expresses
the success of the transformation may be the weakest in the poem.
The lines "In the wind-fondled crucible of his splendour / The dirt
becomes God," seem a grandiose statement for which the alchemical
imagery of the poem is an inadequate preparation. Unless one imports
pantheistic or Jungian meaning into the line, it carries no conviction.
Such lines recall some of the gnomic and pretentious ones in Pound's
late Cantos. Moreover, there has been no preparation for the tone. It
is as if lines expressing spiritual illumination from *Four Quartets* appeared in *The Waste Land*.

To interpret Hughes's poetry as dramatizing Jungian individuation,
one would need to attribute its power to archetypes rather than to
literary art. His own statements about the poet as shaman or about
his symbols engaging the "elemental power circuit of the Universe"
encourage such a reductionist approach to his art. He has said that he
thinks of his jaguar poems not only as descriptions of the animal but
also as "invocations of a jaguar-like body of elemental force, demonic
force. It is my belief that symbols of this sort work. And the more
concrete and electrically charged and fully operational the symbol, the
more powerfully it works on any mind that meets it. The way it works
depends on that mind . . . on the nature of that mind."[29] In these terms,
the symbol "works" not by means of literary art but by some kind of
"electricity"; and its effect is wholly dependent on the receptivity of

the reader. If that is the case, one might say, with Robert Duncan, "Well, I wonder how any poet could be attracted to Jungianism. To me poets use symbols to be initial and in the universe. Jung uses them to be in a psyche and around a center." Although Duncan admires as much as Hughes does Jung's insights into the psyche, he is skeptical of the Jungian system: "I don't disbelieve in the existence of archetypes, but I wouldn't posit their importance in the way Jung does. . . . I think that everything we see is posited in the material world. So that an archetype doesn't get to be very arche. Instead of an archetype, we'd better look at a tree or a particular individual."[30]

Although Bradshaw believes that *Cave Birds* is a successful "psychic drama," he is aware of the difficulty in depending on mythical archetypes to validate Hughes's poetry. He thinks that the critic should be skeptical of Hughes's emphasis on the poet's shamanic role." Before we accept the shaman as a "symbol of psychic integration that exposes Western inadequacies," Bradshaw thinks that we should be ready to ask if we indeed "believe that shamans fly, or that their intestines turn to opal after death? What do we actually know about the incidence of neurosis and schizophrenia in primitive societies?"[31] These questions may seem naïvely direct, but if they cannot be satisfactorily answered, how seriously can we take Hughes's role as a shamanistic healer?

Similarly, we have to accept some radical psychological assumptions to accept Scigaj's claims for Hughes's poetry: "Readers who acknowledge their own demons and desires while participating in the imaginative life of the poetry have a much better chance of integrating their conscious lives with their buried selves, and thus achieving peace. . . . Hughes delights us with his metaphors and formal dexterity as he teaches us how to understand our culture and achieve personal wholeness."[32] Delight and understanding are certainly qualities we can derive from Hughes's poetry. But why should we assume, first, that his poetry can make us aware of our "buried selves" and, second, that such an operation will help us achieve peace or "personal wholeness"? (Some buried selves, one might say, should stay buried.) We ought to question the assumptions both Hughes and his critics make about the efficacy of Jungian archetypes, the priestlike power of the poet, or the nature of the human psyche so that we can evaluate the claims made for the success of *Cave Birds*. Scigaj's answer to such criticism may be seen in his reply to Bradshaw's skepticism about Hughes's shamanism: "From a modernist standpoint these comments are imperceptive. The important point is that whole communities for

many centuries and in very different geographical areas . . . found shamanic techniques psychologically efficacious. . . . The paradigm and its
effects are important, not the performer or methods" (222). An equally
important point, however, is that these techniques would not have
been "efficacious" if these communities had not *believed* they were.

Although Eliot's criticism was applied too narrowly to Yeats, his
principle that a poet's ideas should demonstrate an "absorption into
life" seems valid.[33] In an essay on modern myth making, Philip Rahv
(whose commitments were more political than religious) complained
of "a vague literary compromise between skepticism and dogma, in
essence a form of magico-religious play with antique counters in a
game without real commitments or consequences."[34] Such a play without commitments is what makes some of Hughes's "antique counters," such as the symbolic falcon and the alchemical cauldron, ring
false. If "the road back to genuine mythic consciousness is closed," as
Rahv notes, it is no solution for artists "to deny historical time and
induce in themselves through aesthetic and ideological means a sensation of mythic time" (208, 210). In Hughes's case, the trial and alchemical elements are supposed to create a mythical time in which
the persona's guilt can be transcended. Hughes said that the song of
the primitive hunter was thousands of years off key, and the same
may be said of the ancient myths and rituals he sees as new "Holy
Ground."

Hughes has searched for an alchemy that unites the myths of many
cultures in a narrative that attempts to transcend the limits of historical time and place. The problem is that he strains his metaphor to
the breaking point in turning the alchemical stages into a narrative
scheme in which the quester is reborn. He might well have left his
vision of a personal waste land a "heap of broken images," as Eliot
did. Instead, he attempted to make his own framework for his poem
rather than leave the success or failure of that task to his critics. Yet
many brilliant images and whole poems, such as "In These Fading
Moments," "Something Was Happening," and "Bride and Groom,"
might not exist had not Hughes created a narrative for them. The
occult framework allowed him to express his buried guilt even if it
did not help him fully explore it. Whatever its shortcomings, *Cave
Birds* seems to have helped him focus on the transformational process
that offered hope of a release from his suffering. In the years after
Plath's suicide, Hughes clung to the idea of an alchemical marriage
as a way of healing his wound. *Cave Birds* is a record of this unsuccessful but moving struggle.

The intensity of this struggle also informs his reading of Shakespeare's works, *Shakespeare and The Goddess of Complete Being* (1992). Like Coleridge and Eliot, Hughes discovers his own obsessions at the heart of Shakespeare's poetry. In particular, he finds the "ur-tragedy" of Dido and Aeneas throughout Shakespeare's tragic plays and believes that it appears as an "unconfessed and unfocused centre of guilt" (429) in *The Tempest*, which he describes as "the final product of a long alchemical labor" (447). Hughes refers to Aeneas's rejection and then abandonment of Dido, followed by her tragic suicide, the "strange first 'crime'" (429) that underlies the suffering throughout the tragedies. He senses the "smouldering presence" (423) of Dido's life in Miranda, but in a redeemed and positive form because the Dido figure is now on Prospero's magical island. Although Ferdinand is most clearly the transformed and faithful Aeneas, Hughes believes that Prospero is also an Aeneas figure because he has absorbed the suffering and guilt of Aeneas's crime. As we saw in the Introduction, Hughes believes that Prospero is Shakespeare's portrait of an occult magus. Thanks to his "Hermetic mastery of supernatural powers" (469), Prospero arranges the "ultimate reparation" (421) for Aeneas's guilt in acknowledging Caliban as his own, freeing Ariel, and blessing the union of Ferdinand and Miranda. For Hughes, Prospero is not only the central figure of Shakespeare's plays but also the character most like Shakespeare himself, because the "supreme alchemist Prospero/Shakespeare" (457) expresses the spiritual mastery longed for in Hughes's own work.

Hughes clung to the hope that his work could express the sense of reparation and reconciliation he finds in *The Tempest*. Hughes's later work, however, is far less Hermetic and ambitious than *Cave Birds* or *Gaudete*. Writing to a disciple who was embarked on occult studies, Freud told him he was too influenced by "Jung's complex-mythology" and advised him that one "should not strive to eliminate his complexes but to get into accord with them."[35] Such an accommodation with one's psychological problems and limitations, rather than an attempt to overcome or transcend them, characterizes Hughes's verse after *Cave Birds*. Yeats said of the poets of the nineties that at a certain point they all got down off their stilts, and the same is true of Hughes as he approached the 1980s. *Remains of Elmet* (1979) is an elegy for a depressed region in his native Yorkshire. *Moortown* (also 1979) is largely devoted to a farming diary he kept while working on a Devon farm with his father-in-law, Jack Orchard, to whom the book is dedicated. Like *Remains of Elmet*, *River* (1983) is a book of poems and photographs in which Hughes again concentrates on animals and landscape, as he does in the relatively minor volumes *Flowers and Insects* (1986) and *Wolfwatching* (1989). In *River*, the animals still seem agents of revelation but with a difference. A poem entitled "That Morning" recounts an incident that occurred on a fishing trip with his son Nicholas. Two "gold bears" appear, swimming like men and eating salmon off their talons (72). The poem describes Holy Ground, but it is shared with his child and involves no "new divinity." The bears are simply the sign that "we were where we were." The transformation theme is expressed with similar modesty when the "I" of "Gulkana," a "spectre of fragments," reflects that only death is certain while rebirth is "Unknown, uncertain" (84).

These late poems are Hughes's version of the burying of Prospero's magical book and the breaking of his staff. We have seen this poetic gesture in Yeats's doubt of the "half-read wisdom of daemonic images," Pound's admission that he could not make his work cohere, and Plath's breaking of the wine glass in "Dialogue over a Ouija Board." We see it again in Merrill's shattering of the mirror in his *Changing Light* trilogy. One is left after reading Hughes's work, however, with a question that the work of these other poets does not raise. Has the occult material helped to develop, or has it merely obscured, his poetic themes? Hughes's alchemical themes certainly helped him to treat a painful subject. Yet this material seems to conceal the real burden of his work: that his quester cannot be redeemed because his guilt is too enormous. In James Merrill, we find a poet whose occultism seems to lay bare rather than protect his persona.

James Merrill's
Romantic Unconscious

On this view we should have one distinct theory of the performances of a typical test-medium. They would all be originally due to an odd *tendency to personate*, found in her dream-life as it expresses itself in trance. Most of us reveal such a tendency whenever we handle a 'Ouija board' or a 'planchet' or let ourselves write automatically with a pencil.
—William James,
"Confidences of a Psychical Researcher"

In the work of Robert Duncan, Sylvia Plath, and Ted Hughes, we saw that the development of occult motifs paralleled an exploration of psychological themes, such as Duncan's sexual identity crisis, Plath's obsession with her father, and Hughes's guilt over Plath's death. For these poets, the occult world is a hidden one of unconscious fears and desires. Yet it is explored in terms that psychoanalysis has not merely neglected but often repudiated. In Chapter 4, we saw that Jacques Lacan cited Freud's break with Jung as evidence that the modern conception of the unconscious "is not at all the romantic unconscious of imaginative creation. It is not the locus of the divinities of night." This conception does not encompass, for example, the strange "divinities" that inhabit the afterlife of Plath's Ouija board. Lacan believes that post-Freudian "research into the unconscious moves, on the contrary, in the direction of a certain desiccation." We instinctively turn away from the world of "spiritist, invocatory, necromantic practice,"

of what, in the constructions of the Gnostics, are called the intermediary beings—sylphs, gnomes, and even higher forms of these ambiguous mediators. Furthermore, let us not forget that when Freud began to disturb this world, he gave voice to the line Flectere si nequeo superos Acheronta movebo. It seemed heavy with disturbing apprehensions when he pronounced it, but remarkably enough, its threat is completely forgotten after sixty years of experience. It is remarkable that what was thought to be an infernal opening should have been so remarkably asepticized.[1]

Although therapists such as Lacan naturally approve of this asepsis, poets naturally prefer the "romantic unconscious."

No contemporary poet has explored this area of the psyche more thoroughly than James Merrill in *The Changing Light at Sandover*. Merrill's world of unconscious impulses is the one mapped by Jung rather than Freud, and the Jungian unconscious it unfolds is related to Jung's most daring Gnostic and alchemical speculations. Merrill, as he says in his poem "Bronze," uses the Jungian conception of the dream as a "diving bell."[2] Merrill's world of angels, demons, and dualistic gods— revealed through the medium of the Ouija board—is anything but asepticized. Many literary critics have regarded the strange divinities of his occult epic as if they were symptoms of a mental disease. Harold Bloom complained of his "troublesome and inauthentic" sources "such as Dr. Carl Gustav Jung." Irvin Ehrenpreis scorned Merrill for "sounding like a Gnostic"; Denis Donoghue wrote that the poem reminded him of "a neglected script from 'Star Trek'"; and Hugh Kenner dismissed the "intricate fit of Ouija-board messages from other-world planes of awareness" as "campy, catty cleverness." Even a critic as sympathetic to Merrill as Helen Vendler is uncomfortable with the occult machinery of the poem, and she tries to make the Ouija board device more acceptable to the general reader by saying that "it can stand, we might say, for language itself." She interprets Merrill's board as a "symbol system" rather than as a means of exploring the afterlife, much as she interpreted Yeats's *A Vision* as an aesthetic rather than an occult vision.[3]

This distaste for Merrill's subject matter, which Lacan's comments on modern psychoanalysis might lead us to expect, could not surprise Merrill. We saw in the Introduction that the poet himself is uncomfortable with the amount of what he calls spiritualistic "Popthink" in the poem. He states such misgivings more memorably than his critics have by questioning the validity of his poetic material in witty couplets:

> all this
> Warmed up Milton, Dante, Genesis?

> This great tradition that has come to grief
> In volumes by Blavatsky and Gurdjieff?
> (CLS 136)

Obviously, Merrill uses his occult material far too intelligently and ironically for us to dismiss it as mere cleverness. He explores the world of the unconscious mind with the self-aware seriousness of a major poet. The key passage in understanding the nature of this exploration occurs in section "U" ("U" for "Unconscious"), in which Merrill writes:

> Jung says—or if he doesn't, all but does—
> That God and the Unconscious are one.
> (74)

In section "S" of *The Book of Ephraim* ("S" for Stevens, in part), Merrill had cited the passage in Wallace Stevens's "Final Soliloquy of the Interior Paramour" which states (or almost does) that "God and the imagination are one" (WS 524). The reference to Stevens on the imagination suggests Merrill's ambition to extend the power of his own imagination into the "other world." The source of the Jung passage could be his autobiography *Memories, Dreams, Reflections* (337), which Merrill cites elsewhere in the poem (CLS 229). Jung writes that when he uses mythical language, he is "aware that 'mana,' 'daimon,' and 'God' are synonyms for the unconscious."[4]

The evidence that *The Changing Light* is an exploration of the romantic, Jungian unconscious is nowhere more apparent than in Merrill's use of alchemical lore. As Jung explains in his autobiography, his study of the medieval alchemists was essential to the development of his theories because he found in them an "historical basis" for his own study of the unconscious (200). The alchemists projected the contents of the unconscious mind into the symbols that represented their quest for gold, and Jung was profoundly impressed that their symbols represented the same archetypes that he had discovered. He would no doubt have been equally gratified that such a poet as Merrill, who dares to let his imagination take him wherever it leads, should discover similar alchemical patterns in his researches. The alchemical motifs in *The Changing Light at Sandover*, to which Jung may serve as a guide, help characterize the nature of Merrill's imaginative world.

The reader of this book knows how pervasive alchemy is as a metaphor for poetic art. The appeal of describing a transformation of the base metal of ordinary language into the gold of poetic art is irresistible, as when Wallace Stevens in "The Man on the Dump" describes his poetic *"stanza"* as his alchemical *"stone"* (WS 203). Stevens, Eliot, and Plath all drew upon alchemy for important images, such as Sylvia Plath's "pure gold baby." For Yeats, Pound, and Duncan, alchemy was a source of imagery throughout their poetic careers. H.D. and Ted Hughes, moreover, used alchemical concepts structurally to help them organize long poems. In Merrill's case, the first alchemical reference in *Changing Light* seems casual. It occurs when the voice of Nature is heard describing one of the five immortal spirits (the "LIVE ALEMBICS") who through successive incarnations encourage the progress of humanity (in this case, the evolution of music). She speaks in the capital letters that signify a communication through Merrill's Ouija board: "THUS THE MELODIC SENSE REFINED IN LIVE / ALEMBICS THRU THE CENTURIES WILL GO" (CLS 497). Another seemingly casual alchemical reference appears in the comment that the spirit Michael makes about Merrill's attempt to make supernatural wisdom available through his poetry: "MINING LEAD & PRODUCING QUICKSILVER?" (346). The reference to quicksilver, or mercury, is more than casual, however, because it links other references in the poem both to mercury as the key element of alchemical formulas for transforming lead to silver and gold, and to Mercury (or Hermes) the Roman and Greek god. Such linked references support the lyric structure of this long poem; and mercury is literally the major structural "element."

The importance of the liquid metal mercury to alchemy was related to the god Mercury's importance as a messenger of the gods and a conductor of human souls from the realm of the living to that of the dead. As we saw in the work of H.D. and Duncan, Mercury or Hermes thus mediated between the gods and humanity, and between life and death, much as the element mercury supposedly mediated the transformation of lead and other base metals into silver and gold. Mercury's significance to the alchemists is seen in Jung's description of Mercury as "the divine winged Hermes manifest in matter, the god of revelation, lord of thought and sovereign psychopomp."[5] Thus when the spirits address Merrill and Jackson, they do so under the aegis of Mercury ("WE ARE MERCURY") and tell them that their "province" is "MESSAGES THE TRANSPORTING AND DELIVERY / OF SOULS" (CLS 246).

Mercury as an element is also important because quicksilver was used as the backing for mirrors, which relates it to the transformation of the ordinary world into the miraculous one revealed by the Ouija board. The spirits can see Merrill and Jackson in any reflecting surface, and early in Book 2 of the trilogy, *Mirabell's Books of Number*, the two friends acquire a Victorian mirror (appropriate to the poem's Alice through the looking-glass adventure) that always appears in their sessions. This old, spotted mirror figures in the following address to Mercury, in which Merrill ponders the information that the spirits are "Mercury":

> With new eyes we confront the mirror,
> Look *beyond* ourselves. Does he appear?
> > (CLS 249)

Although the "he" of the passage grammatically appears to be the god or element Mercury, the context suggests that the "he" is also the new teaching spirit, Michael, who is soon to arrive to continue Merrill's lessons.[6] But in either case the function of the spirit is the mercurial one of revelation. But does the spirit appear? The possibility is, Merrill admits, that the mirror and his own work of art merely reflect his own mind and that he is inventing fictions rather than receiving revelations from "beyond ourselves." But further contemplation of the mirror suspends his disbelief. The mirror's quicksilver backing has decayed, and the clouded background suggests the presence of Mercury:

> an alchemical Jekyll
> Mapping the orbit of the long, long trek
> Back? To what?
> > (249)

The "alchemical Jekyll" Mercury is the guide on the "orbit" back to death and dissolution. Mercury's function as psychopomp for the dead has been imaged in the darkening surface of the mirror itself.

To use Lacan's phrase, Mercury is an extremely "ambiguous mediator." Ezra Pound expressed that duality in the final image of "A Song of the Degrees" in describing the god's "two-faced iridescence" (Personae 96). Mercury's duality is also his crucial quality in H.D.'s "Hermes of the Ways" and in Duncan's "After Reading Barely and Widely." In addition to emphasizing Mercury's dual or hermaphroditic nature, Jung comments on the sinister side of this duality: "sometimes he was a ministering and helpful spirit . . . and sometimes the *servus* or *cervus fugitivus* (fugitive slave or stag), an elusive, deceptive, teasing goblin who drove the alchemists to despair and had many of his attributes in common with the devil."[7] Merrill meditates on Mercury's diabolic role in a superb passage on "the lord of chill and fever" who brings the revelation of our mortality:

> You will at his convenience
> Have glimpsed among thousands the five or seventeen
> Or forty year-old self consigned like raiment
> Worn only once, on such-and-such a day,
> To the hope chest that cramps and crystallizes
> The secret backward flow.
>
> (CLS 249)

The euphemistic diction of the passage tells nevertheless of the inevitable dissolution in the grave ("hope chest") in which our bodies flow back into the elements.

   This trip backward into the elements through death is the constant theme of *The Changing Light*. The major purpose of the lessons from the other world is to reconcile Merrill and his friend David Jackson, who is the "medium" for the Ouija sessions, to the loss of their friends and to the prospect of their own deaths. Thus "The First Lessons" that Merrill receives from the elemental spirits, Michael, Gabriel, Raphael, and Emmanuel, will proceed under the sign of Mercury. The following passage serves as the epigraph to "The First Lessons: 5":

> *The schoolroom stretches to a line. It breaks*
> *Cleverly into two floating poles*
> *Of color that in dark 'air' glow and pulse,*
> *Undulate and intertwine like snakes.*
> *Whatever road we travel now, this twinned*
> *Emblem lights, and is both distant guide*
> *And craft we're sealed hermetically inside,*
> *Winged as by fever through the shrieking wind.*
>
> (CLS 336)

The two poles symbolize the multiple dichotomies of the poem—life and death, dark and light, male and female, sun and moon, matter and antimatter—the list is endless. The poles become the twining serpents of Mercury's caduceus, the magical wand that could turn base metals to gold and conduct the dead to the next world (Figure 11). Their spiral form, as in Yeats, will unwind the winding path of spir-

Figure 11. Mercury as a symbol of unity, from Basilius Valentinus, *Musaeum hermeticum*, 1678.

itual illumination during Merrill's lessons. But the passage shows that the caduceus is only a *"distant guide"* and that Merrill is, as expressed in a play on Mercury's Greek name, *"sealed hermetically inside"* the supernatural world, as his image is sealed within a mirror. The diabolic aspect of the winged god as messenger of death appears vividly in the final line: *"Winged as by fever through the shrieking wind."*

Alchemical references are crucial to Merrill's poem because they support its major theme of our need to reconcile ourselves to death. The art of alchemy concerned the breaking down of substances as well as their rebirth through the creation of pure gold or the finding of the alchemist's stone, which makes the transformation into gold possible. The psychological implications of this dual process of destruction and creation are analyzed by Jung in terms relevant to Merrill's poem. For the alchemist "there was first of all an initial state in which opposite tendencies or forces were in conflict; secondly there was the great question of a procedure which would be capable of bringing the hostile elements and qualities, once they were separated, back to unity again."[8] Chaos was not a given; the alchemist had to seek it. It was the *prima materia* on which his art worked; and it could not be achieved until, to use Wallace Stevens's words from "The Man with the Blue Guitar," even "the crust of shape has been destroyed" (WS 183). In psychological terms, Merrill must accept the chaos he feels within at the death of his friends. Through accepting their deaths, he can accept his own, or even discover a kind of immortality he can believe in, which is symbolized by alchemical gold. Thus Jung states that the commonest speculations on the significance of alchemical gold are "the ideas of its permanence (prolongation of life, immortality, incorruptibility)" (xiv). We see this analytic process in what Merrill's principal instructor, "Mirabell," or the Peacock, calls the purpose of Merrill's communications with the other world through the Ouija board. Mirabell speaks in Book 2 of the process by which we accept the loss of all our human qualities: "OUR SEMINAR IS THIS STRIPPING PROCESS" (CLS 211).

The basic personnel of the supernatural seminar are the "scribe" James Merrill, who is referred to in the abbreviated Ouija notation as "JM"; his friend, David Jackson ("DJ"), as the "hand" that transmits the Ouija board messages, who serves Merrill the way Mrs. Yeats served her husband through her mediumship; their Greek friend, Maria Mitsotáki, the key figure in the group; the "senior poet" W. H. Auden; and the Peacock, who symbolizes the *cauda pavonis* (Figure 6) of alchemical transformation. Of the four human members of the seminar, two have recently died, Maria and Wystan. Although Merrill has said that he did not know Auden well in life, he becomes increasingly intimate with him in the afterlife, where Auden is made to regret (as if in penance for his criticism of Yeats's spiritualism) his Anglicanism and faith in the "DREARY DEAD BANG WRONG CHURCH" (CLS 128).

Maria is the spirit most deeply loved by Merrill and Jackson, who came to know her during their winters in Greece. Merrill described their relationship as the "perfection of intimacy, light, airy, without confessions or possessiveness. . . ." Although *The Book of Ephraim* was begun within days of her death, Merrill said that he would have had "to be Jung or Dante to foresee her role in the poem."[9] With the peacock, the five of them represent the elements essential to the alchemical transformation: the maternal Maria is water; W. H. Auden, the poet of limestone landscapes and abandoned lead mines, is earth; Merrill, who belongs to "THE REGION OF STARRY THOUGHT" (CLS 164), is air; Mirabell is fire; and David Jackson represents the quintessence that holds the elements together: "THE SHAPING HAND OF NATURE" (CLS 159). (The four are also represented by metals: David Jackson— "A NICE MIXTURE OF SILVER AND TIN"; Merrill—silver; Auden—platinum; and Maria—gold.)

A series of lyric poems develops the alchemical symbolism of these elements and reveals Merrill's profound understanding of this occult art.[10] One of the lyrics describes the total dissolution of human elements:

> As milkweed, gnat, and fumes of vinegar
>   Chafe in molecular
> Bondage, or dance in and out of it—
> Midnight's least material affairs
> Reconciling to glow faint and far
>   Each atom the sun split,
>   Whose heirs we are who are the air's.
>   (CLS 160)

The stanza leaps from the common elements of some kind of witches' brew to the phenomena of atomic fission—a contemporary equivalent of black magic. The flux of molecules and the splitting or decay of atoms are images for the fate of humanity. Through this imagery, Merrill alludes to Maria's death by cancer after radiation treatments that weakened her without stopping the cancer. The open vowel sounds of the stanza's last line, intensified by the way each half of the line mirrors the other, heighten the concluding statement that we are as insubstantial as the air. Like Maria, we all dwindle "to nothing in one blink of rays" (CLS 209). Some of the most moving lines in the poem occur in a stanza that returns to the imagery of dissolution—this time within an alchemical kiln:

> What must at length be borne
> Is that the sacred bonds are chemical.
> Friend, lover, parent, amphorae that took
> Eons to dream up, to throw and turn—
>   Split-seconds in this kiln.
>   (209–10)

The painless, intense burn is the radiation that has helped to destroy Maria's human identity.

We are to learn, however, that Maria's fate is not yet settled; for the doubleness characteristic of the poem does not allow for anything so final as death. The alchemical symbolism itself implies transformation and rebirth. For example, the image of "milkweed" which "chafe[s] in molecular bondage" itself implies transformation because it is poisonous to humans yet sustains the life of a butterfly—a bit of alchemical lore that Ezra Pound knew when he wrote, "Milkweed the sustenance / as to enter arcanum."[11] There have been hints of Maria's special status in the other world throughout the poem, as when Auden says that she has the "SPECIFIC GRAVITY / OF A CULT FIGURE," which gives him a clue he hopes to "puzzle out" later (CLS 493). The puzzle is solved in the final section of Book 3, *Scripts for the Pageant*, when Maria tells Merrill that when alive she had sought him out to inspire the writing of his poem. When Merrill remembers that Maria died in the same week that he began the first part of the trilogy, Maria states that this was "NO ACCIDENT. . . . CHILDREN: I AM OF THE FIVE" (CLS 465). (The recurrent tag of "NO ACCIDENT" enforces the Freudian principle that mental and physical slips always reveal psychological motivation.)

The "FIVE" are spiritual Masters or Magi who reincarnate in order to guide mankind. The number 5 is appropriate because it signifies the four elements plus the alchemical quintessence. We learn that Maria incarnates Plato's spirit, and she will be reborn once again in Bombay. (Some details about her precocious infancy appear in the poem's "Coda" [CLS 528].) This revelation is almost too astounding for Merrill to accept, and "Love for Maria both suspends / And quickens disbelief." Flowing underneath his "incredulity" is

> Joy, the flash of the unbaited hook—
> *Yes, yes, it fits, it's right, it had to be!*
> Intuition weightless and ongoing
>   Like stanzas in a book
> Or golden scales in the Melodic brook—).
> (466)

The golden scales are an image of Merrill's love for Maria, which will not allow him to believe that her humanity will be lost. Maria pleads "O IMAGES, DEAR ENFANT, IMAGES . . . / NEVER LET THOSE SCALES DROP FROM YOUR EYES" (466). The wordplay on "scales" involves the musical scales of the "Melodic brook" as well as the suggestion that if JM is to weigh the evidence he should let the scales be weighted toward a belief in Maria's continued existence. Further, in the biblical use of the word (Acts 9:18), the scales must never fall from JM's eyes because they are in fact the film of images that arise from his love for Maria. Her final image is golden, which alludes to her "specific density" as one of the Five. A cassia bush that Maria spotted one evening thrives on the terrace of Merrill's house in Athens: "NO TEARS BESIDE / THE GOLDEN WEEPING BUSH MY DEARS" (513).

The image that best captures the poem's mercurial tone, however, is not the golden bush but the scales of right and wrong, true and false, yes and no—balancing but never settling before our eyes. Merrill has spoken of moments when the poem's occultism was "altogether too beautiful not to be true" (Rec 51). Such moments compel belief, as when JM suspends his skepticism at the news of Maria's survival. He spoke of this feeling in an interview: "It's true that in the glow of some of the later messages, when all the themes began to connect, and every last detail added its touch to the whole, there was no question of not assenting to what we were being shown" (Rec 53). The question of assent, however, is balanced by the question of error. If one believes mistakenly in something false, is the belief worthless? The meaning of "error" is a major theme of the *Sandover* trilogy. To appreciate it better, our perspective of the poem should also be double. As in reading H.D., a Freudian as well as a Jungian approach is required.

The Freudian dimension involves the conception of slips and error as signs of unconscious meanings or communications. Merrill begins his poem with an apology: "Admittedly, I err by undertaking / This in its present form" (CLS 3). In one sense, the "error" is his decision to describe his Ouija sessions in a long poem rather than in a novel of "unseasoned telling"; but in a deeper sense, the error is to have described these occult adventures at all. The sense of "error" as a "mistake," however, is qualified by its root meaning, "to wander." The decision to narrate his story as the Ouija board dictates, according to a scheme drawn from the letters and numbers on its face (which recalls the narrative significance of *The Waste Land*'s tarot pack), limits his conscious control over its development. Despite the difference in their poetic styles, Merrill is like Pound in embarking on a poetic voyage that is a "periplum" and not a journey from one point to another. Both know how weak the structures of their long poems are compared with Dante's *Divine Comedy*. Merrill indirectly comments on this problem when his friend Robert Morse, within the poem itself, criticizes the poem in manuscript:

> Everything in Dante knew its place.
> In this guidebook of yours, how do you tell
> Up from down?
>
> (256)

The title under which *The Book of Ephraim* first appeared is *Divine Comedies*, and the plural form of "comedy" itself acknowledges the poem's fragmentation. Merrill could only agree with Pound that the modern world gives the poet no "Aquinas-map" such as Dante's culture gave him.[12] When the tea cup Merrill uses as a pointer began transmitting messages through the Ouija board, it moved "dully, incoherently" before it "swerved, clung, hesitated, / Darted off." Even when he becomes more adept at both following and transcribing its movements, "THIS TOPSYTURVY WILLOWWARE / IGLOO WALTZING WITH THE ALPHABET" delivers anything but an ordered or even rational discourse.[13] Yet the most "fragmentary message" the board spells out is "twice as entertaining, twice as wise / As either of its mediums" (CLS 6–7). With their hands together on the willowware cup, sitting in a room with a Yeatsian "turn of the century dome" (5), the two mediums will follow the cup's wanderings wherever it takes them. Despite his distrust of such a poetic method, Merrill hopes that "wrong things in the right light are fair" (63).

From the sense of error as a "mistake" and then as a "wandering," Merrill relates the word still more widely to a "lapse" and a "fall." (In his poem "The Grand Canyon," he makes a similar play on words by describing the geologic "fault" of the canyon as a "mistake")[14] The "error" of the poem is a "fall" or "lapse" into the bizarre world it explores, and many passages express Merrill's worry that his and Jackson's obsession with the Ouija board may be *"folie à deux"* (CLS 30), or even a dangerous incursion into a daemonic world (9, 73), which would be a fall in an ethical sense. JM considers these possibilities in a passage in section "U" of *The Book of Ephraim*, which I have already briefly quoted. Beginning with a citation of Jung, it ends with an address to the "familiar spirit" who is JM's and DJ's mediator in the afterlife. Despite its Jungian reference, the passage implies a Freudian understanding of their experiences. (The ellipsis mark in the ninth line is in the text).

> Jung says—or if he doesn't all but does—
> That God and the Unconscious are one. Hm.
> The lapse that tides us over, hither, yon;
> Tide that laps us home away from home.
> Onstage, the sudden trap about to yawn—
> Darkness impenetrable, pit wherein
> Two grapplers lock, pale skin and copper skin.
> Impenetrable brilliance, topmost panes

Catching the sunset, of a house gone black . . .
Ephraim, my dear, let's face it. If I fall
From a high building, it's your name I'll call,
OK?

(74)

Despite the uncertain or even dubious tone of the "Hm," Merrill is
nevertheless making a major statement about his poetic subject. One
enters the world of the imagination only through some kind of fall,
as he suggests through a crucial play on the words *lap* and *lapse*. The
word *lapse* emerged from verbal play during the passage's composition. As one sees in the poem's typescript, Merrill first wrote "laps
fallen asleep in; home away from home," which developed into the
phrase "lapse that tides us over."[15] "Laps" was deferred to a new line
and joined with a new sense of the word *tide*, resulting in the brilliant
chiasmus of *lapse/tide, Tide/laps*. In *The Psychopathology of Everyday
Life*, Freud shows how verbal play or mistakes, the famous "Freudian
slips," can reveal the contents of the unconscious mind. (Freud himself
did not use the term *lapse*, but his American disciple A. A. Brill introduced in translation the terms *lapsus linguae, lapsus memoriae*, and *lapsus calami* to indicate slips of the tongue, memory, and pen.) These
slips or lapses are traps that lower us into the "darkness impenetrable" of the unconscious, where the poet can nevertheless glimpse the
struggle of dark and light: "pale skin and copper skin." The "tide that
laps us home away from home" swirls into the unconscious level of
our own minds. Thus there are no innocent or meaningless verbal
slips. Throughout the poem the reiterated phrase "NO ACCIDENT" reminds us that there is a reason, conscious or not, for everything we
say and do. Freud's technique of exploring dreams gives the pattern
of Merrill's explorations through the Ouija board: "In the case of [a
slip of the tongue] the man was asked how he had arrived at the
wrong word '*Vorschwein*' and the first thing that occurred to him gave
him the explanation. Our technique with dreams, then, is a very simple one, copied from this example. . . . The dreamer knows about his
dream; the only question is how to make it possible for him to discover his knowledge and communicate it to us.[16] As in H.D.'s poetry,
the "play of the signifier" lays out the winding path that Merrill will
follow to communicate his vision of life and death. Playing with the
Ouija board allows him both to discover and to communicate his vision.

The reference in "U" to the "house gone back," where the pale- and copper-skinned wrestlers are seen, is elucidated by a passage in Merrill's story "Peru: The Landscape Game." A woman who is said to be Jung's widow has the narrator play a game of "free association," in which he has to interpret the meaning of the contents of an imaginary house: "The house is your own life, your notion of it," and the "wild creature" that inhabits the house "is Yourself—the unconscious."[17] The light of consciousness is the "impenetrable brilliance" of a dark house, its "topmost panes," like the human mind, illumined by a dying light. A similar image is used in Merrill's poem "The House," where the west walls of the house "take the sunset like a blow," and the house contains "wet-faced sleepers" who awaken at the poet's glance.[18] The waking of those who are asleep or dead is ominous in this early poem, but in the *Changing Light*, communication with the dead is more often consoling than frightening. The unconscious is thus the world of the dead, and the "fall"—say, a "fall / From a high building"—is a literal one that could cause Merrill's or anyone's death. On the point of death, it would be Ephraim's name that the poet would call.

Merrill readily admits that this world of the dead may be a projection of his own mind, although he is Jungian enough to add that "consciousness doesn't stop with human beings." He even speculates that there may be a "great untapped mind, if you can call it that, in the natural world itself."[19] The "reality" of his experience can be taken for whatever it is worth—particularly, of course, its poetic worth. It would therefore be pointless to argue that the poem is "really" about the Jungian unconscious, or that the psychoanalytic "level" of the poem is the basic one. Yet the issue of whether the subject matter of the poem is merely a compulsive or neurotic personal experience devoid of the universal qualities necessary for a work of art is essential to Merrill himself. In his novel *The Seraglio* (1957), the interest in occultism of the protagonist, Francis Tanning, is linked to the growth of his neurosis about his sexuality. The possible link between neurosis and occultism is also explored in *The Changing Light*.

In the novel, Tanning castrates himself to escape his family's pressure to marry and raise children. This issue is handled far more lightly in *Ephraim* when JM goes to see his "ex-shrink" after he has lost touch with Ephraim. The doctor's judgment on the matter is expressed in a trimeter couplet in which the simple rhyme and meter emphasize his superficiality: "what you and David do / We call *folie à deux*" (CLS 30). Under the shrink's prodding, JM then states an orthodox interpretation of his experiences: "Somewhere a Father Figure shakes his rod" at JM and DJ because their love is barren, and their creation Ephraim helps them to justify their lives. After the consultation, JM and DJ again try to recall Ephraim, and to their surprise he answers and delivers a terse judgment of his own on the shrink: "FREUD / We learned that evening DESPAIRS / OF HIS DISCIPLES." Their self-doubts have fallen away as Ephraim returns and "clouds disperse / On all sides" (30–31). The issue of Ephraim as a psychological projection is faced and then seemingly resolved. Although Ephraim's disclosures may already lie "at some obscure / Level or another, in our skulls," they stand on their own merits whatever their origins.

Nevertheless, in Books 2 and 3 of the poem, *Mirabell* and *Scripts for the Pageant*, we learn that DJ and JM have not resolved the issues raised by their occult experiences. They are still uncomfortable about their Ouija experiments. As far as they are concerned, "No more spirits, please. . . . Ephraim's book is written now, is shut" (CLS 99). The dangerous power of the spirits was demonstrated in section "U" when DJ's hand felt like it had been stepped on and was sore long afterward. But a passage about the "Age of the Wrong Wallpaper" (a period of time that corresponds to their association with Ephraim) shows that this sinister world is calling them back:

No sooner on our walls, the buds uncurl
In scorn. Compulsively repetitive
Neuroses full-blown and slack-lipped, then whole
Faces surely not intended, peer
Forth—once seen, no question of unseeing
That turbaned mongoloid, that toad with teeth.
(97)

The motif of emergent neuroses is extended by another decorative addition at Stonington, a Chinese carpet of blue cloudlets containing "limber, leotarded, blue-eyed bats" (98). Like the "bat shapes" of Plath's "Dialogue over a Ouija Board," these creatures are a warning that the occult phenomena have become threatening.

After the deaths of certain friends—Maria, Chester Kallman, and Robert Morse—JM and DJ are tempted to recall Ephraim: "Where else to look for sense, comfort and wit?" (CLS 99–100). These friends return accompanied by spirits who describe the afterlife in the traditional terms of occultism. Such descriptions cause JM some embarrassment over the provenance and nature of the revelations. The material on the evolution of the three terrestrial races and the nine stages of reincarnation, for example, seems to come straight out of Blavatsky. More seriously, this material is tainted, if not by a Blavatskian racism, then by an elitism that seems inherent in such theories. As we saw in the Introduction, Merrill himself questioned the validity of a tradition that "came to grief" in the writings of Blavatsky and Gurdjieff. Nevertheless, true to his principle to follow the path of error, he follows the literal dictates of the spirits. In *Mirabell* the reader is faced with a theosophical system of bewildering intricacy, which becomes frankly inconsistent with the advent of a series of unreliable narrators, including primary ones such as Bezelbob (later spirit 741), the peacock Mirabell (a transformation of 741), the hornless unicorn Uni, and the angels Michael and Gabriel—as well as secondary ones such as Jesus, Buddha, and other historical and allegorical figures.

The cosmology these spirits describe has the Gnostic and Jungian features characteristic of occult systems. The two essential elements are the ones George B. Hogenson, in his study of the Gnostic influence on Jung, describes as (1) "the call—from the God beyond who has nothing to do with established theology" and (2) "the primacy of the feminine principle" in redeeming the cosmos.[20] The "call" in *Changing Light* occurs in one of its central and most moving passages in which "God B" (or "Biology") calls to his "brothers" in the cosmic pantheon. The "call" is tuned to "mortal wavelength" by Mirabell:

> BROTHERS HEAR ME BROTHERS SIGNAL ME
> ALONE IN MY NIGHT BROTHERS DO YOU WELL
> I AND MINE HOLD IT BACK BROTHERS I AND
> MINE SURVIVE BROTHERS HEAR ME SIGNAL ME.
>   (CLS 360)

This "pulse of the galactic radio" that fills the void of space comes from God B, who in Wystan's phrase, is "KEEPING UP HIS NERVE ON A LIFERAFT" (362), and it performs the Jungian task of bringing Gnostic enlightenment to the hearer. As JM remarks to Wystan, God B seems utterly unlike the "joyous Architect" (362) that Michael, the angel of light, had described. The call from God B helps to correct what Jung would call the "incompleteness" of such a "God-image." The God we learn about in *The Changing Light* belongs to a Gnostic cosmology in which "good" or positive forces barely stave off the "evil" or negative forces.

In relation to our earth, "2 GODS / GOVERN BIOLOGY & CHAOS" (CLS 113); but there are many more gods in this Gnostic universe. Of them,

God B is the youngest and was allowed to shape the world on condition that he install the "MONITOR" (392) at its heart. Although it is once referred to as a god, the Monitor is not one of the pantheon but appears to represent the destructive power of time. A variety of Gnostic demiurges create life on earth. For example, a race of centaurs created the bat-creatures JM met at the beginning of *Mirabell* and were destroyed by them—hence the bat's punishment (or "damnation" in the Christian sense) by God B. The shaping of the earth and of humankind was the work of the four angels who narrate much of *Scripts*, especially the first book: Michael, Gabriel, Raphael, and Emmanuel. But it was the dark angel Gabriel who gave to humankind the spark of consciousness that transformed them from ape to human—and made them capable of the self-destruction that now threatens the race.

The Monitor seems to wait upon this destruction, but there is also a God who actively opposes God B and is called God A, the Adversary. God A is a void rather than a positive evil and is related to antimatter, black holes, and the negative charge in the atom. God Biology must press back against this "insane / Presence beyond our furthest greenhouse pane" (CLS 398), but the energy needed is enormous and may be declining. This fear is expressed in perhaps the finest lyric passage in the poem. JM and Wystan are reflecting on the strange music that accompanied the lyrics of God B's song. When DJ says, "Dante heard that Song," Wystan asks a question that JM answers:

> WHO WD THINK THAT THE SONG HAD HAD SUCH LYRICS?
> The lyrics may be changing. Dante saw
> The Rose in fullest bloom. Blake saw it sick.
> You and Maria, who have seen the bleak
> Unpetalled knob, must wonder: will it last
> Till spring? Is it still rooted in the Sun?
>
> (363)

After hearing God B's song, DJ laments that their Ouija sessions now seem so "Manichaean" (362). Although Evil has been redefined as negativity or a void or a black hole, it is just as threatening to humankind's existence. God B is assisted by his "TWIN SISTER" Nature, but her concern for the earth's survival is questionable because she is both a creative and a destructive force.

This balance between good and evil, creation and destruction, and positive and negative is reflected in the titles of the three sections of *Scripts*: "Yes," "&," and "No," which are marks on the Ouija board.

In answer to the question of the survival of humankind, the cup wavers throughout between the "yes" and "no," with the "&" serving as a "bridge" (CLS 362). The hope for survival is centered in the "feminine principle," but not in the figure of Nature. With the possible exception of Wystan Auden, Maria Mitsotáki is the major character in the poem, and Maria represents the reconciling and redeeming feminine force.

Reflecting on Merrill's cosmology, Irwin Ehrenpreis disapprovingly but accurately states that Merrill "presents us with inversions of Biblical myth and Christian morality that suggest the tradition of gnosticism."[21] Ehrenpreis thinks that Merrill's Gnosticism is incoherent because it does not oppose matter to the spirit; but Ehrenpreis's conclusion is based on a far too narrow (and Manichaean) understanding of the Gnostic tradition. It is true that Madame Blavatsky and the Russian mystic G. I. Gurdjieff raided Gnostic traditions and that their formulations of spiritualistic doctrines were less than coherent. It is also true that Merrill's occultism is a strange jumble of material—stranger, even, than the eclectic myths in Pound's *Rock-Drill* or Hughes's *Cave Birds*. But it is just this jumble of beliefs that make up occultism. Even if one rejects Merrill's occult donnée, one has to admit he has adopted it with a sophisticated awareness of the risks he is taking. His self-consciousness and humor save him from the prophetic or shamanistic pose that rings false in Hughes' *Cave Birds*.

James Merrill began his poem with the feeling that using his Ouija board fantasies was an error. It was a mistake for a poet whose art was lush and descriptive (CLS 4) to begin a long narrative; a mistake for a poet who strives for a sensibility "no idea violates" (14) to create a "seminar" in which such "great ideas" as the existence of God and the destiny of humankind are debated; and it was a mistake, or at least a lapse in taste, to plunge into Gnostic traditions: "Raw revelation typed to maximum / Illegibility" (256), as his friend Robert Morse described the poem. Moreover, the revelations speak pessimistically of the ultimate extinction of humankind and of a universe void of human meaning. Yet out of such mistakes, and out of the fall into the dark materials of the unconscious mind, Merrill creates deeply humane and sympathetic figures like Maria and Auden as well as images of perfection such as the rose and the circle. But he never forgets the incompleteness out of which such images arise. The circle is also the "o o o" of the galactic void (360) and the rose a "bleak / Unpetalled knob" (363). The presence of the spirits implies their absence in ordinary life as well as their inevitable departure from the world Merrill has helped to make for them.

The departure of the spirits is planned at the conclusion to the first section ("Yes") of *Scripts*. The spirits "see" JM and DJ through a mirror always present at the séances. Wystan and Maria are the spirits present at this time, and JM feels that he and DJ could well be on their side of the mirror thanks to their growing intimacy. Maria warns him, however, that when the "lessons" are finished, he must break the mirror and let them go. JM's and DJ's shocked reactions to this news are clear from Auden's command that they dry their eyes. When Maria suggests that it might be a gentler farewell if the ritual of departure used water poured out into a plant, JM insists that the poem's logic calls for the breaking of a glass. The glass recalls the epigraph of *Scripts* from Proust's *Jean Santeuil*, in which the breaking of a vase is interpreted as a good omen, like the shattering of a glass at a Jewish wedding: "'*Ce sera comme au temple le symbole de l'indestructible union*'" (278).

Throughout sections 2 and 3 of *Scripts*, the changes of the moon bring us closer to the moment when JM and DJ must release the spirits. Everything that has happened in these two sections has been conditioned by the knowledge that the spirits must soon depart. Maria appoints the time as three days after a new moon. At DJ's suggestion, they will use a marble doorstop to break the mirror into a bowl of water and pour it over a cassia bush that Maria discovered and which still blooms on JM's terrace in Athens. The bowl, "brimming with water, / Lobs an ellipse of live brilliance" (CLS 515), which recalls the elliptic shape of the new moon and the pattern of the letters on the Ouija board as it also anticipates the shapes of the fragmented glass. JM will speak the ritual words and break the mirror into the cup that DJ holds, which will then be poured into the golden branches of the cassia bush:

> Our eyes meet. DJ nods. We've risen. Shutters
> Click at dreamlike speed. Sky. Awning. Bowl.
> The stylus lifted. Giving up its whole
> Lifetime of images, the mirror utters

> A little treble shriek and rides the flood
> Or tinkling mini-waterfall through wet

Blossoms to lie—and look, the sun has set—
In splinters apt, from now on, to draw blood,

Each with its scimitar or bird-beak shape
Able, days hence, aglitter in the boughs
Or face-down, black on soil beneath, to rouse
From its deep swoon the undestroyed heartscape

—Then silence.

(517)

The elliptic phrasing in the first three lines is appropriate to a ritual of shattering in which a virtual lifetime is lost in an instant or the snap of a shutter. Much earlier, in section "V" of *Ephraim*, JM recalled that he was lucky when he lost his camera during a tour because its loss would teach him never to "overlook a subject for its image, / To labor images till they yield a subject" (76). The implied poetics of these lines clarifies Merrill's ambition (resembling Ezra Pound's in *The Cantos*) to write a long poem that would be more than a "batch of images" (CLS 75). Now that the poem is finished, he reminds us (as Yeats did in "The Phases of the Moon") that poetry is "mere images." Although they are fragments, the pieces of the mirror assume recognizable shapes of "scimitar" or "bird-beak" that can recall their friends and reopen the wounds of their loss.

Wystan Auden and Maria are the principal spirits freed by the breaking of the mirror, but among the many other departing spirits, one must particularly note W. B. Yeats. We learn in *Ephraim* that Merrill had been studying *A Vision* early in his occult explorations, and a number of allusions to Yeats (such as the gyre diagrams [CLS 475]) remind us of his formative influence. But it is not until *Mirabell* that we learn that Yeats's spirit dwells in the very hand that DJ rests on the Ouija board and provides the "energy that activates / These very messages" (217). (One might recall the precedent that John Milton entered William Blake's left foot in *Milton*, Book 1, Plate 15.) Yeats is thus literally the guiding hand behind the poem, and he compliments DJ by telling him he was as good a medium as his own wife (CLS 481). Yeats's poetry often expressed the feeling, as in "The Choice," that his imaginative and occult researches were sapping his own life. His frequent use of Heraclitus's statement that we and the gods "die each other's life, live each other's death" is paralleled when the spirits tell JM: "WE ARE U YOU ARE WE EACH OTHER'S DREAM" (117).[22] In

"Meditations in Time of Civil War," Yeats admits that he is "caught / In the cold snows of a dream" (Poems 204). Similarly, JM and DJ feel that they have traversed a "door / Shutting us off from living" (CLS 217). Both Yeats and Merrill thus acknowledge what Auden's meditation on *The Tempest*, his poem *The Sea and the Mirror*, presents as the necessary end of the poet's career: the renunciation of magic.

This renunciation, however, is not unreserved. Yeats was "content to live it all again" (Poems 236), and his late works *Purgatory* and "The Death of Cuchulain" dwell on reincarnation. The gesture of renunciation, or the admission of failure, is sincere. Yet there is always the chance of a new beginning. For Merrill, the shattering of the mirror is a beginning as well as an end. It signifies the "giving up" of a "whole lifetime of images" in the creation of a poem. The marble wedge, which was merely a door stop, now becomes a "stylus" that frees images through writing. In signifying the departure of his friends, it also reminds us that the transmigration of their spirits has begun. As the poem's coda tells us (526–28), Maria is incarnated in Bombay as a child (male) with extraordinary mental gifts. (In Merrill's final work, *A Scattering of Salts* [1995], the poem "Nine Lives" tells of JM and DJ's unsuccessful attempt to contact the child when he visits Athens at age eight with his family.) Maria commands her friends to

> SEND OUR IMAGINED SELVES
> FALLING IN SHARDS THRU THE ETERNAL WATERS
> (DJ CUPBEARER) & INTO THE GOLDEN BOUGH
> OF MYTH   ON INTO LIFE.
>
> (CLS 516)

The shattering is like Prospero's breaking of his staff, drowning of his book, and freeing of the elemental spirits Ariel and Caliban. Merrill's "Pageant," like Prospero's in *The Tempest*, is necessarily "insubstantial" as the dead, or the memories of them, begin to fade. Merrill is as haunted as Ted Hughes by the figure of Prospero. In Merrill's poem "Dreams of Clothes" (1972), Prospero inspires the poet's dreams. The narrator of his experimental novel *The (Diblos) Notebook* refers to himself as a Prospero (133) and sets the action of his novel on a Greek island where the "illusory lightness" recalls the enchanted island of *The Tempest* (47). The novel's imagery of sea and light is a preview of the dazzling imagery of *The Changing Light at Sandover*. Merrill also recalls Shakespeare's island in Section "F" of "Ephraim" where "Miranda's island" is a controlled environment for a sign-making chimpanzee named Miranda. Despite her lack of self-consciousness, Miranda is groping like the poet for some higher existence. In *Mirabell*, JM alludes to *The Tempest* in asking a spirit to help him "drown the double-entry book / I've kept these fifty years" (CLS 122). After Maria is freed, she is addressed as "Ariel" in the opening lyric of the poem's coda. The most revealing reference to *The Tempest* is Maria's remark to JM that the release will make him seem "QUITE LIKE PROSPERO" (364). Merrill seems to have meditated more profoundly than any of the poets of the occult except Hughes on the significance of *The Tempest* and of Prospero's rough magic. Unlike Hughes, however, Merrill identifies with Prospero more in his gesture of renunciation than in his magical power. His awareness that the power necessarily fades keeps Merrill's touch light—*his* tempest is spelled out by a tea cup. Although more comprehensive in his treatment of occult themes than any poet since Yeats, he also uses them more deftly thanks to a poetic tone that ranges from the sublime to the intentionally ridiculous. As I suggest in my conclusion, no poet has used the magician's staff as wisely as James Merrill.

Conclusion

... we reveal our status
with twin-horns, disk, erect serpent.
— H.D., *The Walls Do Not Fall* (CP 516)

Borrowing a phrase from T. S. Eliot, one could say that the poets of the occult all lusted after strange gods. Violating the traditional boundaries of religious discourse and ritual, they trespassed into what Eliot called the "wrong spiritual world." Instead of a monotheistic and benevolent Creator whose ways are just if mysterious, the world of these poets reveals pagan gods whose arbitrary behavior deprives humanity of free will. In religious terms, the "error" of these poets is that they become prophets of these false gods; in aesthetic terms, it is simply that they become prophets. Much as they violate the bounds of conventional religion, they also violate the conventions of modern poetry in a style that Eliot dismissed as a "worn-out poetical fashion." Their conception of poetry as prophecy or a witness to transcendent truths seemed dead with the Romantics and pardonable only in Yeats because he was a transitional figure. The conception of poetry as an art or craft seems barely relevant to their conception of poetry as a magical invocation of spirits or archetypes. At a time when poets rarely speak in a prophetic voice, when the "I" of the poem is modest, or decentered, or entirely effaced, they speak with the bardlike tones of Shakespeare's Prospero when boasting of commanding the elements and opening graves. Wallace Stevens wrote, "To say more than human things with human voice" cannot be, nor "to say human things with more / Than human voice" (WS 300). Yet the poets of the occult speak in that voice and so, from

Stevens's point of view, fail to speak the "acutest speech," which is simply human.

Despite his scruples, Eliot could nevertheless respect Yeats's sincere if heretical attempt to approach the "religious sources of poetry." But many readers and critics are far less receptive to the occult style than Eliot. Robert Duncan recalls the contempt that greeted H.D.'s *The Walls Do Not Fall* from critics who found her belief in the reality of the ancient gods silly and irrelevant, especially in wartime. He compares this reception with the praise for Robert Lowell's *Land of Unlikeness*, which was "intellectually discrete" in finding God absent from the world. Duncan argues that poets like H.D., who write of a living and affirmative religious experience, will not be taken as seriously by the "consensus of opinion of reasonable men" as a poet who, like Lowell, despairs of having such an experience.[1]

Perhaps Merrill was anticipating this kind of incomprehension when he confessed to an interviewer that he "must have some kind of awful religious streak just under the surface" (Rec 44). The negative reviews he received when *The Changing Light* was first published only turned to an acceptance as Helen Vendler and other critics interpreted the Ouija board as a language game. In the case of Pound and especially Yeats, critics have interpreted their spiritual beliefs as aesthetic positions. But they are not only aesthetic. As Duncan says of Pound and H.D., their spiritual experiences are too real to them to be described as merely "fictive certainties" in the manner of Wallace Stevens.[2] To Duncan, Stevens's voice seems less moving than Pound's because Stevens communicates a "melodious poetic respectability, eminently sane in [its] restriction of poetic meaning to the bounds of the literary, of symbol and metaphor, but at the cost of avoiding facts and ideas that might disturb."[3] Although Pound no less than Yeats could sound crazed or disturbed, this tone was inseparable from the passion and conviction of their poetry.

Yet the critics are often right about the aesthetic sins of occult poets. The bardic note does inflate the poetry of Yeats, Pound, and Ted Hughes; and even Duncan's readers might be confused by his passionate swings between esoteric and politically engaged poetry. H.D has finally been recognized as a major poet but, as in the case of Sylvia Plath, not because of her esoteric or religious vision but for her feminist rereadings of myth. Occult poets may also be faulted for their obscurity—not the kind one expects from poets who reflect the difficulty and diversity of the modern age—but the kind generated from literally "occult" or "secret" doctrines, such as reincarnation or the cycles of history, which Yeats, H.D., Hughes and even Merrill seem to appreciate for their sheer complexity.

As we have seen, Merrill apologized for his involved exegeses of occult lore (such as the Blavatsky-like descriptions of the creation of the universe or the spiritual evolution of humanity) in admitting that they are the fragments of a "great tradition that has come to grief." His justification is that he has vowed to follow the path of "error" wherever it leads, which is deep into the unconscious mind. This path allows him to approach the hidden sources of poetry and to use material most readers would consider "inauthentic" (to use Harold Bloom's term). The very fragmented quality of the material seems to emphasize its inauthenticity. A character in Merrill's novel *The (Diblos) Notebook*, when lecturing on Tennyson and Eliot, tells his students that he prefers Eliot's religious poetry to Tennyson's. Whereas Tennyson is content to echo Anglican hymns, Merrill's lecturer says that *The Waste Land*, Eliot's "'magnificent collage of faith and faiths,'" is more meaningful because Eliot is "'aware in his sophistication that the fragments he has "shored up" are valid *because* of their flaws, their inefficacy as living doctrine—'"(101). The lecturer adopts the paradoxical strategy Merrill himself uses in valuing spiritual experiences for their "inefficacy." Merrill's ironic distance from his poem's religious material is even greater than Eliot's; but, like Eliot, he has acknowledged the crucial importance to him and the world he lives in of religious experience. In the last poem he wrote about his Ouija sessions, "Nine Lives" (*A Scattering of Salts*, 1995), he casts JM and DJ in the role of the magi before an empty manger when they fail to meet Maria as a reincarnated Indian boy of eight (15). Yet as magi they are more akin to Eliot's in "Journey of the Magi" rather than Yeats's "pale unsatisfied ones." When they complain to their Ouija spirit that the boy never arrived at the promised location, the reply is that the light of early evening they admired while waiting was a sufficient revelation. In his memoir, *A Different Person* (1993), Merrill confesses that he is beginning to take Christ seriously enough to pray to him (217). The religious strain is deep in his nature, and it surfaces in circuitous and fascinating ways throughout his works.

In *The Changing Light*, it of course surfaces from his unconscious. Although he seems to approve Jung's equation of God and the unconscious, Merrill conceives of the unconscious rather as a path through which to approach the divine. As we saw in discussing H.D., a Jungian hypothesis about a *spiritus mundi*, or repository of archetypes, is an essential occult belief. After a lifetime of interest in psychic research, William James could come to just one firm conclusion: "that we with our lives are like islands in the sea, or like trees in the forest. . . . But the trees also commingle their roots in the darkness underground, and the islands also hang together through the ocean's bottom."[4] Whatever the worth of the belief, Merrill can trust the metaphor that James uses. The key to interpreting it, however, is Freudian rather than Jungian. The root system is language and is revealed by its verbal alchemy: the play of language and the slips and errors that reveal the hidden. As W. H. Auden tells JM in the script of the spirits,

> IS NOT ARCADIA TO DWELL AMONG
> GREENWOOD PERSPECTIVES OF THE MOTHER TONGUE
> ROOTSYSTEMS UNDERFOOT WHILE OVERHEAD
> THE SUN GOD SANG & SHADES OF MEANING SPREAD
> & FAR SNOWCAPPED ABSTRACTIONS GLITTERED NEAR
> OR FAIRLY MELTED INTO ATMOSPHERE?
>
> (CLS 262)

The passage suggests that the way to God and the unconscious is through this root system; or we might read this passage as confirmation that the revelations of the Ouija board are just a language game that can lead to nothing beyond the game. Merrill would not let the scales fall on either end of such an either/or argument. He is opposed to "dogmatic disbelief," as Eliot wrote of William James, and has "the exceptional quality of always leaving his reader with the feeling that the world is full of possibilities."[5] For Merrill, all questions of doubt and belief are answered by "Yes & No."

Notes

Introduction: Literary Occultism

[1]Lewis Carroll, *Through the Looking Glass*, 251 and n. 5. Tertullian's phrase is from *On the Body of Christ*, vol. 5. See Richard H. Popkin, "Kierkegaard and Scepticism," 367.

[2]Compare, for example, Merrill's interview with Helen Vendler (Rec 49–52) with the one with Fred Bornhauser (Rec 53–61).

[3]I. A. Richards, "Doctrine in Poetry," 258. Eliot replied to Richards's conception of belief in poetry in *The Use of Poetry and the Use of Criticism* after Richards claimed that Eliot dissociated the poetry of *The Waste Land* from all beliefs.

[4]Elisa New, *The Regenerate Lyric*, 9.

[5]Richard Rorty, *Contingency, Irony, and Solidarity*, 104.

[6]John Keats to George and Thomas Keats, December 21, 1817. *The Letters of John Keats: 1814–1818*, vol. 1 (Cambridge: Cambridge University Press, 1958), 193–94.

[7]Richard Ellmann, *The Identity of Yeats*, 238.

[8]Wallace Stevens, *The Necessary Angel*, 115–16. Stevens uses this phrase from Alfred North Whitehead to characterize a "central poetry."

[9]Leon Surette, *Birth of Modernism*, 161, 5; also ix, 164. As Robert Duncan put it in "From *The H.D. Book*, Part II, Chapter 5," to Pound, the gods were living "presences," but he was a "pagan fundamentalist. . . . Helios and even Ra-Set may come into the poem, but not Christ" (45).

[10]Jeffrey M. Perl, *Skepticism and Modern Enmity*, 92

[11]T. S. Eliot, "Eeldrop and Appleplex, I," 8.

[12]T. S. Eliot, "The Pensées of Pascal," in *Selected Essays*, 363.

[13]See Popkin, "Kierkegaard and Scepticism," 366. For Eliot on Montaigne, see "Pensées of Pascal," 364–65.

[14]William James, *The Will to Believe and Other Essays in Popular Philosophy*, 20, 29, 33.

[15]Sigmund Freud, "Psycho-analysis and Telepathy (1941 [1921])," 18: 177–78.

[16]Peter Gay, *Freud*, 354–55, 443–45; Ernest Jones, *The Life and Work of Sigmund Freud*, 3:374.

[17]Jones, *Life and Work of Sigmund Freud*, 2: 427, 429; Eliot, as quoted in Perl, *Skepticism and Modern Enmity*, 92.

[18]Freud, "Psycho-analysis and Telepathy," 193.

[19]As quoted by Jones, *Life and Work of Sigmund Freud*, 3: 403.

[20]Sigmund Freud, *Totem and Taboo*, (1950), 77. All further references to *Totem and Taboo* are to the same edition.

[21]John Milton, "Of Education," 637.

[22]Frank Kermode, Introduction to *The Tempest*, xi; Frances Yates, *The Occult Philosophy in the Elizabethan Age*, 160–61; Ted Hughes, *Shakespeare and the Goddess of Complete Being*, 22.

[23]D. G. James, *The Dream of Prospero*, 66; see Yates, *Shakespeare's Last Plays*, 7–8, 18–19. See also Noel Cobb, *Prospero's Island*.

[24]See Margaret C. Jacob, *The Radical Enlightenment*; chaps. 4 and 5 of Douglas Brooks-Davies, *Pope's "Dunciad" and the Queen of Night*; and Anya Taylor, *Magic and English Romanticism*.

[25]"New Age Harmonies," *Time*, 7 December 1987, 62; see also John Naisbitt and Patricia Aburdene, "Religious Revivals of the Third Millennium," chap. 9.

[26]In *The American Religion*, Harold Bloom characterizes the New Age movement by the conviction that "one's own consciousness is God" and by "the lunatic apotheosis that one's very own spirit guide is built into the ecology of one's own mind" (185).

[27]Theodor W. Adorno, "The Stars Down to Earth," 84.

[28]Theodor Adorno, "Theses against Occultism," 8; and "Stars Down to Earth," 83.

[29]Adorno, "Stars Down to Earth," 83, 85. Adorno's criticism of occultism resembles Harold Bloom's criticism of the fatalism in Yeats's *A Vision*; see Bloom, "Conclusion: The Composite God," in his *Yeats*, 470–71.

[30]W. H. Auden, "Yeats as an Example," 188–89.

[31]Concerning Auden's interest in the occult, see Richard Ellmann, *Eminent Domain: Yeats among Wilde, Joyce, Pound, Eliot, and Auden*, 111; and Dorothy Farnam, *Auden in Love*.

[32]H.D.'s description of her experience with a tripod table that once belonged to William Morris is described in her "H.D. by Delia Alton."

[33]See Freud's remarks in "Psycho-analysis and Telepathy," 18: 177–81, as well as the essay's conclusion, 18: 220.

[34]Samuel Hynes, *The Edwardian Turn of Mind*, 139–46. The membership list included bishops, philosophers, and famous authors, including Arthur Conan Doyle, W. B. Yeats, May Sinclair, and Gilbert Murray. H. G. Wells, William James, Jung, and Freud were corresponding members.

[35]Northrop Frye, "Yeats and the Language of Symbolism," in *Fables of Identity*, 221.

[36]Ezra Pound, *Ezra Pound, John Theobald*, 40.

[37]See Nicholas Goodrick-Clarke, *The Occult Roots of Nazism*, 17–31.

³⁸See James Villas, *Gérard de Nerval*, for a thorough account of occult inter-
pretations of Nerval's poetry.
³⁹William York Tindall, *Forces in Modern Literature* (1947), 254.
⁴⁰Frank Kermode, *The Romantic Image*, 110–11.
⁴¹Arthur Symons, *The Symbolist Movement in Literature*, 1.
⁴²The text was *Le Comte de Gabalis* by Abbé Montfaucon de Villars; see James
Longenbach, *Stone Cottage*, 86–87.
⁴³H.D., *End to Torment*, 45–46.
⁴⁴A sketch of Pound's relationship with Heyman appears in Demetres P.
Tryphonopoulos, *The Celestial Tradition*, 60–64. In *Ezra Pound: The Solitary Volcano*, John Tytel says that Heyman introduced Pound to "Swedenborg, to
Balzac's *Seraphita*, yoga, and Freud" (37).
⁴⁵Ezra Pound, *Ezra Pound and Dorothy Shakespear*, 302.
⁴⁶For a full account of Pound's acquaintance with Mead, see Tryphonopoulos, *Celestial Tradition*, 82–92.
⁴⁷T.S. Eliot, "A Commentary," and *After Strange Gods*, 48.
⁴⁸Robert Duncan, "Chapter 4, *The H.D. Book*, Part Two: 'Nights and Days,' "
28, 33; and " 'Occult Matters,' *The H.D. Book*, Part Two: 'Nights and Days,'
Chapter 5."
⁴⁹Sylvia Plath, *Letters Home*, 280. Plath also tried to consult Yeats's spirit
when she was trying to decide if she should move into a London house once
inhabited by him; she decided to move in when she flipped through his *Collected Plays* to a passage that read, "Get the wine and food to give you strength
and courage, and I will get the house ready." See Paul Alexander, *Rough
Magic*, 291, 307–8.

Chapter 1: Daemonic Images

¹Ann Braude, *Radical Spirits*.
²Quoted in William M. Murphy, "Psychic Daughter, Mystic Son, Skeptic
Father," 12–13.
³See William H. Pritchard, ed., *W. B. Yeats: A Critical Anthology*, 108–10,
113–35, 187–93. See also Pritchard's introduction, 17–28.
⁴Murphy, "Psychic Daughter," 12.
⁵Helen Hennessy Vendler, *Yeats's "Vision" and the Later Plays*, vii.
⁶Richard Ellmann, *The Identity of Yeats*, xvii.
⁷Marion Meade, *Madame Blavatsky*, 439.
⁸Virginia Moore, *The Unicorn*, 172.
⁹For the relationship of metaphor and magic, see Anya Taylor, *Magic and
English Romanticism*, 44–50.
¹⁰W. B. Yeats, "Magic," in *Essays and Introductions*, 28.
¹¹R. P. Blackmur, "The Later Poetry of W. B. Yeats," 123.
¹²T. S. Eliot, "Baudelaire," in *Selected Prose of T. S. Eliot*, 234.
¹³W. B. Yeats, Introduction to *The Oxford Book of Modern Verse, 1892–1935*,
xxxv.
¹⁴Ezra Pound, "Status Rerum."
¹⁵Richard Ellmann, *Eminent Domain*, 80, 86.
¹⁶Hugh Kenner, *The Poetry of Ezra Pound*, 210.
¹⁷Donald Davie, *Ezra Pound: Poet as Sculptor*, 181.

¹⁸For an example of how Pound could both dismiss and affirm—depending on whom he was addressing—occult interests, see James Longenbach, *Stone Cottage*, 20–21. In *The Celestial Tradition*, Demetres P. Tryphonopoulos argues that Pound's interest in occultism never waned; see esp. 20 n. 15.

¹⁹Ellmann, *Identity of Yeats*, 152.

²⁰See my "Pound's 'Vortex' " and William French and Timothy Materer "Far Flung Vortices and Ezra's 'Hindoo' Yogi." For an argument concerning the Neoplatonic tradition in Pound, see Sharon Mayer Libera, "Casting His Gods Back into the NOUS"; and Carroll F. Terrell, *Ideas in Reaction*, esp. chap. 5, "The Divine Mystery."

²¹Eva Hesse, "On the Source of Pound's 'Vortex.' "

²²See William French and Timothy Materer, "Far Flung Vortices." They write of Dorothy Pound that owing to "her exposure through her mother Olivia to Yeats, Mead, and others of that circle, she already had the references to the Ramacharaka books written in her pocket address book when she passed them on to Wm French in 1953" (47). French's correspondence with Pound is in the Beinecke Library, Yale University. The identification of Yogi Ramacharaka was made on the basis of William French's conversations with Pound at St. Elizabeths Hospital.

²³Yogi Ramacharaka, *Raja Yoga*, 78. "Ramacharaka" was not a "hindoo Yoga" but a Chicago journalist, William Walker Atkinson (1862–1932). He was generally believed to be Indian, but his books on yoga and occultism were published by the Yogi Publication Society in Chicago. His Yogi works were extremely popular, and some titles have remained in print since approximately 1903.

²⁴As quoted in French and Materer, "Far Flung Vortices," 48.

²⁵For an excellent discussion of this aspect of Yeats, and of his vorticist imagery, see Ian F. A. Bell, *Critic as Scientist*.

²⁶Ezra Pound, "Vortex: Pound," in *Ezra Pound and the Visual Arts*, 151–52; Vasilii Kandinsky, "On the Spiritual in Art," 69, 73, 79.

²⁷See Mike Weaver, *Alvin Langdon Coburn, Symbolist Photographer, 1882–1966*, 57.

²⁸Similarly, when he wrote to his patron, the no-nonsense lawyer John Quinn, Pound discounted Kandinsky's influence; see his comments on Kandinsky and mysticism in Ezra Pound, *The Selected Letters of Ezra Pound to John Quinn, 1915–1924*, 63.

²⁹See Eric Shanes, *Constantin Brancusi*, 77.

³⁰On the mystical and occult background of other artists, for instance, Kandinsky and Mondrian, see Maurice Tuchman, *The Spiritual in Art*. This background has been neglected or even ignored in art history just as it has been in studies of modern poetry. Influential art critics Alfred Barr and Clement Greenberg have stressed the modern artist's abstract use of color and form for its own sake. Harold Rosenberg turned Kandinsky into the "patron saint of formalism," who constructed "purely plastic elements that were to signify nothing but themselves," and he associated Kandinsky with an art devoid of the "support of metaphysics" ("Mondrian: Meaning in Abstract Art I," in *Art on the Edge*, 42, 40; and "Olitski, Kelly, Hamilton: Dogma and Talent," in ibid., 67). Kandinsky himself, on the contrary, believed that "when, finally, art grows up, its grammar will prove to be built not so much on physical laws

as people have maintained as on the *laws of inner necessity*, which I calmly designate by the word *psychic*" ("On the Spiritual in Art," 82).

[31] As quoted in Longenbach, *Stone Cottage*, 237.

[32] Ezra Pound, *Selected Letters of Ezra Pound, 1907–1941*, 210.

[33] Ellmann, *Eminent Domain*, 78.

[34] Leon Surette, *The Birth of Modernism*, 63–64.

[35] See Forrest Read, *'76: One World and the Cantos of Ezra Pound*, 126.

[36] Longenbach, *Stone Cottage*, 39. Blavatsky discusses the occult meaning of the "churning of the ocean" in H. P. Blavatsky, *The Secret Doctrine*, 135.

[37] For the butterfly image, see Carroll F. Terrell, *A Companion to the "Cantos" of Ezra Pound*, 2:401, 557; for the Faust reference, see 2:401–2.

[38] Read, *'76: One World*, 192.

[39] My discussion of Canto 90 is indebted to chap. 6 of James Wilhelm, *The Later Cantos of Ezra Pound*, and *Dante and Pound: The Epic of Judgment*. I am also indebted throughout this chapter to William French's studies of Pound's occultism.

[40] In *The Secret Doctrine*, Blavatsky shows why occult thinkers relate the sphere and snake images: "The symbol of an egg also expresses the fact taught in Occultism that the primordial form of everything manifested, from atom to globe, from man to angel, is spheroidal, the sphere being with all nations, the emblem of eternity and infinity—a serpent swallowing its tail" (1:132).

[41] Queen Arsinoe II died in 270 B.C. and was worshiped as Arsinoe Aphrodite; see Massimo Bacigalupo, *The Formèd Trace*, 441.

[42] Read, *'76: One World*, 424. In *Later Cantos of Ezra Pound*, Wilhelm writes of this passage: "The notion of man imprisoned in his self-made environment is then contrasted with Plotinus' idea that the soul envelops the body in an incandescent shroud that animates and nurtures it. Yeats has observed this phenomenon in the Cathedral of Notre Dame" (189).

Chapter 2: Ezra Pound as Magus

[1] George Mills Harper, *Yeats's Golden Dawn*, 122–23.

[2] G. R. S. Mead, "The Quest," as quoted in Demetres P. Tryphonopoulos, *The Celestial Tradition*, 85.

[3] Ezra Pound, *Selected Letters of Ezra Pound, 1907–1941*, 25.

[4] Richard Ellmann, *Eminent Domain*, 69. In a letter to John Theobald in 1957, Pound wrote, "I don't think Mead mucked with the psychical research gang" (Ezra Pound, *Ezra Pound, John Theobald*, 32).

[5] Ezra Pound, *Translations of Ezra Pound*, 236.

[6] Ezra Pound, *Ezra Pound and Dorothy Shakespear*, 61, 118.

[7] This is a rare use of a Buddhist conception in Pound's poetry. In the China Cantos, he scorns Buddhistic thought in his eagerness to praise Confucianism. In the cases of both Pound and Yeats, their conceptions of reincarnation are influenced by Neoplatonic rather than Eastern sources.

[8] James Wilhelm, *Ezra Pound in London and Paris, 1908–1925*, 45.

[9] See P. L. Surette, "Helen of Tyre."

[10]James Longenbach, *Stone Cottage*, 88; see also chap. 7, "Dialogues with the Dead."

[11]Quoted in Harper, *Yeats's Golden Dawn*, 11.

[12]Mrs. Yeats in an interview with Richard Ellmann, in his *Eminent Domain*, 71.

[13]Ezra Pound, "Interesting French Publications" (1906), as quoted in Leon Surette, *A Light from Eleusis*, 35. According to Surette, "What Pound takes from Péladan is the conception of this mystery cult . . . and the idea of formulating history in terms of such a secret cult" (37). See also Akiko Miyake, *Ezra Pound and the Mysteries of Love*, for comments on Péladan and also the influence of Gabriel Rossetti.

[14]Peter Makin, *Provence and Pound*, 242; Leon Surette, *The Birth of Modernism*, 142.

[15]N. Christoph de Nagy, *The Poetry of Ezra Pound: The Pre-Imagist Stage*, 102. De Nagy writes that traditionally the beryl contains "prophesying spirits," and "the chrysoprase imparts the magic powers of poetry." In referring to the "opal," Pound uses a symbol of vision that was associated with Yeats and Æ, whom Stephen Dedalus refers to in *Ulysses* as the "opal hush poets." Hugh Witemeyer disagrees with de Nagy because he claims "the whole point of the passage is that vision does *not* depend on occult aids" (*The Poetry of Ezra Pound*, 100). De Nagy is not arguing that the poet is "dependent," however, but that he symbolizes the poetic vision according to the way gemstones are used in "various occult traditions." Witemeyer's book is the best introduction to Pound's early poetry, but like the other major critics of Pound (Kenner, Davie, Herbert Schneidau), he prefers Pound practical to Pound mystical.

[16]See chapter 1, the text immediately following n. 32.

[17]H. P. Blavatsky summarizes many aspects of the belief in mystical adepts as guides in *The Secret Doctrine*. In vol. 5, see sec. 4, "The Secrecy of Initiates"; sec. 13 and 14 for her defense of Simon Magus; and sec. 17 on another of Pound's favorite spiritual masters, Apollonius of Tyana. For a full exposition of this conception of spiritual masters, see Dion Fortune, *The Esoteric Orders and Their Work*. Fortune (pseud. of Violet Mary Firth, 1891–1946)) reorganized the remnants of the Society of the Golden Dawn into the Fraternity of the Inner Light.

[18]For a discussion of reincarnation in *Oisin*, see Frank Kinahan, *Yeats, Folklore, and Occultism*, 100–107.

[19]Pound's remark on mere "theorizing" echoes Mead's preface to a Plotinus volume: "that Plotinus was not a mere theorist but did actually attain unto such a state of consciousness is testified by Porphyry" (G. R. S. Mead, Preface to *Select Works of Plotinus*.

[20]Bruce Fogelman, *Shapes of Power*, 109.

[21]The most thorough treatment of Yeats's alchemy appears in Thomas R. Whitaker, *Swan and Shadow*; see esp. chap. 3.

[22]Ian F. A. Bell, *Critic as Scientist*, 143.

[23]The complete sequence of "Xenia" is reprinted in Hans-Joachim Zimmerman, "Ezra Pound, 'A Song of the Degrees,'" 240–41.

[24]Miyake, *Ezra Pound*, 61.

[25]Ezra Pound, "Three Cantos: III," 248–49. The Latin passage quoted by Heydon is from Porphyry's *De occasionibus*; see Longenbach, *Stone Cottage*, 241–43, for an analysis of Heydon's significance in this early Canto.

[26]Ezra Pound, *Ezra Pound, John Theobald*, 71.

[27]James Joyce, *Ulysses*, 609. The "secret master" is an advanced degree in Freemasonry. For a challenge to the view that Joyce only scoffed at occultism, see Robert D. Newman, "*Transformatio Coniunctionis*," 168–86.

[28]See Miyake, *Ezra Pound*, chap. 7.

[29]For an argument that this interest was unwavering, see Tryphonopoulos, *Celestial Tradition*, 20 n. 15.

[30]See Tryphonopoulos, *Celestial Tradition*, 8–15; on Swedenborg, see 46–48.

[31]Pound, *Selected Letters of Ezra Pound*, 327.

[32]Ibid., 328–29.

[33]Leon Surette, *Birth of Modernism*, 99.

[34]Ibid., 155; Walter Baumann, "Ezra Pound and Magic: Old World Tricks in a New World Poem."

[35]This last voyage is described in Dante's *Inferno*, Canto 26.

[36]Virginia Moore, *The Unicorn*, 137–38.

[37]William French helped Pound proofread *The Spirit of Romance* and has told me that Pound's rereading of the work revived his interest in esoteric lore.

[38]K. K. Ruthven, *A Guide to Ezra Pound's Personae* (1969), 33.

[39]Walter Baumann, "Secretary of Nature, John Heydon," 309. As Baumann observes, Pound "delighted in making fun of Yeats's fascination with the occult," and yet "Pound himself obviously made much greater use of works like Heydon's than did Yeats" (311).

[40]See Miyake, *Ezra Pound*, 209, for a discussion of Pound's use of Heydon in this passage.

[41]See Thomas Grieve, "The Séraphin Couvreur Sources of *Rock-Drill*." The San Ku is mentioned on 481.

[42]Baumann, "Secretary of Nature, John Heydon," 316. Pound's spelling of "Selloi" in Canto 92 is "cellua" (619).

[43]Terrell, *Companion to the "Cantos*," 496.

[44]Ibid., 496. William French mentioned this apparition to Pound in a letter sent to St. Elizabeths, January 6, 1954. I am grateful to Mr. French for showing me a copy. French's letters to Pound are in the Pound Archive at the Beinecke Library, Yale University.

[45]Ibid., 546–47.

[46]Donald Davie, *Ezra Pound: Poet as Sculptor*, 223, 225.

[47]As quoted in Terrell, *Companion to the "Cantos*," 546. See also chap. 5, "The Subtle Body," in Tryphonopoulos, *Celestial Tradition*.

[48]In the *Companion*, Terrell defines the arcanum as "the mysterium, or final secrets, unrevealed in the rites of Eleusis except symbolically, and also the final or secret aspirations of esoteric alchemy" (553). Pound also uses the term *arcanum* in "Notes for CXVII et seq." when he refers to milkweed as the substance that allows the butterfly to enter the arcanum (Cantos 802). In alchemical lore, the butterfly is a symbol of the soul, which can live on the poisonous milkweed and thus overcome any obstacle.

Chapter 3: T. S. Eliot

[1]T. S. Eliot, "Isolated Superiority." The reference to hormones refers to Pound's enthusiasm about Dr. Berman's theory of hormones. Pound recommended that Dr. Berman examine Mrs. Eliot. See Ezra Pound, *The Selected Letters of Ezra Pound to John Quinn, 1915–1924*, 210, 214 n.

[2]Ezra Pound, "Credo" (1930), in *Selected Prose, 1909–1965*, 53; "Axiomata" (1921), in ibid., 51.

[3]For Blake's use of occult material, see Kathleen Raine, *Blake and Tradition*.

[4]T. S. Eliot, "A Foreign Mind." Both the style and substance of Eliot's criticism of occultism seems influenced by Bradley. See Bradley's "The Evidence of Spiritualism," 595–617, which is particularly interesting and witty on the "gratuitous chimera of a spiritual body" (599). Evidently reacting to his criticism of spiritualism, Yeats referred to Bradley as an "arrogant sapless man" (Vision 219).

[5]T. S. Eliot, "Tradition and the Practice of Poetry."

[6]In *The Use of Poetry and the Use of Criticism*, T. S. Eliot wrote, "With the influence of the devil on contemporary literature I shall be concerned in more detail in another book" (137). He was looking ahead to *After Strange Gods*, where he analyzed the "operation of the Evil Spirit" (57) in Hardy and claimed that "the daemonic powers found an instrument of far greater range" (65), by comparison, in Lawrence.

[7]Dorothy Farnam, *Auden in Love*, 71, 153, 159; Robert Craft, *Memories and Commentaries*, 147.

[8]Richard Ellmann, *Eminent Domain*, 111.

[9]W. H. Auden, *Collected Shorter Poems, 1927–1957*, 180–81.

[10]Harold Bloom's criticism of Yeats's Gnosticism runs throughout his *Yeats*; see esp. 46–47, 74–75, 77–78, 378–79 ("God occupies the place of death in the Yeatsian vision"), and 470–71. W. B. Yeats, *Mythologies*, 332; Auden, *Collected Shorter Poems*, 181.

[11]See W. H. Auden, *The Dyer's Hand*, 27, for Auden's remarks on art as magic.

[12]W. H. Auden, "Prospero to Ariel," in *Collected Longer Poems*, 203–10.

[13]T. S. Eliot, "A Commentary."

[14]Peter Ackroyd, *T. S. Eliot*, 113.

[15]Tom Gibbons, "*The Waste Land* Tarot Identified." See also chap. 11 of John Senior, *The Way Down and Out*.

[16]Jessie L. Weston, *From Ritual to Romance* (1957): 7, 204–5. Fortune-telling through cards (this time an ordinary deck) also occurs in Eliot's *Sweeney Agonistes*.

[17]See chap. 4 of Leon Surette, *The Birth of Modernism*, 231–79.

[18]Jessie L. Weston, *The Quest of the Holy Grail* (1964), 137–38.

[19]On the influence of occultists on Weston, see Senior, *Way Down and Out*, 176–78.

[20]Leon Surette, *Birth of Modernism*, 261. Surette observes that the most striking aspect of Weston's occultism is the Blavatskian belief that religions consist of the remnants of the superhuman thinkers of a lost civilization (253).

[21]Lyndall Gordon, *Eliot's Early Years*, 86.

[22]T. S. Eliot, "A Dialogue on Dramatic Poetry," in *Selected Essays*, 39.

[23]Ellmann, *Eminent Domain*, 95.

[24]Harold Bloom, *The Anxiety of Influence*, 147.

[25]T. S. Eliot, *After Strange Gods*, 48.

[26]Eliot, "Commentary."

[27]Bloom, *Yeats*, 470–71.

[28]James Longenbach, "Uncanny Eliot," 47–69, and esp. 56–57; John T. Mayer, *T. S. Eliot's Silent Voices*, 124.

[29]T. S. Eliot, "Poetry and Drama," in *On Poetry and Poets*, 90.

[30]See Alwyn Rees and Brinley Rees, *Celtic Heritage*, 336.

[31]The information in this paragraph is from Grover Smith, *T. S. Eliot's Poetry and Plays*, 217–20.

[32]See Smith, *T. S. Eliot's Poetry and Plays*, 226; see also Agnes Sibley, *Charles Williams*

[33]Paul Murray, *T. S. Eliot and Mysticism*, 156.

[34]Helen Gardner, *The Composition of Four Quartets*, 85; Murray, *T. S. Eliot and Mysticism*, 171.

[35]T. S. Eliot, "Yeats," in *On Poetry and Poets*, 301, 303.

[36]One of *Four Quartets'* epigrams from Heraclitus states that although the word, or logos, is common to all, men act as if they had a wisdom of their own.

[37]Eliot de-emphasized the mystical and occult subjects in his own poetry as he did in Yeats's when he wrote, in 1956, "It was just, no doubt, that I should pay my tribute to the work of Miss Jessie Weston; but I regret having sent so many enquirers off on a wild goose chase after Tarot cards and the Holy Grail" ("The Frontiers of Criticism," in *On Poetry and Poets*, 122).

[38]Ellmann, *Eminent Domain*, 95.

[39]Ibid. Richard Ellmann's reading of the "reconciliation" in *Four Quartets* supports his attempt in *The Identity of Yeats* to minimize the importance of occultism in Yeats's poetry.

[40]W. B. Yeats, Introduction to *The Oxford Book of Modern Verse, 1892–1935*, xxiii.

[41]CPP 139. It is tempting to see in this reference to the ashes of a rose an allusion to Yeats's experiments (referred to in Chapter 1) with trying to resurrect a flower from its ashes with the help of an air pump.

[42]Eliot, "Isolated Superiority," 7.

[43]W. H. Auden, "Yeats as an Example," 191.

[44]Ibid., 190.

Chapter 4: H.D.'s Hermeticism

[1]See Jane Augustine, *"The Mystery* Unveiled."

[2]Susan Stanford Friedman, *Penelope's Web*, 345.

[3]Dianne Chisholm, *H.D.'s Freudian Poetics*, 75.

[4]Susan Stanford Friedman, *Psyche Reborn*, 149.

[5]Leon Surette, *The Birth of Modernism*, 86–88.

[6]Barbara Guest, *Herself Defined*, 328.

[7]Friedman, *Psyche Reborn*, 304n.8; Norman Holmes Pearson, Introduction to *Hermetic Definition*, by H.D., vi.

[8]Norman H. Holland, *Poems in Persons*, 31; Deborah Kelly Kloepfer, *The Unspeakable Mother*, 129. Although Holland refers basically to the Greek god Hermes, and Kloepfer to Hermes Trismegistus, the two are virtually the same figure in H.D.'s poetry—as I show. Gary Burnett refers to Hermes as the "patron of Imagism" in *H.D. between Image and Epic*, 175.

[9]The best account of Hermeticism is in Frances A. Yates, *Giordano Bruno and the Hermetic Tradition*. For an example of the subversive power of Hermeticist thought, see Yates's account of the career of Giordano Bruno, 338–59. On the later development of Hermeticism, see Ernest Lee Tuveson, *The Avatars of Thrice Great Hermes*. The history of the Hermetic Society of the Golden Dawn is told in George Mills Harper, *Yeats's Golden Dawn*.

[10]See Friedman, *Psyche Reborn*, 171.

[11]Friedman, *Psyche Reborn*, 73–74.

[12]Rachel Blau Duplessis, *H.D.*, 124.

[13]Friedman, *Psyche Reborn*, 185.

[14]Hermes Trismegistus, "Tractatus aureus," quoted in C. G. Jung, *Psychology and Alchemy*, 358. Although the text is ascribed to Hermes Trismegistus, Jung writes that it was "regarded as of Arabic origin even in the Middle Ages."

[15]Jung, *Psychology and Alchemy*, 65.

[16]Friedman, *Psyche Reborn*, 253, 250. Although it has the obvious limitations of a medieval tradition, alchemy is not as patriarchal a tradition as Friedman implies. Although a major trope is the marriage of the king and queen, sexual identity is not fixed. This issue is discussed further in my chapters on Robert Duncan and James Merrill.

[17]Friedman, *Psyche Reborn*, 250.

[18]Janice S. Robinson, *H.D.*, 325.

[19]On the alchemical symbolism of ash, see C. G. Jung, *Mysterium Coniunctionis*, 112.

[20]As quoted in Friedman, *Psyche Reborn*, 192.

[21]See ibid.

[22]Jacques Lacan, *The Four Fundamental Concepts of Psycho-analysis*, 24.

[23]H.D., *Selected Poems*, 104.

[24]Jacques Derrida, *Dissemination*, 93. See Duplessis's analysis of H.D.'s use of the "punning metonymic chain of connections" (*H.D.*, 91–92).

[25]Holland, *Poems in Persons*, 35.

Chapter 5: Robert Duncan and the Mercurial Self

[1]W. B. Yeats, "Rosa Alchemica," in *The Secret Rose* 126.

[2]For an analysis of the alchemy in "Sailing to Byzantium," see Thomas R. Whitaker, *Swan and Shadow*, 274.

[3]In agreeing with Kenneth Rexroth about the importance of his parents' occultism to his poetry, Duncan said that the occultism came naturally to him and that he "didn't have to be an initiate" (Michael André Bernstein and Burton Hatlen, "Interview with Robert Duncan," 109).

[4]Robert Duncan, "From *the H.D. Book*, Part I: 'Beginnings'; Chapter 5, 'Occult Matters'," 9.

⁵Robert Duncan, "Chapter 4, *The H.D. Book*, Part Two: 'Nights and Days,' 28, 33.

⁶Robert Duncan, "The Lasting Contribution of Ezra Pound," 23–24.

⁷For example, the colleagues of electrochemist John Bockris at Texas A&M asked for his resignation after he received a grant to change various elements into gold. See Robert Pool, "Alchemy Altercation at Texas A&M."

⁸John Donne, *The Complete Poetry of John Donne*, 48.

⁹C. G. Jung, *Psychology and Alchemy*, 34.

¹⁰Robert Duncan, "Two Chapters from *The H.D. Book*," 67. Duncan shows why he has a natural preference for the work of the poet rather than the psychologist when he writes, "We saw for a moment in Plato's imagination the old cosmology transformed into or give way to a new ideology. Now, everywhere, cosmology and ideology give way to psychology" (74).

¹¹Ben Jonson, *The Alchemist*, 49 (3. 162–65).

¹²C. G. Jung, *Mysterium Coniunctionis*, 41.

¹³Jung, *Psychology and Alchemy*, 42.

¹⁴Duncan, "Two Chapters," 74. Mercury or Hermes was a prominent figure in his family occult circle. In "From *The H.D. Book*: 'Occult Matters'," Duncan writes that he was told that "true teachers, like Christ, Buddha, Hermes, or Lao-Tse, were Light Beings, messengers of the Sun Itself. Hermes, Mercury, was the one with winged helmet and winged scandals I have seen in the bronze figure that stood on the piano at Aunt Fay's. He was the god of the high air, of those helium fields, carrying a rod around which two snakes twisted. This wand or *caduceus* meant, Aunt Fay explained, that he was god of Life, systole and diastole of the heart beat" (5).

¹⁵Jung, *Psychology and Alchemy*, 65.

¹⁶Ibid., 65–66. Robert Kelly, a poet associated with Duncan, is also fascinated with the figure of Mercury; see his collection of poems *The Alchemist to Mercury*. Kelly's letters to Duncan in the Bancroft Library, University of California–Berkeley, express the two poets' sense of a revival of "occult matters."

¹⁷Johannes Fabricius, *Alchemy*, 76.

¹⁸See also Robert Duncan, "After Reading H.D.'s Hermetic Definition," in *Roots and Branches*, 81–84. For an analysis of H.D.'s role in the volume, see Burton Hatlen, "Robert Duncan's Marriage of Heaven and Hell," 207–26.

¹⁹Concerning Duncan's translation of Nerval's *Chimeras*, see Mark Andrew Johnson, *Robert Duncan*, 117–18. See also Georges Le Breton, *Nerval, poéte alchimique*. The "Prince d'Aquitaine" is of course also referred to in Eliot's *The Waste Land*.

²⁰Robert Duncan, "*The H. D. Book*, Part Two, Chapter 2," 17.

²¹Thomas Gardner, *Discovering Ourselves in Whitman*, 7–8.

²²Robert Duncan, *Fictive Certainties*, 219–20. In this linguistic speculation, he is heavily influenced by Ludwig Wittgenstein's *Philosophical Investigations*. For an excellent account of Wittgenstein on "The Indispensability of Persons and Person-Words," see Dallas M. High, *Language, Persons, and Belief*, 113–26.

²³Charles Nicholl, *The Chemical Theatre*, 103.

²⁴Jung, *Psychology and Alchemy*, 289.

²⁵Robert Duncan, "Interview," 72.

²⁶Jacques Lacan, *Écrits*, 33.

²⁷Jung, *Mysterium Coniunctionis*, 125.

[28]For more on Stevens's alchemy, see Leonora Woodman, *Stanza My Stone* See Duncan's comments on Stevens in Bernstein and "Interview with Robert Duncan," 109.

Chapter 6: Sylvia Plath

[1]"Ted Hughes and Crow" (interview with Ekbert Faas), in Faas, *Ted Hughes*, 205.
[2]I am grateful to Paul Alexander for reading an early draft of this chapter and sharing his knowledge with me.
[3]Jon Rosenblatt, *Sylvia Plath*, xi.
[4]Sylvia Plath, *Letters Home*, p. 25.
[5]Linda Wagner-Martin, *Sylvia Plath*, 28, 58–59.
[6]William Wordsworth, *The Prelude*, 6.l.638.
[7]Wagner-Martin, *Sylvia Plath*, 75.
[8]Paul Alexander, *Rough Magic*, 196–97.
[9]Ted Hughes, *Lupercal*, 55.
[10]Mary Kurtzman, "Plath's 'Ariel' and Tarot."
[11]Faas, *Ted Hughes*, 41.
[12]Steven Axelrod, *The Wound and the Cure of Words*, 163.
[13]T. S. Eliot, *The Waste Land: A Facsimile*, 126n.5.
[14]The specific rivalry in "The Wishing Box" concerns which spouse has the more vivid dreams. The story appears in Sylvia Plath, *Johnny Panic and the Bible of Dreams and Other Prose Writings*, 54–61.
[15]Plath, *Johnny Panic*, 28.
[16]Sylvia Plath, *The Journals of Sylvia Plath*, 244.
[17]Ted Hughes, "Sylvia Plath and Her Journals," 155.
[18]Plath, *Journals of Sylvia Plath* (entry for December 17, 1958), 279.
[19]Philip Rieff, *Freud*, 361, 377.
[20]Sigmund Freud, "Psycho-analysis and Telepathy (1941 [1921])," 18:177.
[21]Ibid., 18:177.
[22]Wagner-Martin, *Sylvia Plath*, 240; Anne Stevenson, *Bitter Fame*, 289–90, 296.
[23]See esp. sec. "I" of "The Book of Ephraim," 29–32.
[24]Sigmund Freud, "Mourning and Melancholia," 156.
[25]Sigmund Freud, "A Neurosis of Demoniacal Possession in the Seventeenth Century," in *On Creativity and the Unconscious*, 278.
[26]Sigmund Freud, "The 'Uncanny,'" in *On Creativity and the Unconscious*, 143.
[27]Ted Hughes, "Notes on the Chronological Order of Sylvia Plath's Poems," 81–82. This version of Hughes's "Notes" differs slightly from the one in *The Art of Sylvia Plath: A Symposium*, ed. Charles Newman (Bloomington: Indiana University Press, 1970).
[28]Paul Alexander, *Rough Magic*, 44.
[29]Plath, *Journals of Sylvia Plath*, 222.

Chapter 7: Ted Hughes's Alchemical Quest

[1]In a 1970 interview, Hughes said of the American spiritualitst Edgar Cayce (1877–1945) that he was a "healer and prophet" who could take shamanistic flights: "And of course he returned with the goods" (Ekbert Faas, *Ted Hughes*, 206). In a review of books on astrology and divining in 1964, Hughes wrote that the American astrologer Evangeline Adams (1872?-1932) proved her powers "under test conditions and repeatedly" ("Superstition," in *Ted Hughes, Winter Pollen*, 51). It is unlikely, however, that the "test conditions" of the early twentieth century would meet the present criteria for such standards. On Edgar Cayce's supposed cures, see Martin Gardner, *Fads and Fallacies in the Name of Science*, 188–91.

[2]Ted Hughes, Preface to *The Journals of Sylvia Plath*, xiii; and "Sylvia Plath," in Faas, *Ted Hughes*, 181.

[3]Sagar and Tabor, *Ted Hughes: A Bibliography*, 90.

[4]Nor does Hughes adopt the sophisticated historical perspective on magical lore of Geoffrey Hill. On Hill's use of magic, especially alchemy, see chap. 4 in Vincent Sherry, *The Uncommon Tongue*

[5]As revealed in Paul Alexander's biography of Plath, *Rough Magic*, the woman for whom Hughes left Plath, Assia Gutman Wevill, also committed suicide. Although I believe the passages I cite concern Plath's death, it is obvious that the fates of both women are relevant.

[6]Faas, *Ted Hughes*, 37.

[7]Ted Hughes, "Myth and Education," 77–94.

[8]C. G. Jung, *Mysterium Coniunctionis*, 180.

[9]"Ted Hughes and Crow" (interview), in Faas, *Ted Hughes*, 205.

[10]T. S. Eliot, *The Waste Land: A Facsimile*, xxxiii.

[11]C. G. Jung, *Alchemical Studies*, 32; "Ted Hughes and Crow," 212.

[12]Hughes has said that he had a "cult" of the White Goddess, which Plath "immediately took up"; see Judith Kroll, *Chapters in a Mythology*, 40 and chap. 3. I am indebted to Leonard Scigaj for showing me a transcript of *Difficulties of a Bridegroom*.

[13]Hughes, quoted in Terry Gifford and Neil Roberts, *Ted Hughes*, 152.

[14]Cleanth Brooks, *Modern Poetry and the Tradition*, 136.

[15]T. S. Eliot, *On Poetry and Poets*, 122.

[16]Leonard M. Scigaj, *The Poetry of Ted Hughes*, 15.

[17]Anne Stevenson, *Bitter Fame*, 301.

[18]Ibid., 56, 129.

[19]Sigmund Freud, *The Interpretation of Dreams (Second Part)*, 509–10.

[20]Scigaj, *Poetry of Ted Hughes*, 230.

[21]C. G. Jung, *Symbols of Transformation*, 202.

[22]C. G. Jung, *Memories, Dreams, Reflections*, 334, 338.

[23]Keith Sagar, *The Art of Ted Hughes*, 183.

[24]Graham Bradshaw, "Creative Mythology in *Cave Birds*," 237.

[25]Gifford and Roberts, *Ted Hughes*, 231.

[26]Scigaj, *Poetry of Ted Hughes*, 213.

[27]Craig Robinson, *Ted Hughes as Shepherd of Being*, 145. See also Nick Bishop, *Re-Making Poetry*, 201–3.

²⁸Scigaj, *Poetry of Ted Hughes*, 206.
²⁹"Ted Hughes and Crow," 199.
³⁰Robert Duncan, "Interview," 72.
³¹Bradshaw, "Creative Mythology in *Cave Birds*," 212.
³²Scigaj, *Poetry of Ted Hughes*, 19.
³³See Chapter 3, for Eliot on Blake and Pound.
³⁴Philip Rahv, "The Myth and the Powerhouse," 202.
³⁵Ernest Jones, *The Life and Work of Sigmund Freud*, 167.

Chapter 8: James Merrill's Romantic Unconscious

¹Jacques Lacan, *The Four Fundamental Concepts of Psycho-analysis*, 24, 30. The line from Virgil quoted by Sigmund Freud in chap. 7, sect. E, of *The Interpretation of Dreams* is from *The Aeneid* (7.312): "If I cannot bend the Higher Powers, I will move the infernal regions."
²James Merrill, "Bronze," in *Late Settings*, 51.
³Harold Bloom, *James Merrill*, 1; Irvin Ehrenpreis, "Otherworldly Goods"; Denis Donoghue, "What the Ouija Board Said"; Hugh Kenner, "Poetize or Bust," 69; Helen Hennessy Vendler, "'Mirabell': Books of Number," 220–21. Concerning Vendler's interpretation of Yeats, see my Introduction.
⁴In *The Consuming Myth* Stephen Yenser says that the reference is to a similar passage in Jung's "Answer to Job" (239).
⁵C. G. Jung, *Psychology and Alchemy*, xiv.
⁶James Merrill considers Ephraim and Michael the "ultimate composite voice" and notes that the meaning of Ephraim's name is "double fruitfulness"; see his interview with Fred Bornhauser in *Recitative*, 56. Jacob's preference for Ephraim, the younger son, over Manaseh in Genesis 48 is also relevant to the theme of doubleness.
⁷Jung, *Psychology and Alchemy*, 65–66.
⁸C. G. Jung, *Mysterium Coniunctionis*, xiv.
⁹James Merrill, "The Art of Poetry XXXI," 189.
¹⁰See my "Death and Alchemical Transformation in James Merrill's *The Changing Light at Sandover*." In a letter to me of November 29, 1985, Merrill said that whatever knowledge of alchemy he had came from his reading of Goethe's *Faust*. But he added that if he had known more about alchemy, its use in the poem would have been psychologically "overdetermined." His conclusion about the alchemy in *The Changing Light* was that "a lot of subliminal iconography surfaces." Merrill treats the Faust legend in *Mirabell*, Book 2.
¹¹Ezra Pound, *The Cantos of Ezra Pound*, 802. The butterfly also appears in this passage: "to have heard the farfalla [It.: "butterfly"] gasping / as toward a bridge over worlds."
¹²Ezra Pound, *Selected Letters of Ezra Pound, 1907-1941*, 323.
¹³James Merrill, "The Will," in *From the First Nine*, 343.
¹⁴James Merrill, "The Grand Canyon," in *Water Street*, 14.
¹⁵The typescripts are in the Olin Library of Washington University, St. Louis.
¹⁶Sigmund Freud, *Introductory Lectures on Psychoanalysis*, 105.

[17]The image of the house in Merrill's poetry usually signifies, as he put it in "An Urban Convalescence," some experience that has been lived through (*Water Street*, 6).

[18]Merrill, "The House," in *From the First Nine*, 35–36.

[19]Ross Labrie, "James Merrill at Home," 24, 35.

[20]George B. Hogenson, *Jung's Struggle with Freud*, 37.

[21]Irwin Ehrenpreis, "Otherworldly Goods," 48. His criticism recalls Shaun's facile dismissal of Shem in *Finnegans Wake* (170:11) as a "gnawstick." In his essay collection, *James Merrill*, Bloom calls the poet a "curious kind of religious poet, 'curious' because the religion is a variety of Gnosticism" (1).

[22]This line reads, in one of Yeats's versions, "The immortals are mortal, the mortals immortal, each living the other's death and dying the other's life." See A. Norman Jeffares and A. S. Knowland, *A Commentary on the Collected Plays of W. B. Yeats*, 195.

Conclusion

[1]Robert Duncan, "From *The H.D. Book*, Part II, Chapter 5," 39–40.

[2]Michael Andrè Bernstein and Burton Hatlen, "Interview with Robert Duncan," 109.

[3]Duncan, "From *The H.D. Book*, Part II," 47.

[4]William James, "The Confidences of a Psychical Researcher (1909)," 372.

[5]T. S. Eliot, "William James on Immortality."

Works Consulted

Ackroyd, Peter. *T.S. Eliot: A Life*. New York: Simon and Schuster, 1984.

Adorno, Theodor W. "The Stars Down to Earth: *The Los Angeles Times* Astrology Column." *Telos: A Quarterly Journal of Radical Social Theory*, no. 19 (spring 1974): 13–90.

———. "Theses against Occultism." *Telos: A Quarterly Journal of Radical Social Theory*, no. 19 (spring 1974): 7–12.

Alexander, Paul. *Ariel Ascending: Writings about Sylvia Plath*. New York: Harper and Row, 1985.

———. *Rough Magic: A Biography of Sylvia Plath*. New York: Viking Penquin, 1991.

Ambelain, Robert. *Dans l'ombre des cathédrales*. Paris: Editions Adyar, 1939.

Auden, W. H. *Collected Longer Poems*. New York: Random House, 1965.

———. *Collected Shorter Poems, 1927–1957*. New York: Random House, 1964.

———. *The Dyer's Hand*. New York: Vintage, 1968.

———. "Yeats as an Example." *Kenyon Review*, 10 (winter 1948): 187–95.

Augustine, Jane. "*The Mystery* Unveiled: The Significance of H.D.'s 'Moravian' Novel." *H.D. Newsletter*, 4 (spring 1991): 9–17.

Axelrod, Steven. *The Wound and the Cure of Words*. Baltimore: Johns Hopkins University Press, 1992.

Bacigalupo, Massimo. *The Formèd Trace: The Later Poetry of Ezra Pound*. New York: Columbia University Press, 1980.

Banta, Martha. *Henry James and the Occult*. Bloomington: Indiana University Press, 1972.

Baumann, Walter. "Ezra Pound and Magic: Old World Tricks in a New World Poem." *Paideuma*, 10 (fall 1981): 209–24.

———. "Secretary of Nature, John Heydon." In *New Approaches to Ezra Pound*, ed. Eva Hesse.

Bell, Ian F. A. *Critic as Scientist: The Modernist Poetics of Ezra Pound.* London: Methuen, 1981.

Bernstein, Michael André, and Burton Hatlen. "Interview with Robert Duncan," *Sagetrieb,* 7 (January 1969): 16–38.

Besant, Annie, and C. W. Leadbeater. *Thought-Forms.* 1901. Reprint, Adyar, Madras, India: The Theosophical Publishing House, 1941.

Bishop, Nick. *Re-Making Poetry: Ted Hughes and a New Critical Psychology.* New York: St. Martin's, 1991.

Blackmur, R. P. "The Later Poetry of W. B. Yeats." In *W. B. Yeats: A Critical Anthology,* ed. William H. Pritchard.

Blavatsky, H. P. *The Secret Doctrine.* 1888. Vols. 1–6. The Adyar Edition. Adyar, India: Theosophical Publishing House, 1938.

Bloom, Harold. *The American Religion: The Emergence of a Post-Christian Nation.* New York: Simon and Schuster, 1992.

——. *The Anxiety of Influence: A Theory of Poetry.* New York: Oxford University Press, 1973.

——. *Yeats.* New York: Oxford University Press, 1970.

——, ed. *James Merrill.* New York: Chelsea House, 1985.

Bradley, F. H. "The Evidence of Spiritualism." In *Collected Essays.* Oxford: Clarendon, 1969.

Bradshaw, Graham. "Creative Mythology in *Cave Birds.*" In *The Achievement of Ted Hughes,* ed. Keith Sagar.

Bragaglia, Anton Giulio. Ed. Giulio Einaudi. *Fotodinamismo futurista.* 1911. Reprint, Turin: Centro Studi Bragaglia, 1970.

Braude, Ann. *Radical Spirits: Spiritualism and Women's Rights in Nineteenth-Century America.* Boston: Beacon, 1989.

Brivic, Sheldon. *Joyce between Freud and Jung.* Port Washington, N.Y.: Kennikat, 1980.

Brooks, Cleanth. *Modern Poetry and the Tradition.* Retrospective ed. Chapel Hill: University of North Carolina Press, 1967.

Brooks-Davies, Douglas. *Pope's "Dunciad" and the Queen of Night: A Study in Emotional Jacobitism.* Manchester: Manchester University Press, 1985.

Burnett, Gary. *H.D. between Image and Epic: The Mysteries of Her Poetics.* Ann Arbor: UMI Research Press, 1990.

Carroll, Lewis. *Through the Looking Glass.* In *The Annotated Alice,* ed. Martin Gardner. Cleveland: World Publishing, 1960.

Chaboseau, Jean. *Le tarot.* Paris: Nielans, 1946.

Chisholm, Dianne. *H.D.'s Freudian Poetics.* Ithaca: Cornell University Press, 1992.

Cobb, Noel. *Prospero's Island: The Secret Alchemy at the Heart of the Tempest.* London: Coventure, 1984.

Craft, Robert. *Memories and Commentaries.* Garden City, N.Y.: Doubleday, 1960.

Davie, Donald. *Ezra Pound: Poet as Sculptor.* New York: Oxford University Press, 1964.

de Nagy, N. Christoph. *The Poetry of Ezra Pound: The Pre-Imagist Stage.* Bern: Francke, 1966.

Derrida, Jacques. *Dissemination.* Trans. Barbara Johnson. Chicago: University of Chicago Press, 1981.

Donne, John. *The Complete Poetry of John Donne.* Ed. John T. Shawcross. Garden City, N.Y.: Doubleday, Anchor, 1967.

——. *The Life and Letters of John Donne.* Rev. and collected by Edmund Gosse. Vol. 2. Gloucester, Mass.: Peter Smith, 1959.

Donoghue, Denis. "What the Ouija Board Said." *New York Times Book Review,* 15 June 1980, 11.

Duncan, Robert. *Bending the Bow.* New York: New Directions, 1968.

——. "Chapter 2, *The H.D. Book,* Part II." *Caterpillar,* 6 (January 1968): 6–29.

——. "Chapter 4. *The H.D. Book,* Part Two: 'Nights and Days.'" *Caterpillar,* 7 (April 1969): 27–55.

——. *Fictive Certainties.* New York: New Directions, 1985.

——. "From *The H.D. Book,* Part I: 'Beginnings'; Chapter 5, 'Occult Matters'." *Stony Brook,* 3/4 (fall 1968): 4–19.

——. "From *The H.D. Book,* Part II, Chapter 5." *Sagetrieb,* 4 (Robert Duncan Special Issue, fall/winter 1985): 39–85.

——. *Ground Work: Before the War.* New York: New Directions, 1984.

——. *Ground Work II: In the Dark.* New York: New Directions, 1987.

——. "*The H.D. Book,* Part Two, Chapter 2." *Caterpillar,* 7 (January 1969): 16–38.

——. "Interview." In *Towards a New American Poetics: Essays and Interviews,* ed. Ekbert Faas.

——. "The Lasting Contribution of Ezra Pound," *Agenda,* 4 (October/November 1965): 23–26.

——. *The H.D. Book,* Part Two: 'Nights and Days,' Chapter 5." *Stony Brook,* 3/4 (fall 1969): 336–47.

——. *The Opening of the Field.* 1960. Reprint, New York: New Directions, 1973.

——. *Roots and Branches.* 1964. Reprint, New York: New Directions, 1968.

——. "Two Chapters from *The H.D. Book.*" *TriQuarterly,* 12 (spring 1968): 67–98.

Duplessis, Rachel Blau. *H.D.: The Career of That Struggle.* Bloomington: Indiana University Press, 1986.

Eco, Umberto. *Foucault's Pendulum.* Trans. William Weaver. San Diego: Harcourt Brace Jovanovich, 1983.

Ehrenpreis, Irwin. "Otherworldly Goods." *New York Review of Books,* 22 (January 1981): 48.

Eliot, T. S. *After Strange Gods: A Primer of Modern Heresy.* New York: Harcourt, Brace, 1933.

——. *The Cocktail Party.* Ed. Nevill Coghill. London: Faber and Faber, 1974.

——. "A Commentary." *Criterion,* 14 (January 1935): 261.

——. *The Complete Poems and Plays: 1909–50.* New York: Harcourt, Brace, 1964.

——. "Eeldrop and Appleplex, I." *Little Review,* 4 (May 1917): 7–11.

——. "A Foreign Mind." *Athenaeum,* no. 4653 (4 July 1919): 552.

——. Introduction to *Revelation,* ed. John Baillie and Hugh Martin. New York: Macmillan, 1937.

——. "Isolated Superiority." *Dial*, 84 (January 1928): 4–6.

——. *On Poetry and Poets*. New York: Farrar, Straus and Giroux, 1961.

——. *The Sacred Wood*. 1920. Reprint, London: Methuen, 1960.

——. *Selected Essays*. New York: Harcourt, Brace, 1964.

——. *Selected Prose of T. S. Eliot*. Ed. Frank Kermode. New York: Harcourt Brace Jovanovich, 1975.

——. "Tradition and the Practice of Poetry." Introduction and Afterword by A. Walton Litz. *Southern Review*, 21 (October 1985): 873.

——. *The Use of Poetry and the Use of Criticism*. London: Faber and Faber, 1933.

——. *The Waste Land: A Facsimile and Transcript*. Ed. Valerie Eliot. New York: Harcourt Brace Jovanovich, 1971.

—— (unsigned). "William James on Immortality." *New Statesman*, 9 (8 December 1917): 547.

Ellmann, Richard. *Eminent Domain: Yeats among Wilde, Joyce, Pound, Eliot, and Auden*. New York: Oxford University Press, 1970.

——. *The Identity of Yeats*. London: Oxford University Press, 1954.

——. *Yeats: The Man and the Masks*. 1948. Reprint, New York: Norton, 1979.

Faas, Ekbert. *Ted Hughes: The Unaccommodated Universe. With Selected Critical Writings by Ted Hughes and Two Interviews*. Santa Barbara: Black Sparrow, 1980.

——, ed. *Towards a New American Poetics: Essays and Interviews*. Santa Barbara: Black Sparrow Press, 1978

Fabricius, Johannes. *Alchamy: The Medieval Alchemists and Their Royal Art*. Copenhagen: Rosenkild og Bagger, 1976.

Farnam, Dorothy. *Auden in Love*. New York: Simon and Schuster, 1984.

Flannery, Mary Catherine. *Yeats and Magic*. Gerrards Cross: Smythe, 1977.

Fogelman, Bruce. *Shapes of Power: The Development of Ezra Pound's Poetic Sequences*. Ann Arbor: UMI Research Press, 1988.

Fortune, Dion [Violet Mary Firth]. *The Esoteric Orders and Their Work*. 1928. Reprint, St. Paul, Minnesota: Llewellyn Publications, 1978.

French, William, and Timothy Materer. "Far Flung Vortices and Ezra's 'Hindoo' Yogi." *Paideuma*, 11 (spring 1982): 39–53.

Freud, Sigmund. *The Interpretation of Dreams (Second Part)*. Vol. 5 of *The Standard Edition of the Complete Psychological Works of Sigmund Freud*, ed. James Strachey. London: Hogarth, 1953.

——. *Introductory Lectures on Psychoanalysis*. Vol. 15 of *The Standard Edition of the Complete Psychological Works of Sigmund Freud*, ed. James Strachey. London: Hogarth, 1961.

——. "Mourning and Melancholia." In *The Standard Edition of the Complete Psychologial Works of Sigmund Freud*, ed. James Strachey, vol. 15. London: Hogarth, 1955.

——. *Sigmund Freud on Creativity and the Unconscious*, ed. Benjamin Nelson. New York: Harper and Row, 1958.

——. "Psycho-analysis and Telepathy (1941 [1921])." In *The Standard Edition of the Complete Psychological Works of Sigmund Freud*, ed. James Strachey, vol. 18. London: Hogarth, 1955.

——. *Psychopathology of Everyday Life*. Trans. A. A. Brill. New York: Macmillan, 1915.

——. *Totem and Taboo: Some Points of Agreement between the Mental Lives of Savages and Neurotics*. 1913. Trans. James Strachey. New York: Norton, 1950.

——. "The Uncanny." 1919. In *Sigmund Freud on Creativity and the Unconscious*, ed. Benjamin Nelson. New York: Harper and Row, 1958.

Friedman, Susan Stanford. *Penelope's Web: Gender, Modernity, H.D.'s Fiction*. Cambridge: Cambridge University Press, 1990.

——. *Psyche Reborn*. Bloomington: Indiana University Press, 1981.

Frye, Northrop. *Fables of Identity: Studies in Poetic Mythology*. New York: Harcourt, Brace, 1963.

Gardner, Helen. *The Composition of Four Quartets*. Oxford University Press, 1978.

Gardner, Martin. *Fads and Fallacies in the Name of Science*. New York: New American Library, 1957.

Gardner, Thomas. *Discovering Ourselves in Whitman: The Contemporary American Long Poem*. Urbana: University of Illinois University Press, 1989.

Gay, Peter. *Freud: A Life for Our Time*. New York: Norton, 1988.

Gibbons, Tom. "*The Waste Land* Tarot Identified." *Journal of Modern Literature*, 2 (November 1972): 560–65.

Gifford, Terry, and Neil Roberts. *Ted Hughes: A Critical Study*. London: Faber and Faber, 1981.

Goodrick-Clarke, Nicholas. *The Occult Roots of Nazism: The Ariosophists of Austria and Germany, 1890–1935*. Wellingborough, England: Aquarian 1985.

Gordon, Lyndall. *Eliot's Early Years*. New York: Oxford University Press, 1977.

Grieve, Thomas. "The Séraphin Couvreur Sources of *Rock-Drill*." *Paideuma*, 4 (fall/winter, 1975): 361–508.

Guest, Barbara. *Herself Defined: The Poet H.D. and Her World*. New York: Doubleday, 1984.

Hallberg, Robert von. *American Poetry and Culture: 1945–1980*. Cambridge: Harvard University Press, 1985.

Harper, George Mills. *Yeats's Golden Dawn*. New York: Barnes and Noble, 1974.

Hatlen, Burton. "Robert Duncan's Marriage of Heaven and Hell: Kabbalah and Rime in *Roots and Branches*." In *World, Self, Poem: Essays on Contemporary Poetry from the "Jubilation of Poets*," ed. Leonard M. Trawick. Kent, Ohio: Kent State University Press, 1990.

H.D. [Hilda Doolittle]. *Collected Poems, 1912–44*. Ed. Louis L. Martz. New York: New Directions, 1982.

——. *End to Torment: A Memoir of Ezra Pound*. New York: New Directions, 1979.

——. *The Gift*. New York: New Directions, 1982.

——. *Hermetic Definition*. New York: New Directions, 1972.

——. "H.D. by Delia Alton." *Iowa Review*, 16 (H.D. Centennial Issue, fall 1968): 179–221.

——. *Selected Poems*. Ed. Louis L. Martz. New York: New Directions, 1988.

——. *Tribute to Freud*. 1956. Reprint, Boston: Godine, 1974.

Hesse, Eva, "On the Source of Pound's 'Vortex.'" *Paideuma*, 9 (fall 1980): 329–31.

——. ed. *New Approaches to Ezra Pound*. Berkeley: University of California Press, 1969.

High, Dallas M. *Language, Persons, and Belief: Studies in Wittgenstein's Philosophical Investigations and Religious Uses of Language*. New York: Oxford University Press, 1967.

Hogenson, George B. *Jung's Struggle with Freud*. Notre Dame, Ind.: University of Notre Dame Press, 1983.

Holland, Norman H. *Poems in Persons: An Introduction to the Psychoanalysis of Literature*. New York: Norton, 1973.

Hough, Graham. *The Mystery Religion of W. B. Yeats*. New York: Barnes and Noble, 1984.

Hughes, Ted. *Cave Birds: An Alchemical Cave Drama*. 1975. Revised ed., New York: Viking Penguin, 1978.

——. *Gaudete*. London: Faber and Faber, 1977.

——. *Lupercal*. New York: Harper & Brothers, New York: Harper and Row, 1971.

——. "Myth and Education." In *Writers, Critics, and Children*, ed. Geoff Fox *et al*. New York: Agathon, 1976.

——. "Notes on the Chronological Order of Sylvia Plath's Poems." *TriQuarterly*, 7 (fall 1966): 81–88.

——. *River: Poems by Ted Hughes, Photographs by Peter Keen*. London: Faber and Faber, 1983.

——. *Shakespeare and the Goddess of Complete Being*. New York: Farrar, Straus and Giroux, 1992.

——. "Sylvia Plath and Her Journals." In *Ariel Ascending: Writings about Sylvia Plath*, ed. Paul Alexander.

——. *Winter Pollen: Occasional Prose*. Ed. William Scammel. London: Faber and Faber, 1994.

——. *Wodwo*. New York: Harper and Row, 1967.

Hynes, Samuel. *The Edwardian Turn of Mind*. Princeton: Princeton University Press, 1968.

Jacob, Margaret C. *The Radical Enlightenment: Pantheists, Freemasons, and Republicans*. Winchester, Mass.: Allen and Unwin, 1981.

James, D. G. *The Dream of Prospero*. Oxford: Clarendon Press, 1967.

James, William. "The Confidences of a Psychical Researcher." 1909. In *Essays in Psychical Research: The Works of William James*, ed. Frederick H. Burkhardt. Cambridge: Harvard University Press, 1986.

——. *The Will to Believe and Other Essays in Popular Philosophy*. Cambridge: Harvard University Press, 1979.

Jeffares, A. Norman, and A. S. Knowland. *A Commentary on the Collected Plays of W. B. Yeats*. London: Macmillan, 1975.

Johnson, Mark Andrew. *Robert Duncan*. Boston: Twayne, 1988.

Jones, Ernest. *The Life and Work of Sigmund Freud*. Vols. 2 and 3. New York: Basic Books, 1955 and 1957.

Jonson, Ben. *The Alchemist.* Ed. Douglas Brown. New York: Hill and Wang, 1965.

Joyce, James. *Ulysses.* New York: Vintage, 1961.

Jung, C. G. *Alchemical Studies.* Trans. R. F. C. Hull. New York: Bollingen Foundation, 1967.

———. *Collected Papers on Analytical Psychology.* Ed. Constance E. Long. 2d ed. New York: Moffat, Yard, 1917.

———. *Memories, Dreams, Reflections.* Recorded and edited by Aniela Jaffè. Trans. Richard Winston and Clara Winston. New York: Vintage, 1965.

———. *Mysterium Coniunctionis: An Inquiry into the Separation and Synthesis of Psychic Opposites in Alchemy.* Trans. R. F. C. Hull. New York: Bollingen Foundation, 1963.

———. *Psychology and Alchemy.* Trans. R. F. C. Hull. New York: Bollingen Foundation, 1968.

———. *Symbols of Transformation: An Analysis of the Prelude to a Case of Schizophrenia.* Trans. R. F. C. Hull. New York: Pantheon, 1956.

Kandinsky, Vasilii. "On the Spiritual in Art." In *The Life of Vasilii Kandinsky in Russian Art,* ed. John E. Bowlt and Rose-Carol Washton Long. Newtonville, Mass.: Oriental Research Partners, 1980.

Kelly, Robert. *The Alchemist to Mercury.* Ed. Jed Rasula. Richmond, Calif.: North Atlantic, 1981.

Kenner, Hugh. "Poetize or Bust." *Harper's Magazine,* September 1983; 67–70.

———. *The Poetry of Ezra Pound.* Norfolk, Conn.: New Directions, 1951.

———. *The Pound Era.* Berkeley and Los Angeles: University of California Press, 1971.

Kermode, Frank. "Introduction." *The Tempest* (The Arden Shakespeare). Cambridge: Harvard University Press, 1954.

———. *The Romantic Image.* New York: Vintage, 1957.

Kinahan, Frank. *Yeats, Folklore, and Occultism: Contexts of the Early Work and Thought.* Winchester, Mass.: Unwin Hyman, 1988.

Kloepfer, Deborah Kelly. *The Unspeakable Mother: Forbidden Discourse in Jean Rhys and H.D.* Ithaca: Cornell University Press, 1989.

Kroll, Judith. *Chapters in a Mythology: The Poetry of Sylvia Plath.* New York: Harper and Row, 1976.

Kurtzman, Mary. "Plath's 'Ariel' and Tarot." *Centennial Review,* 32 (summer 1988): 286–95.

Labrie, Ross. "James Merrill at Home: An Interview." *Arizona Quarterly,* 38 (1982): 19–36.

Lacan, Jacques. *Ecrits: A Selection.* Trans. Alan Sheridan. New York: Norton, 1977.

———. *The Four Fundamental Concepts of Psycho-analysis.* Trans. Alan Sheridan. New York: Norton, 1978.

Le Breton, Georges. *Nerval, poéte alchimique: La clef des chimères.* Paris: Curandera, 1982.

Libera, Sharon Mayer. "Casting His Gods Back into the NOUS." *Paideuma,* 2 (winter 1973): 355–77.

Longenbach, James. *Stone Cottage: Pound, Yeats, and Modernism.* New York: Oxford University Press, 1988.

——. "Uncanny Eliot." In *T. S. Eliot: Man and Poet,* ed. Laura Cowan. Orono, Maine: National Poetry Foundation, 1992.

Makin, Peter. *Provence and Pound.* Berkeley and Los Angeles: University of California Press, 1978.

Materer, Timothy. "Death and Alchemical Transformation in James Merrill's *The Changing Light at Sandover.*" *Contemporary Literature,* 29 (spring 1988): 82–104.

——. "Pound's 'Vortex.'" *Paideuma,* 6 (fall 1977): 175–76.

Mayer, John T. *T. S. Eliot's Silent Voices.* New York: Oxford University Press, 1989.

Mead, G. R. S. Preface to *Select Works of Plotinus.* Trans. Thomas Taylor. London: Bell, 1895.

Meade, Marion. *Madame Blavatsky: The Woman behind the Myth.* New York: Putnam's, 1980.

Merchant, Carolyn. *The Death of Nature: Women, Ecology, and the Scientific Revolution.* New York: Harper and Row, 1980.

Merrill, James. "The Art of Poetry xxxi," *Paris Review,* 84 (1982): 189.

——. *The Changing Light at Sandover: Including the Whole of the Book of Ephraim, Mirabell's Books of Number, Scripts for the Pageant, and a New Coda, The Higher Keys.* New York: Atheneum, 1983.

——. *The (Diblos) Notebook.* New York: Atheneum, 1965.

——. *A Different Person: A Memoir.* New York: Knopf, 1993.

——. *From the First Nine: Poems, 1946–74.* New York: Atheneum, 1984.

——. *Late Settings.* New York: Atheneum, 1985.

——. "Peru: The Landscape Game." *Prose* (spring 1971): 105–14.

——. *Recitative: Prose by James Merrill.* Ed. J. D. McClatchy. Berkeley: North Point, 1986.

——. *A Scattering of Salts.* New York: Knopf, 1995.

——. *The Seraglio.* New York: Knopf, 1957.

——. *Water Street.* 1962. Reprint, New York: Atheneum, 1980.

Milton, John. "Of Education." In *John Milton: Complete Poems and Major Prose,* ed. Merritt Y. Hughes. New York: Odyssey, 1957.

Miyake, Akiko. *Ezra Pound and the Mysteries of Love: A Plan for the Cantos.* Durham: Duke University Press, 1991.

Moore, Virginia. *The Unicorn: William Butler Yeats' Search for Reality.* New York: Macmillan: 1954.

Murphy, William M. "Psychic Daughter, Mystic Son, Skeptic Father." In *Yeats and the Occult,* ed. George Mills Harper. Toronto: Macmillan, 1975.

Murray, Paul. *T. S. Eliot and Mysticism: The Secret History of Four Quartets.* New York: St. Martin's, 1991.

Naisbitt, John, and Patricia Aburdene. "Religious Revivals of the Third Millennium." In *Megatrends 2000.* New York: William Morrow, 1990.

New, Elisa. *The Regenerate Lyric: Theology and Innovation in American Poetry.* New York: Cambridge University Press, 1993.

Newman, Robert D. "*Transformatio Coniunctionis*: Alchemy in *Ulysses*." In *Joyce's Ulysses: The Larger Perspective*, ed. Robert D. Newman and Weldon Thornton. Newark: University of Delaware Press, 1987.

Nicholl, Charles. *The Chemical Theatre*. Boston: Routledge and Kegan Paul, 1980.

Olney, James. *The Rhizome and the Flower: The Perennial Philosophy, Yeats and Jung*. Berkeley: University of California Press, 1980.

Pearson, Norman Holmes. Introduction. *Hermetic Definition*, by H.D.

Perl, Jeffrey M. *Skepticism and Modern Enmity: Before and after Eliot*. Baltimore: Johns Hopkins University Press, 1989.

Plath, Sylvia. *The Collected Poems*. Ed. Ted Hughes. New York: Harper and Row, 1981.

——. *Johnny Panic and the Bible of Dreams and Other Prose Writings*. London: Faber and Faber, 1977.

——. *The Journals of Sylvia Plath*. Ed. Ted Hughes and Frances McCullough. New York: Ballantine, 1982.

——. *Letters Home: Correspondence, 1950–1963*. Ed. Aurelia Schober Plath. New York: Harper and Row, 1975.

Pool, Robert. "Alchemy Altercation at Texas A&M." *Science*, (26 November 1993, 1367(1).

Popkin, Richard H. "Kierkegaard and Scepticism." In *Kierkegaard: A Collection of Critical Essays*, ed. Josiah Thompson. Garden City, N.Y.: Doubleday, Anchor, 1972.

Pound, Ezra. *The Cantos of Ezra Pound*. New York: New Directions, 1973.

——. *The Collected Early Poems of Ezra Pound*. Ed. Michael King. New York: New Directions, 1976.

——. *Ezra Pound and Dorothy Shakespear: Their Letters 1909–1914*. Ed. Omar Pound and A. Walton Litz. New York: New Directions, 1984.

——. *Ezra Pound, John Theobald: Letters*. Ed. Donald Pearce and Herbert Schneidau. Redding Ridge, Conn.: Black Swan Books, 1984.

——. *Gaudier-Brzeska: A Memoir*. 1916. Reprint, New York: New Directions, 1970.

——. *Guide to Kulchur*. 1938. Reprint, New York: New Directions, 1968.

——. *The Literary Essays of Ezra Pound*. Ed. T. S. Eliot. 1954. Reprint, New York: New Directions, 1968.

——. *Personae: The Shorter Poems*. Rev. ed. Ed. Lea Baechler and A. Walton Litz. New York: New Directions, 1990.

——. *Selected Letters of Ezra Pound: 1907-1941*. Ed. D. D. Paige. 1954. Reprint, New York: New Directions, 1971.

——. *The Selected Letters of Ezra Pound to John Quinn: 1915–1924*. Ed. Timothy Materer. Durham: Duke University Press, 1991.

——. *Selected Prose, 1909–1965*. Ed. William Cookson. New York: New Directions, 1973.

——. *The Spirit of Romance*. 1910. Reprint, New York: New Directions, 1968.

——. "Status Rerum." *Poetry*, 1 (January 1913): 125.

——. "Three Cantos: III." *Poetry*, 10 (August 1917): 248–54.

———. *Translations of Ezra Pound*. Ed. Hugh Kenner. 1953. Reprint, New York: New Directions, 1963.

Pritchard, William H., ed. *W. B. Yeats: A Critical Anthology*. Baltimore: Penguin, 1972.

Rachewiltz, Boris de. "Pagan and Magic Elements in Ezra Pound's Works." In *New Approaches to Ezra Pound*, ed. Eva Hesse.

Rahv, Philip. "The Myth and the Powerhouse." In *Literature and the Sixth Sense*. New York: Houghton Mifflin, 1969.

Raine, Kathleen. *Blake and Tradition*. London: Routledge and Kegan Paul, 1969.

———. *Yeats the Initiate: Essays on Certain Themes in the Work of W. B. Yeats*. London: George Allen, 1986.

Ramacharaka, Yogi. *Fourteen Lessons in Yogi Philosophy and Oriental Occultism*. Chicago: Yogi Publications Society, 1903; reprinted, 1931.

———. *Raja Yoga*. Chicago: Yogi Publications Society, 1905; reprinted, 1931.

Richards, I. A. "Doctrine in Poetry." In *Practical Criticism*. New York: Harcourt, Brace and World, 1963.

Read, Forrest. *'76: One World and the Cantos of Ezra Pound*. Chapel Hill: University of North Carolina Press, 1981.

Rees, Alwyn, and Brinley Rees. *Celtic Heritage: Ancient Tradition in Ireland and Wales*. New York: Thames and Hudson, 1961.

Rieff, Philip. *Freud: The Mind of a Moralist*. 3d ed. Chicago: University of Chicago Press, 1979.

Riffaterre, Hermine, ed. *The Occult in Language and Literature*. New York: New York Literary Forum, 1980.

Roberts, Marie. *Gothic Immortals: The Fiction of the Brotherhood of the Rosy Cross*. London: Routledge, 1990.

Robinson, Craig. *Ted Hughes as Shepherd of Being*. New York: St. Martin's, 1989.

Robinson, Janice S. *H.D.: The Life of an American Poet*. Boston: Houghton Mifflin, 1982.

Rorty, Richard. *Contingency, Irony, Solidarity*. New York: Cambridge University Press, 1989.

Rosenberg, Harold. *Art on the Edge: Creators and Situations*. Chicago: University of Chicago Press, 1983.

Rosenblatt, Jon. *Sylvia Plath: The Poetry of Initiation*. Chapel Hill: University of North Carolina Press, 1979.

Ruthven, K. K. *A Guide to Ezra Pound's Personae*. 1926. Reprinted, Berkeley and Los Angeles: University of California Press, 1969.

Sagar, Keith. *The Art of Ted Hughes*. 2d. ed. London: Cambridge University Press, 1978.

———, ed. *The Achievement of Ted Hughes*. Manchester: Manchester University Press, 1983.

Sagar, Keigh, and Stephen Tabor. *Ted Hughes: A Bibliography 1946–1980*. London: Mansell, 1983.

Saurat, Denis. *Literature and the Occult Tradition*. London: Bell, 1930.

Scigaj, Leonard M. *The Poetry of Ted Hughes: Form and Imagination*. Iowa City: University of Iowa Press, 1986.

Senior, John. *The Way Down and Out: The Occult in Symbolist Literature.* Ithaca: Cornell University Press, 1959.

Shanes, Eric. *Constantin Brancusi.* New York: Abbeville, 1989.

Sherry, Vincent. *The Uncommon Tongue: The Poetry and Criticism of Geoffrey Hill.* Ann Arbor: University of Michigan Press, 1987.

Sibley, Agnes. *Charles Williams.* Boston: Twayne, 1982.

Smith, Grover. *T. S. Eliot's Poetry and Plays: A Study in Sources and Meaning.* 2d ed. Chicago: University of Chicago Press, 1974.

Stevens, Wallace. *Collected Poems.* New York: Random House, 1954.

———. *The Necessary Angel.* New York: Vintage, 1951.

Stevenson, Anne. *Bitter Fame: A Life of Sylvia Plath.* Boston: Houghton Mifflin, 1989.

Surette, Leon. *The Birth of Modernism: Ezra Pound, T. S. Eliot, W. B. Yeats, and the Occult.* Montreal: McGill-Queen's University Press, 1993.

———. *A Light from Eleusis: Ezra Pound's "Cantos."* Oxford: Clarendon, 1979.

Surette, P. L. "Helen of Tyre." *Paideuma,* 2 (winter 1972): 419–21.

Symons, Arthur. *The Symbolist Movement in Literature.* 1899. Rev. ed., New York: Dutton, 1919; reprinted, 1958.

Taylor, Anya. *Magic and English Romanticism.* Athens: University of Georgia Press, 1979.

Terrell, Carroll F. *A Companion to the "Cantos" of Ezra Pound.* Vols. 1 and 2. Berkeley and Los Angeles: University of California Press, 1984.

———. *Ideas in Reaction: Byways to the Pound Arcana.* Orono, Maine: Northern Lights, 1991.

Tindall, William York. *Forces in Modern Literature.* Freeport, N.Y.: Books for Libraries, 1947; reprinted, 1970.

Tryphonopoulos, Demetres P. *The Celestial Tradition: A Study of Ezra Pound's "The Cantos".* Waterloo, Ont.: Wilfrid Laurier University Press, 1992.

Tuchman, Maurice, ed. *The Spiritual in Art: Abstract Painting, 1890–1985.* New York: Abbeville, 1986.

Tuveson, Ernest Lee. *The Avatars of Thrice Great Hermes: An Approach to Romanticism.* Lewisburg, Pa. Bucknell University Press, 1982.

Tytel, John. *Ezra Pound: The Solitary Volcano.* New York: Doubleday, 1987.

Unger, Leonard. *Eliot's Compound Ghost: Influence and Confluence.* University Park: Pennsylvania State University Press, 1981.

Varia, Radu. *Brancusi.* Trans. Mary Vaudoyer. New York: Rizzoli, 1986.

Vendler, Helen Hennessy. "'Mirabell': Books of Number." In *Part of Nature, Part of Us: Modern American Poets.* Cambridge: Harvard University Press, 1980.

———. *Yeats's "Vision" and the Later Plays.* Cambridge: Harvard University Press, 1963.

Villas, James. *Gérard de Nerval: A Critical Bibliography.* Columbia: University of Missouri Press, 1968.

Wagner-Martin, Linda. *Sylvia Plath: A Biography.* New York: Simon and Schuster, 1987.

Weaver, Mike. *Alvin Langdon Coburn: Symbolist Photographer, 1882–1966: Beyond the Craft.* An Aperture Monograph. Oxford: Phaidon, 1986.

Weston, Jessie L. *From Ritual to Romance.* 1920. Reprint, New York: Doubleday, Anchor, 1957.

——. *The Quest of the Holy Grail.* 1913. Reprint, London: Cass, 1964.

Whitaker, Thomas R. *Swan and Shadow: Yeats's Dialogue with History.* Chapel Hill: University of North Carolina Press, 1964.

Wilde, Alan. *Horizons of Assent: Modernism, Postmodernism, and the Ironic Imagination.* Baltimore: Johns Hopkins University Press, 1981.

Wilhelm, James. *Dante and Pound: The Epic of Judgment.* Orono, Me.: University of Maine Press, 1974.

——. *Ezra Pound in London and Paris, 1908–1925.* University Park: Pennsylvania State University Press, 1990.

——. *The Later Cantos of Ezra Pound.* New York: Walker, 1977.

Williams, Charles. *All Hallows' Eve.* 1945. Introduction T. S. Eliot. Reprint, New York: Farrar, Straus and Giroux, 1969.

——. *Descent into Hell.* London: Faber and Faber, 1937.

Wilson, Edmund. *Axel's Castle.* 1931. Reprint New York: Scribner's, 1959.

Witemeyer, Hugh. *The Poetry of Ezra Pound: Forms and Renewal, 1908–1920.* Berkeley and Los Angeles: University of California Press, 1969.

Woodman, Leonora. *Stanza My Stone: Wallace Stevens and the Hermetic Tradition.* West Lafayette, Ind.: Purdue University Press, 1983.

Yates, Frances A. *Giordano Bruno and the Hermetic Tradition.* Chicago: University of Chicago Press, 1964.

——. *The Occult Philosophy in the Elizabethan Age.* London: Routledge and Kegan Paul, 1979.

——. *Shakespeare's Last Plays: A New Approach.* London: Routledge and Kegan Paul, 1975.

Yeats, W. B. *The Autobiography of William Butler Yeats.* 1953. Reprint, New York: Macmillan, 1971.

——. *Essays and Introductions.* New York: Macmillan, 1961.

——. Introduction to *The Oxford Book of Modern Verse, 1892–1935,* ed. W. B. Yeats. New York: Oxford University Press, 1936.

——. *Mythologies.* 1959. Reprint, London: Macmillan, 1962.

——. *The Secret Rose: Stories by W. B. Yeats.* A Variorium Edition. Ed. Phillip L. Marcus, Warwick Gould, and Michael J. Sidnell. Ithaca: Cornell University Press, 1981.

——. *The Poems: A New Edition.* Ed. Richard J. Finneran. New York: Macmillan, 1983.

——. *A Vision: A Reissue with the Author's Final Revisions.* 1937. Reprint, New York: Macmillan, 1956.

Yenser, Stephen. *The Consuming Myth: The Work of James Merrill.* Cambridge: Harvard University Press, 1987.

Zimmerman, Hans-Joachim. "Ezra Pound, 'A Song of the Degrees': Chinese Clarity versus Alchemical Confusion." *Paideuma,* 10 (fall 1981): 225–41.

Zinnes, Harriet, ed. *Ezra Pound and the Visual Arts.* New York: New Directions, 1980.

Index